SPATIAL FORM
in NARRATIVE

SPATIAL FORM
in NARRATIVE

Edited by

JEFFREY R. SMITTEN

and

ANN DAGHISTANY

with a Foreword by Joseph Frank

CORNELL UNIVERSITY PRESS
Ithaca and London

First published 1981 by Cornell University Press.
Published in the United Kingdom by Cornell University Press Ltd.,
Ely House, 37 Dover Street, London W1X 4HQ.

International Standard Book Number 0-8014-1375-3
Library of Congress Catalog Card Number 81-3244
Printed in the United States of America
*Librarians: Library of Congress cataloging information appears
on the last page of the book.*

Contents

Foreword

This volume of essays is a gratifying testimony to the vitality of the ideas first published more than thirty years ago in my article "Spatial Form in Modern Literature." It has occurred to me that, as an introduction to the following scholarly discussions, a few personal details about the writing and the reception of the essay may not be without general interest to those concerned with the issues it raises.

The work as a whole originated in my fascination with Djuna Barnes's *Nightwood,* which I read shortly after its publication in 1937. The book haunted me for some reason—perhaps because it was so difficult to understand, yet so impressive even at first contact—and I began to define for myself the difference between it and more conventional novels. I recall thinking of some such term as "counterrealism," with which I played for a while without getting very far; but I was struck by T. S. Eliot's comparison in the preface between the prose of the novel and poetry, and began to feel that perhaps some progress could be made by working in this direction. What is important, though, as I see it now, is that my preoccupation was never abstract or theoretical. I did not set out to write a theory of modern literature—far from it—and the idea that I might be engaged in doing so, given my sense of my general ignorance, never crossed my mind. I only wished to see if I could say something helpful and enlightening about a particular work; and I remained focused on that work and that aim throughout.

This explains the somewhat lopsided character of the essay, which I am sure must have struck a good many readers; works of such great scope as *Ulysses* and *Remembrance of Things Past* are disposed of in a few paragraphs, while *Nightwood* gets a full treatment. Part of the reason is that much work on Joyce and Proust had already been done, and I was not out to duplicate it; another part is simply that even when my original perspective had greatly expanded, I still remained attached to my initial purpose. Perhaps out of a sense of gratitude to the book that had got me started, and which had been relatively neglected, I insisted on giving *Nightwood* a place of honor.

For a number of years after reading *Nightwood* I thought about some of the problems it had suggested, and I jotted down quotations from my reading. None of them fitted any particular pattern that I could yet see, but they struck me as in some way relevant to my concerns. Most of them were later incorporated into the text, though I did not find a place for others. I distinctly recall, for example, writing down the famous passage from G. Wilson Knight's *The Wheel of Fire* (which several commentators have quite rightly spotted as related to my own point of view) where he asserts that "a Shakespearian tragedy is set spatially as well as temporally in the mind," and that there are in the plays "a set of correspondences which are related to each other independently of the time-sequence of the story."[1] I also remember reading over and over again, with great admiration, an essay on Virginia Woolf by William Troy (one of the best and most original critics of his generation), which asserted that Woolf's symbolic structure contradicts the laws of narrative. Taking down his *Selected Essays* from the shelf now, I discover: "The symbol may be considered as something *spatial*" (italics in original); and the remark that in poetry, "whether separate or integrated into a total vision, symbols are capable of being grasped, like other aspects of space, by a single and instantaneous effort of perception."[2]

1. Knight, *The Wheel of Fire* (London, 1930; New York: Meridian Books, 1957), p. 3.
2. Troy, *Selected Essays* (New Brunswick: Rutgers University Press, 1967), p. 76.

Suggestions of this kind no doubt came pouring in from all directions, and I have been much interested in the efforts that have been made to reconstruct the intellectual and cultural atmosphere of the post–World War I period so far as it posed issues that led to some of my formulations.[3] But I really did not know how to use these hints and pointers for a long time. Perhaps I began to get my first glimpse when I applied myself to reading art criticism. I had begun quite early with Roger Fry, Herbert Read, and Clive Bell, and had studied modern art with Meyer Schapiro at the New School for Social Research. Heinrich Wölfflin certainly taught me something about the possibilities of formal analysis; and of course I was led to Wilhelm Worringer by his influence on T. E. Hulme and the constant reference to him in English criticism. But I recall vividly that my ideas began to take coherent shape only after I finally read Lessing's *Laocoön,* which I may have decided to look into because of the discussion of time and space in Edwin Muir's now classic *Structure of the Novel.*

I have a distinct recollection that I felt a shock of recognition and exhilaration after going through Lessing in the little Everyman edition, whose crimson cover I still see before my eyes. Somehow this gave me the systematic clue I had been searching for without really knowing it; and I believe that I began to take my ideas seriously only after this discovery, convinced now that I really knew what I was doing and had something to say that I had found nowhere else among all the critics I admired and from whom I had learned.

My work was greatly aided by the fact that, through a presumptuous letter to Archibald MacLeish, then Librarian of Congress, I managed to obtain a desk in the stacks of the Library (to which I had no right, lacking both academic qualifications and official status), and could thus use the resources of the Library and take out books. Indeed, the essay is irrevocably associated in my mind with the Library of Congress, not only because much of the reading for it was done there, but also because Allen Tate was then Consultant in Poetry at that institution.

3. The article by James Curtis in the present volume gives a wide-ranging survey of the general climate of ideas. An excellent reconstruction of the literary-critical background can be found in Chapter III of Ronald Foust's unpublished Ph.D. dissertation, "The Place of Spatial Form in Modern Literary Criticism" (University of Maryland, 1975).

By a stroke of luck, the first part of my essay was shown to Tate by a friend to whom I had lent the manuscript; and I remember as a great event receiving an invitation from Tate to call upon him at lunchtime. With a generosity and kindliness I shall never forget, this distinguished poet and critic, whose work I had long esteemed, expressed a great interest in what he had read and launched at once into a discussion of it. No one could have been more encouraging, not so much because of anything specifically said in praise, but because of a conversational tone that showed he assumed a mutual participation in the literary enterprise and implicitly accepted the awed neophyte as a valuable interlocutor. This was only the first of my many debts to Allen Tate, who never ceased to believe that one of the important functions of a man of letters in the modern world is to put himself out unceasingly for others in whom he can discern a spark of talent, and who never allowed differences in background or opinion to interfere with this obligation.

If not at this first meeting, then shortly thereafter, he told me that he was soon to become the editor of *The Sewanee Review*, and that if I would finish my article as I had outlined it to him in conversation, he would publish it in the early issues of the periodical he planned to rejuvenate. Several letters from him during the months following his departure from Washington kept urging me to get on with the job, and I remember writing my analysis of *Nightwood* and the final pages under the stimulus of this spur. I often wonder whether I should have gone on without this encouragement; certainly the task would have been much more difficult, and I might well have given up after a certain point. Nor do I recall whether the manuscript had been completed when the first installment began to appear. In any event, this is how it was launched on its career.

Shortly after the first installment was published, I received a telephone call from New York asking for the right to translate a condensed version of the entire work into Spanish. The caller was the editor of *La revista belga*, a monthly journal in the format of *Reader's Digest*, financed at that time by the Belgian government and published in this country for Latin American readers. Naturally, I was very pleased and hastened to agree; if I am not mistaken, the latter part of the essay appeared in Spanish even *before* the English edition. I have often wondered who read it and whether it came to the attention of any of the recent Latin American novelists who seem to exemplify its principles so well.

Nonetheless, Latin America was very remote, and the response I had received from it seemed accidental and almost imaginary. I did know that in the United States publication was greeted only by a resounding silence. The sole reaction I recall was a letter from someone in Texas informing me (accurately) that I had made a mistake in the use of a French phrase. Two or three years passed before I received another letter; this one was from Mark Schorer, asking if he could reprint the essay, in shortened form, in his proposed anthology, *Criticism: The Foundations of Modern Literary Judgment* (1948). I assented eagerly; and the inclusion of my text in a volume side by side with the most eminent critics of the past and present brought it to the attention of a wider audience. In the same year it was also mentioned and cited in René Wellek and Robert Penn Warren's *Theory of Literature*. Since then, to my surprise and pleasure, it has continued to arouse interest, stimulate further work, and, salubriously, provoke disagreement and refutation. Critical ideas are even more notoriously short-lived than most of the literature that gives rise to them; but the stubborn longevity of my youthfully audacious conjectures seems to indicate that they managed to hit on something central to the modern (and even postmodern) situation of literature in our time.

JOSEPH FRANK

Princeton, New Jersey

Editors' Preface

Although the introduction to this collection attempts to define "spatial form," it may be helpful to the reader to have a concise definition of the term before beginning that more complex discussion. As used in this book, "spatial form" in its simplest sense designates the techniques by which novelists subvert the chronological sequence inherent in narrative. We read narratives one word after another, and in this sense all narratives are chronological sequences. But the novelist's arrangement of events within this linear flow of words often departs in varying degrees from strict chronological order. Also, portions of a narrative may be connected without regard to chronology through such devices as image patterns, leitmotifs, analogy, and contrast. "Spatial form" is simply the general label for all these different narrative techniques. We must remember, moreover, that technique implies the creation of an effect in the reader's mind, and thus "spatial form" includes not only objective features of narrative structure but also subjective processes of aesthetic perception. These processes may be stimulated by narrative technique or they may exist even prior to technique. In either case, however, contributors to this book often conceive of them as working in opposition to the linear flow of words in narrative. In its fullest significance, then, "spatial form" embraces both a set of narrative techniques and the reading process itself.

Several other terms also need brief definition since, as they are used in the following essays, they are nearly synonymous with "spatial form." "Modernist" refers to works written between the end of the nineteenth century and World War II—works that are experimental and often involve spatial form. "Contemporary" designates a similar class of works written since World War II. Two additional terms are not so tied to chronology but nonetheless refer to experimental—and thus spatial-form—narratives: "avant-garde" and "modern" may be applied to works from various literary periods, though they always denote the common trait of narrative experiment.

We gratefully acknowledge the following permissions to reprint previously published material: Joseph Frank, "Spatial Form: Thirty Years After," reprinted from *Critical Inquiry*, 4 (1977), 231–252, and 5 (1978), 275–290, by permission of The University of Chicago Press; Eric Rabkin, "Spatial Form and Plot," reprinted from *Critical Inquiry*, 4 (1977), 253–270, also by permission of The University of Chicago Press; lines 1–11 from "The Waste Land" in *Collected Poems 1909–1962* by T. S. Eliot, copyright 1936 by Harcourt Brace Jovanovich, Inc.; copyright © 1963, 1964 by T. S. Eliot, reprinted by permission of the publisher and of Faber and Faber Ltd.

JEFFREY R. SMITTEN
ANN DAGHISTANY

Lubbock, Texas

Introduction: Spatial Form
and Narrative Theory

Jeffrey R. Smitten

I

Joseph Frank's essay "Spatial Form in Modern Literature," since its first appearance in 1945, has aroused considerable interest and controversy. A glance at the bibliography of this volume shows that it has evoked scores of applications, replies, and extensions—the sort of response accorded major books, not articles. Oddly enough, in the Foreword here published, Frank reveals that he had no theoretical purpose in writing the essay; he simply wished to account for his reaction to Djuna Barnes's *Nightwood*. As a result, the theoretical insights that have aroused greatest excitement over the years—notably the ones concerning narrative—are only suggested or implied, and the work as a whole provokes a great many more questions about the nature of narrative than it answers. For most essays such limitations would prove fatal; but because Frank's filled a need, it soon found its way into the classroom, and critics have been returning to it with increasing frequency over the last fifteen years as the interest in literary theory has grown. What is the need that "Spatial Form in Modern Literature" meets? It is the reader's and critic's need to see united under a single rubric three fundamental aspects of narrative: language, structure, and reader perception.

Frank's essay only hinted at the complicated interrelationship of these three, but as several decades of readers have sensed but never articulated, it provides a crucial first step toward a comprehensive theory of narrative.

The potential for theoretical comprehensiveness in Frank's early work is the reason for publishing the present collection of new essays. Because of the extraordinary suppleness of his theory of spatial form, its striking potential for being defined in many different ways, an organized collection by various hands seemed the best way to reveal the true character and utility of the theory. To provide a unity of purpose, all the essays in this book concern narrative fiction, the genre with which spatial form has been most closely and fruitfully associated. On the one hand, the chapters explore the connections between spatial form and language, structure, and reader perception in narrative more thoroughly and systematically than has been done before; on the other, they map out new implications of spatial form, showing, most dramatically perhaps, how it relates to major forms of modern criticism and theory, including New Criticism, Formalism, Structuralism, phenomenology, myth criticism, and linguistics. These essays demonstrate that spatial form is far from being a mere period aesthetic that accounts for the practice of a few avant-garde writers during the first decades of the twentieth century. It is a critical theory applicable to the entire genre of narrative fiction, and at the same time it is situated squarely in the mainstream of Modernist criticism. These qualities of spatial form, which have never been adequately recognized, account for the long-standing interest in the theory and earn it an important place in the history of literary criticism.

Although the essays in this collection interconnect in many ways, they have been arranged according to the predominant issue they address. The first three parts, on language, structure, and reader perception, are analytical, breaking down in their respective ways the general concept of spatial form. Each of the essays in these parts defines spatial form in terms of one of these three aspects and applies that definition to particular groups of narratives. The fourth part, "The Theoretical Context of Spatial Form," is synthetic, placing spatial form in the context of Modernist aesthetics and contemporary literary theory and measuring it against opposing views. This part particularly stresses the theoretical comprehensiveness of the theory.

The following two sections of this introduction analyze the presentation of language, structure, and reader perception in Frank's
essay, further justifying the arrangement of the present volume, and
then describe how the three topics are treated in the various essays.
These two sections are therefore a guideline to how this book may be
used to expand one's understanding of spatial form in narrative.

II

In "Spatial Form in Modern Literature," Frank postulates a seamless connection between language, structure, and reader perception.
Citing Lessing's *Laocoön*, he argues that modern aesthetic theory has
evolved not from a set of fixed categories imposed on the work of art
but from the relation between the work of art and the conditions of
human perception. Aesthetic form and perceiving mind mutually
implicate one another. But for purposes of analysis here it is necessary to separate language, structure, and perception; in so doing we
will see more clearly how they are connected. Let us consider language first.

Spatial form rests upon a linguistic basis (see the discussion of
spatial form and linguistic theory by James Curtis, below, Chapter
7, and the comments by Frank on Saussure and Jakobson). To
expose this basis, Frank begins his essay by discussing modern
poetry, which he uses as a paradigm for narrative. He finds that
much modern poetry—that of Eliot and Pound, for example—undermines the inherent consecutiveness of language, forcing the reader
to perceive the elements of the poem not as unrolling in time but as
juxtaposed in space.[1] This undermining is accomplished primarily
by the suppression of causal/temporal connectives, those words and
word groups by which a literary work is tied to external reality and
to the tradition of mimesis. The suppression of these connectives
alters the whole character of the literary work and forces the reader
to perceive it in a new, unconventional way. The reader's new task
involves two aspects.

(1) The reader faces a puzzling text. Because causal/temporal
connectives are suppressed, the reader cannot locate characters and
events in space and time. The words he reads do not describe a

1. Frank, "Spatial Form in Modern Literature," in his *The Widening Gyre:
Crisis and Mastery in Modern Literature* (New Brunswick: Rutgers University
Press, 1963), p. 10.

coherent dramatic situation referring immediately to external reality.
Consider the opening lines of *The Waste Land*:

> April is the cruellest month, breeding
> Lilacs out of the dead land, mixing
> Memory and desire, stirring
> Dull roots with spring rain.
> Winter kept us warm, covering
> Earth in forgetful snow, feeding
> A little life with dried tubers.
> Summer surprised us, coming over the Starnbergersee
> With a shower of rain; we stopped in the colonnade,
> And went on in sunlight, into the Hofgarten,
> And drank coffee, and talked for an hour.[2]

The reader does not know who is speaking or (except for the season)
where in time the events occurred. Of course, the denotation of
words like "stirring / Dull roots with spring rain" is clear enough,
but what is the context of the words? This is obviously not a poem
on agriculture, but it is hard to see what they have to do with what
"we" did in the "Hofgarten." There is an especially perplexing break
between lines 7 and 8 where the theme shifts from natural description (with the ironic evocation of Chaucer) to the human activities of
summer. Where is the poem going?

(2) The reader must work out a syntax for the text. If conventional
connectives no longer exist, the reader, to make sense of the text,
must discover for himself what connections are to be made among
the seemingly disconnected words and word groups. Once we have
succeeded in that task, we can then see what the individual words
symbolize and how they relate to one another and to the whole. But
the meaning of the text emerges only after the reader has discovered
its internal relationships, its syntax. One reader of *The Waste Land*
describes the process of comprehending its opening lines this way:

> Having . . . grasped that beneath the fragmentary surface of *The
> Waste Land* there does indeed exist a "method," a recognizable plan,
> it is time to see how that unity emerges in the elaboration of the
> poem. The opening section, *The Burial of the Dead*, brings into play
> the various themes of the whole conception: themes at this stage
> apparently separate and incoherent, but possibly destined—though

---

2. Eliot, *The Complete Poems and Plays, 1909–1950* (New York: Harcourt,
Brace, 1958), p. 37.

not before the end, if then—to assume "meaning" through repetition
and development as parts of what may emerge as a unified creation.[3]

Only by seeing parts in terms of the whole, only by working out in a
novel way the relationships among the seemingly disconnected word
groups, can the reader comprehend the poem. He does not follow
the connections between the parts of the poem as supplied by familiar tradition; he makes them for himself as best he can.

At this point we should extend Frank's comments by noting that
what is true for the language of poetry is equally true for the language of narrative fiction. Any time the novelist suppresses causal/
temporal connectives or—what amounts to the same thing—makes
his work self-referential or nonreferential (as Jerome Klinkowitz
explains in Chapter 1), he forces the reader to discover the syntax of
the work by paying extraordinary attention to the synchronic relationship among the seemingly disconnected word groups. Roland
Barthes made this point in describing Butor's *Mobile*: "Michel Butor
has conceived his novels as a single structural investigation whose
principle might be this: it is by *tying* fragments of events together
that meaning is generated, it is by tirelessly transforming these
events into functions that the structure is erected: the writer (poet,
novelist, chronicler) *sees* the meaning of the inert units in front of
him only by *relating* them."[4] The units of the narrative, in Frank's
words, must be seen as juxtaposed in space, not unrolling in time.

Once this linguistic model is established, Frank proceeds to the
question of narrative structure (parts III and IV of his essay). The
same principle operating among the words and word groups of a
poem Frank finds among the paragraphs and chapters of a novel.
Causal/temporal *transitions* are again the trouble spots, for they
require establishment of the narrative line. Frank shows how traditional narrative syntax can be disrupted in several ways: cutting back
and forth between simultaneous actions (as in the country fair scene
in *Madame Bovary*), using distributed exposition (as in *Ulysses*),
presenting events or characters discontinuously (as in *Remembrance
of Things Past*; the essays in this collection will add considerably to

3. Derek Traversi, *T. S. Eliot: The Longer Poems* (New York: Harcourt Brace
Jovanovich, 1976), p. 23.
4. Barthes, "Literature and Discontinuity," in *Critical Essays,* trans. Richard
Howard (Evanston: Northwestern University Press, 1972), pp. 182–183.

the list of techniques). To qualify the starkness of these categories, we should note what is always assumed in Frank's actual discussion: no novel is perfectly temporal or spatial, for they all involve simultaneity, flashbacks, or jumps in time, and they almost never ignore time completely. Some novels—for example, *Can You Forgive Her?*—rely primarily on chronological sequence for their principle of structure with only brief, clearly marked violations of chronology. Others—say, *Mrs. Dalloway*—move more slowly in time and rely heavily on simultaneity of events. Still others—like *Flanders Road*—involve dense mosaics of past and present the interrelations of whose parts completely displace concern with temporal progression in the present. What the concept of spatial form does is to call attention to the departures from pure temporality, from pure causal/temporal sequence. When these departures are great enough, the conventional causal/temporal syntax of the novel is disrupted and the reader must work out a new one by considering the novel as a whole in a moment of time. That is, the reader must map out in his mind the system of internal references and relationships to understand the meaning of any single event, because that event is no longer part of a conventional causal/temporal sequence. One organizing schema must replace another that is no longer applicable.

In Frank's essay, these linguistic and structural considerations are finally connected to the reader's perception. The reader plays a crucial role throughout Frank's discussion because Frank attributes to him the key to spatial form—reflexive reference. This term designates the reference of one part of the work to another; it is by means of reflexive reference that the syntax of a narrative is worked out. But the question arises: where does reflexive reference reside? In the work? Or is it something perceived or created by the reader? Frank speaks of it both ways, as in this passage:

> There is a striking analogy . . . between Proust's method and that of his beloved Impressionist painters; but this analogy goes far deeper than the usual comments about the "impressionism" of Proust's style. The Impressionist painters juxtaposed pure tones on the canvas, instead of mixing them on the palette, in order to leave the blending of colors to the eye of the spectator. Similarly, Proust gives us what might be called pure views of his characters—views of them "motionless in a moment of vision" in various phases of their lives—and allows the sensibility of the reader to fuse these views into a unity. Each view must be apprehended by the reader as a unit; and

Proust's purpose is achieved only when these units of meaning are referred to each other reflexively in a moment of time. [p. 25]

Like the Impressionist painter, Proust has constructed his work in a particular way with particular structural characteristics. Yet the completion of the work rests with the reader/spectator. In the case of the painting, the spectator's processes of visual perception pull the discrete points of the picture into a whole. In the case of the reader, his alertness to reflexive reference, his ability to construct a syntax for the work, creates a whole out of the discrete parts of the narrative. The implication lurking in this passage—as throughout Frank's essay—is that spatial-form narratives place a greater burden on the reader's synthesizing power than do more conventional temporal narratives.

Reader perception has important theoretical implications for spatial form which do not get fully explained in "Spatial Form in Modern Literature." It should be clear that Frank's assumption about reader perception parallels the far more detailed discussions of such aestheticians and critics as Roman Ingarden and Wolfgang Iser. Both of these theorists argue that words, sentences, and larger units in narrative acquire full meaning only when connected to their surrounding contexts. No element in written discourse is understood in isolation. As Ingarden says, "In a reading which is properly carried out, the content of the work is organized quasi-automatically into an internally coherent, meaningful whole of a higher order and is not merely a random conglomeration of separate sentence meanings which are completely independent of one another."[5] Iser analyzes this process of meaning formation in terms of "gaps," those points in the narrative where the reader himself must make a connection or fill out a relationship.[6] Although Frank never deals explicitly with any of these theories, he makes similar assumptions about reader perception with phenomenological and Gestaltist implications. Reflexive reference is a part of every reader's process in making sense of a narrative. However, the reader's capacity for reflexive reference is

5. Ingarden, *The Cognition of the Literary Work of Art*, trans. Ruth Ann Crowley and Kenneth R. Olson (Evanston: Northwestern University Press, 1973), p. 35.
6. Iser, *The Act of Reading: A Theory of Aesthetic Response* (Baltimore: The Johns Hopkins University Press, 1978). For additional psychological and philosophical background to Iser's ideas (including the role of Gestalt psychology), see Aron Gurwitsch, *The Field of Consciousness* (Pittsburgh: Duquesne University Press, 1964).

taxed far more by many late nineteenth- and early twentieth-century narratives than by others. More of the synthesizing, the discovery of narrative syntax, is left to the reader; there are more and greater gaps to be filled in. Ultimately, then, language and structure in narrative implicate reader perception, and we can see that there is a seamless connection between the three, as Frank had postulated. From this schematic outline of the issues raised by "Spatial Form in Modern Literature," we can proceed to a summary of how the essays in this collection address these issues.

III

Although the two essays treating spatial form and language in this volume do not use formal linguistic theory, both build their particular insights from a consideration of referentiality in narrative language. Jerome Klinkowitz's "The Novel as Artifact: Spatial Form in Post-Contemporary Fiction," Chapter I, has a complex two-stage argument resting ultimately on the role of language in spatial form. We saw in the example from *The Waste Land* that reflexive reference among word groups is forced on the reader from the start because he cannot understand the meaning of events until he has grasped the poem as a whole. Klinkowitz makes self-reflexiveness of language the controlling idea in his essay and ties it to the function of time in fiction. In his view, "contemporary fiction" (defined as the avant-garde fiction written since World War II) has finally achieved a pure spatiality by eliminating time and sequence from narrative. Of course, the reader's perceptual time has not been eliminated, but the representation of time in the narrative has. Fiction has become an artifact like architecture: although a work of contemporary fiction—like a building—cannot be seen simultaneously as a single, complete whole, it—no more than a building—does not represent a chronological sequence. With the elimination of time and sequence in contemporary fiction has come the elimination of verisimilitude, the representation of familiar reality that operates according to causal/temporal patterns. Since contemporary fiction does not represent time, it does not render this traditional image of the world that is dependent upon time and causation. And, having discarded time and with it verisimilitude, contemporary fiction has altered the role of language in fiction. Here is the crux of Klinkowitz's argu-

ment. Instead of being in a sense invisible, leading the reader immediately to the represented reality, the words in contemporary
fiction become their own reality: the fiction is entirely self-reflexive.
Fiction is now wholly independent of, not dependent upon, external
reality, thus realizing Alain Robbe-Grillet's program: "I do not
transcribe. I construct. This had been even the old ambition of
Flaubert: to make something out of nothing, something that would
stand alone, without having to lean on anything external to the work;
today this is the ambition of the novel as a whole."[7] Contemporary
fiction is not mimetic; it is only itself, the act of putting words on the
page. Thus Klinkowitz shows us how adaptable—even prophetic—
Frank's essay is, because it accommodates fiction more radically
spatial than *Ulysses* and other Modernist works. Taken with some of
Frank's own comments on recent French fiction in this book (Chapter 9), Klinkowitz's essay demonstrates that spatial form is the
theory central to the development of recent fiction both in America
and abroad.

By contrast with Klinkowitz's emphasis on very recent fiction,
Ann Daghistany and J. J. Johnson's Chapter 2 is on a literary tradition beginning as early as Aristophanes. "Romantic irony"—the
deliberate destruction of illusion in a literary work—is a term often
applied to this tradition, though it has special relevance to literature
of the Romantic and pre-Romantic periods (*Don Juan, Tristram
Shandy*). Daghistany and Johnson argue that the effect produced by
romantic irony—a momentary perception of the relatedness of all
things—is a type or version of spatial form. (In this respect, their
discussion anticipates Part III of the present volume, because one of
their major concerns is reader perception.) However, the connection
between spatial form, as Frank has defined it, and romantic irony is
not based simply on similarity, for once the essential affinity has
been grasped, it becomes clear that the spatiality involved in romantic irony is different from that involved in Frank's theory. Daghistany and Johnson use the terms "closed," to designate the form
entailed by Frank's theory, and "open," to designate that by romantic irony. Closed spatial form is a system of reflexive references that
interlock perfectly, all bearing upon a single theme or core. Open
spatial form—the type created by romantic irony—has been sug-

7. Robbe-Grillet, "From Realism to Reality," in *For a New Novel: Essays on
Fiction,* trans. Richard Howard (New York: Grove Press, 1965), p. 162.

gested, in a different context, by Roland Barthes: in the ideal plural text

> the networks are many and interact, without any one of them being able to surpass the rest; this text is a galaxy of signifiers, not a structure of signifieds; it has no beginning; it is reversible; we gain access to it by several entrances, none of which can be authoritatively declared to be the main one; the codes it mobilizes extend *as far as the eye can reach,* they are indeterminable (meaning here is never subject to a principle of determination, unless by throwing dice); the systems of meaning can take over this absolutely plural text, but their number is never closed, based as it is on the infinity of language.[8]

In open spatial form relations extend infinitely outward from a given point; they do not turn inward to focus on a core. In the more particular case of romantic irony, the infinite network of relations does extend as far as the eye can reach, for it operates not only in the text but beyond the text, incorporating the reader himself and his world. Like Klinkowitz's analysis of pure space in contemporary fiction, Daghistany and Johnson's analysis of romantic irony finally rests on a linguistic basis. Using the "Proteus" section of *Ulysses* as an illustration, they show that the novel plays closed and open types of spatiality against each other. The former is achieved through devices such as leitmotifs and epiphanies, the latter through the destruction of illusion (romantic irony). The destruction of illusion means that the reader is forcibly reminded of the textuality of the book, that he is merely reading words on a page. The integrity of *Ulysses* rests on the novel's recognition that it is only writing and that it cannot naively pretend to be more. Paradoxically, however, as Daghistany and Johnson show, by the novel's recognition of its limited nature as mere "signs on a white field" it gains integrity and expressive power. Language, then, is the key not only to reflexive reference (closed spatial form) but also to romantic irony (open spatial form). Furthermore, Daghistany and Johnson's identification of spatial form with the long literary tradition of romantic irony opens a fruitful vein of further investigation and demonstrates the centrality of Frank's theory to literary history as well as to recent literature.

8. Barthes, *S/Z,* trans. Richard Miller (New York: Hill and Wang, 1974), pp. 5–6.

The three essays on structure explore one of the best-known aspects of spatial form, but they employ new taxonomies for describing spatial-form narratives. All three essays describe the ways in which narratives depart from "pure chronology" or "pure linearity." In so doing, all three establish varying degrees of spatiality discriminated by different narrative techniques. These essays add substantially to sections III and IV of "Spatial Form in Modern Literature."

David Mickelsen's classification in Chapter 3, "Types of Spatial Structure in Narrative," is based on formalism, and in this respect his essay complements that by Ivo Vidan on reader perception. At the same time, since Mickelsen assumes a mimetic function for language, he does not allow completely for the more radical formulation of spatiality based on self-reflexive language which is to be found in Klinkowitz's examination of contemporary fiction. Within these boundaries Mickelsen provides a wide-ranging classification touching upon three formal problems: narrative structure, narrative unity, and style. He addresses the same question in connection with each problem: what are the means by which an author can slow or stop the progression seemingly inherent in narrative? Structures slowing narrative progression may be found in genres as unexperimental as detective and picaresque fiction, the former often referring back in time to earlier events, the latter simply juxtaposing events without strong causal connections. Leitmotifs and multiple narrative lines are also ways in which fiction can work against forward progression. Then, of course, there are narratives which actively try to eliminate time. Mickelsen shows that time can be eliminated from narrative (or at least severely attenuated) by the use of a very brief time period for the whole narrative, the use of a series of uneventful incidents over a longer time period, the removal of temporal indicators, and the scrambling of the time scheme. But once the critic has identified the structures by which narrative progression is lessened, he still must treat the second of Mickelsen's major problems—narrative unity. The seemingly disconnected fragments of the narrative must cohere by some means, or else the narrative will be merely chaotic. Mickelsen argues that the only available means of coherence for spatial-form narrative is theme, of which there are two essential types: portraits of individuals and tableaux of societies. This division suggests that spatial-form narratives, which have rejected actions evolving through time, are concerned with rendering a multiplicity of events all existing at about the same time. Spatial-form narrative is premised, in short, on what Joseph Warren Beach called "breadthwise cutting."[9] The final problem that Mickelsen addresses is style. Not only can the structure of narrative slow forward progression, but also the type of language employed can significantly affect its movement. Here Mickelsen comes close to Klinkowitz by analyzing fictional techniques that complement and even to an extent underlie contemporary fiction. Word play, extended imagery, syntactic complication, and incremental repetition are all stylistic devices that retard narrative progression. By means of his various classifications, Mickelsen has enlarged the technical dimension of Frank's "Spatial Form in Modern Literature" and, like the other writers in this volume, has extended the applicability of spatial form to the whole genre of narrative fiction.

The second essay in the part on structure, Eric Rabkin's "Spatial Form and Plot," Chapter 4, has a number of important connections with the other chapters in this volume. For one thing, Rabkin relates structure to reader perception. Although his primary emphasis is formalist and therefore focused on narrative structure, he is very much aware of the effect of structure on reader perception. For another, Rabkin expands the previous discussions of language and style in narrative. Borrowing concepts from the Russian Formalists, he considers in detail the ways in which language affects the forward progress of narrative. Plot—Rabkin's main concern—has two dimensions: synchronic and diachronic. The latter is the forward progression of narrative, linear and sequential; the former is the context in which a given event in the plot is perceived. All plots have both synchronic and diachronic aspects, but the relations between them shift with different types of narratives. Covering a wide extent of literary history, the body of Rabkin's chapter is a series of discriminations of the varying relations of the synchronic and diachronic in plot and consequently of the different perceptual demands placed on the reader. He begins with folktales, continues through medieval romance and the early novel (*Tristram Shandy*), and finishes with Faulkner, whose narratives are said to be the ones

9. See Beach, *The Twentieth-Century Novel: Studies in Technique* (New York: Century, 1932), esp. section 5.

best described as spatial. In the course of this survey, Rabkin introduces another distinction between types of plots, which nicely characterizes what he sees as spatial form. The distinction is between hypotactic and paratactic plots, with the latter as the more purely spatial. Thus spatial form for Rabkin is associated with pure juxtaposition, like that found in *The Sound and the Fury* and *Absalom, Absalom!* Narratives that employ flashbacks, frame stories, motifs, and the like, although departing from straight chronology are still best classed as hypotactic. But this conclusion does not mean that spatial form is a metaphor useful only in describing a limited number of narratives written in the twentieth century. As Rabkin tells us at the close of his essay: "The metaphor of spatial form, which arose in response to modern narrative experimentation, can thus help provide us with insights into technical problems throughout literary history." Spatial form directs the critic to essential aspects of *all* narratives.

Rather than dealing with spatial form and narrative structure in strictly literary terms, the third chapter in Part II employs an analogy between literature and the visual arts. Joseph Kestner's "Secondary Illusion: The Novel and the Spatial Arts" develops an idea that is merely implicit in Frank's "Spatial Form in Modern Literature," but that, as Kestner demonstrates, is essential both to the concept of spatial form and to the novel as a genre. Frank argued that Lessing's separation of the visual and the narrative arts (the arts of juxtaposition and of sequence) was broken down by Modernist literature; and scattered through Frank's essay are various allusions to analogies between literature and the visual arts (such as the comparison of Proust and the Impressionists cited above). Frank did not emphasize these interart relations, however, and in his contribution to this collection he says that he specifically did not suggest that modern literature was imitating the effects of the visual arts; they only underwent parallel development in the early part of this century (see section VI of "Spatial Form in Modern Literature"). But Kestner's argument is more subtle than the old *ut pictura poesis* theory, which Frank rightly rejects. Through a survey of critical and authorial commentary, Kestner shows that artists and critics have conceived of the novel as primarily temporal and as secondarily spatial. In other words, inherent in the novel as a genre is a degree of spatiality. (Conversely, in the spatial arts there is an inherent degree of temporality.) Thus the novel is inextricably tied to the spatial arts, the spatial arts to the novel. Kestner proceeds from this theoretical position to define three aspects of the novel's spatial secondary illusion. The first of these is pictorial. Kestner sees an interpenetration of painterly and literary concepts. For example, he discusses frame narratives, which Rabkin and Mickelsen had treated in literary terms, and shows that the spatializing function of the frame narrative can be illuminated by theoretical consideration of framing and perspective in painting. The conclusion he implies is that although frames in narrative create only a secondary illusion, they have much more importance in the creation of spatial form than either Rabkin's or Mickelsen's analysis suggests. The second aspect of secondary illusion is sculptural. Here Kestner concentrates on the role of character in fiction (complementing Mickelsen's discussion) and on point of view (complementing Rabkin's). The final aspect is architectural secondary illusion, which takes in the broader aspects of narrative structure (chapters, volumes, etc.) as well as the narrower (style, word placement). In his consideration of style, Kestner again touches upon matters raised by Mickelsen and Rabkin, though his conclusions about the realization of spatial form are not as qualified as theirs. Thus, although Kestner begins with an idea that may, at first glance, seem to contradict Frank's position, we can see that he deals with a number of crucial points in common with the other chapters in this section. Moreover, it is certainly no accident that both Frank (below, in "Spatial Form: Thirty Years After") and Kestner agree that the criticism of Gérard Genette embodies the central ideas involved in spatial form. Their agreement on this point indicates their underlying agreement on the larger question of the nature of spatial form and its importance to the entire genre of narrative.

Bearing upon the subject of "Spatial Form and Reader Perception in Narrative," Ivo Vidan's Chapter 6, "Time Sequence in Spatial Fiction" ultimately relies upon the phenomenological aesthetics of Roman Ingarden to make its distinctions among types of time sequence. Vidan addresses an extremely important problem in the theory of spatial form. Critics like Reuben Brower and Walter Sutton, who are hostile to spatial form, have complained that a novelist's scrambling of his time sequence does not necessarily result in something that can reasonably be called spatial form. Even though events may be out of chronological order, they argue, the reader is still expected to make connections between events in temporal terms. As Brower has said, "As soon as one says 'juxtaposed in an instant of time,' the game is up, since only in space are objects set side by side. Nor is the theory made more consistent by introducing, as Frank does, 'the principle of reflexive reference.' A reader who refers back to word groups in a poem or to narrative units in a novel is thinking not in a 'spatial form,' but in a sequence of time."[10] Vidan readily concedes that the scrambled time sequences or the framed narratives of some novels do not create spatial form, and he cites *Wuthering Heights* as an example of a narrative with a complex temporal structure that is not spatial form (contrast his treatment of this novel with Kestner's). Vidan goes on to argue, however, that certain ways of managing temporal sequence in fiction can create spatial form. Accordingly, he directs his analysis to the type of fictional structure most problematic for his position: novels having "a continuous fable which develops in an ascertainable way." The task Vidan sets for himself is to distinguish the novels in this class which have an intricate temporal structure but which retain their dependence on temporality from those which attenuate or arrest time through their structure. Both types of novel play temporal against spatial, but only one actually creates spatial form. The theoretical key to Vidan's distinction lies in Ingarden's *The Cognition of the Literary Work of Art*. Vidan's premise is that spatial form is a matter of effect—the reader's noesis or cognition that comprehends the entire narrative. Vidan tells us that the decisive factor in the creation of spatial form "is whether the order and relationship of time sequences functionally contribute to the impact of the novel's totality." Ultimately, in Ingarden's terms, this distinction rests on the way in which the reader—interacting with narrative structure—retains and concretizes the work. With its emphasis on the reader's consciousness, Vidan's essay not only complements the more formalistic analyses of the preceding section, but also integrates spatial form with the much larger subject of the perception of narrative, once again showing the centrality of spatial form to narrative genre and to critical theory.

Though not a history of spatial form, the three essays making up the concluding section on the theoretical context of spatial form are perhaps the best available materials toward such a history. Virtually

10. Brower, "The Novel as Poem: Virginia Woolf Exploring a Critical Metaphor," in *The Interpretation of Narrative: Theory and Practice*, ed. Morton W. Bloomfield (Cambridge: Harvard University Press, 1970), p. 233.

the only previous sustained efforts to place spatial form in the context of modern thought are Ronald Foust's dissertation, "The Place of Spatial Form in Modern Literary Criticism," and Ricardo Gullón's article "On Space in the Novel."[11] The three essays in turn survey the Modernist roots of spatial form; examine the parallel of spatial form with various contemporary critical theories, including Structuralism, phenomenology, and myth criticism; and reply to critics hostile to the theory. Thus these essays give the reader both a chronological view of spatial form's development as well as a deeper sense of the explanatory power of the theory itself.

James M. Curtis discusses in Chapter 7 the intellectual origins of spatial form in the philosophy and literary criticism of the late nineteenth and early twentieth centuries—roughly the Modernist period. As Frank notes in the preface to this volume, some Modernist works, like those by Eliot, Knight, Muir, Troy, and Hulme as well as the great novels by Proust and Joyce, were very influential in shaping his ideas. To explain this influence on Frank, Curtis borrows the notion of a "paradigm shift" from Thomas Kuhn's well-known study *The Structure of Scientific Revolutions*. A paradigm in Kuhn's terms is a model that provides a coherent interpretation of phenomena; a paradigm shift is the change from one explanatory model to another as a result of an accumulation of "unexplainable" phenomena. Curtis notes a crisis in early twentieth-century criticism (a crisis still apparent in Frank's own puzzlement over *Nightwood*, which led to the writing of "Spatial Form in Modern Literature") in which important narratives like *Ulysses* and *Remembrance of Things Past* could not be adequately understood in terms of the prevailing critical paradigms. Modernist critics therefore were searching for new paradigms, and they fell back on space and time as major categories on which to found their new theories. As Curtis acutely points out, however, these early critics were not able to formulate a consistent and coherent interpretation of Modernist works, because they had not sufficiently freed themselves from older paradigms. Frank's "Spatial Form in Modern Literature," appearing toward the end of this period of Modernist speculation, succeeded for the first time in presenting a critical theory that would account consistently for Modernist works. In short, as Curtis tells us, Frank was the first

11. Foust, unpub. Ph.D. diss., Univ. of Maryland, 1975, and Gullón, *Critical Inquiry*, 2 (1975), 11–28.

to apply Modernist theory successfully to Modernist practice. At the same time, Frank's conception of spatial form was allied to strands of Modernist thought that would come to prominence after 1945 and that are still enormously influential today. For example, Curtis finds significant parallels between Frank's theory and the Structuralist linguistics of Saussure and the Structuralist anthropology of Lévi-Strauss. By placing spatial form in its Modernist context, Curtis has added a new dimension to our understanding of the theory, for not only does he illuminate Frank's own situation in developing spatial form, but he also locates the concept squarely in the main path of the development of modern criticism.

Ronald Foust's Chapter 8, a study of the parallels between the theory of spatial form and contemporary myth criticism, phenomenology, and Structuralism, is one of the most ambitious essays in this volume. Like Curtis, Foust places spatial form in a context of modern thought, and in so doing he develops with clarity and fullness a comprehensive view of its explanatory power. Foust's purpose in citing the parallels between spatial form—a late Modernist theory, as Curtis has shown—and more recent critical theories is not to give it a relevance that might prove specious for the 1970s. Rather, Foust argues, spatial form provides the foundation for a properly synthetic criticism, a criticism of complementarity. Taking his cue from Paul de Man, he describes the aporia that has resulted because critics have naively opted for only one pole in what is actually a dialectical relationship between the "interior" and "exterior" aspects of a literary work. Critics have stressed either content or form, subject or object, history or myth, time or space. Virtually all of the preceding essays in this volume have alluded to this situation with the suggestion—more or less explicit—that the critic must take into account both poles of this dialectical relationship when dealing with narrative. Foust expands and develops these scattered suggestions into a coherent, persuasive argument for a critical theory that encompasses both poles simultaneously; he refuses to make a separation of concepts that must be seen as one whole. Because of its extraordinary flexibility and comprehensiveness, spatial form offers the critic the best means of establishing a critical theory based on complementarity. Through each of the three sections of his essay, Foust carefully discriminates parallels and contrasts between spatial form and other theories, and then describes how spatial form involves a dialectical method that prevents it from dwindling into merely an early anticipation of one of these other theories. Spatial form consistently leads to a complex synthesis, mediating between competing critical theories. This extraordinary quality is perhaps best illustrated in Foust's remarks on spatial form and Structuralism:

> By interpreting Frank's theory structurally, we can see reflexive reference as a process of self-regulation whereby one system (the reader) interpenetrates the significance formed by the consciousness latent in another system (the text) through the transformational device of the juxtaposition of word groups. Viewed solely as element or "things," these word groups are, of course, static; but they are not just elements, they are elements of a synergic whole. The reader's active response to the latent life of the text, or system, initiates a process from which existential as well as logical significance is derived by participation in the re-creation of the text. What is resurrected is a heterocosm consisting of the subjectivity of the reader, the "subjectivity" of the "author," and the objectivity of the spatial "thing," the book itself.

Opposed aspects of a work of art are here brought into complementary relationship, and, Foust maintains, it is only through such relationships that a fuller, truer criticism will be formed. Extending Curtis's discussion, Foust places spatial form in the mainstream of contemporary critical theory. Indeed, for Foust spatial form holds the key to the future of literary criticism.

Joseph Frank's Chapter 9, "Spatial Form: Thirty Years After," eloquently gathers together many of the themes touched upon in this volume, in an effort to accomplish two things: to reply to critics hostile to the theory of spatial form and to describe the modern critical tradition that has developed the insights contained in the theory. In the first half of the essay, Frank points out that only a few hostile critics have addressed specific questions of literary analysis in "Spatial Form in Modern Literature." Most have concentrated on broad cultural issues that have little to do with the literary terms he wished to establish. Accordingly, he maintains this two-part division, responding first to the few critics like G. Giovannini and Walter Sutton who have actually questioned literary analysis, then dealing with Philip Rahv and Robert Weimann, who address the larger cultural question of the relation of avant-garde literature and spatial form generally. The climax of Frank's reply to his critics is his discussion (which combines literary and cultural issues) of Frank

Kermode's attack in *The Sense of an Ending*. Here Frank connects the debate surrounding spatial form not only with Kermode's own development as a critic but also with the cultural and intellectual tradition of modern literature and criticism. Frank's analysis of how hostility to spatial form developed provides an essential addition to the discussion by Curtis and Foust of spatial form's affinities. Not only does Frank treat a body of criticism in depth which is handled only in passing elsewhere in this volume, but he also provides a masterful historical account of how and why hostility to the concept evolved: he takes spatial form out of a strictly literary context and connects it with major intellectual and cultural changes in prewar and postwar Europe and America. There could be no better evidence than this essay of the importance of spatial form in modern thought.

In the second half, Frank turns from his critics to the critical tradition that has best developed the ideas expressed in "Spatial Form in Modern Literature"—namely, French Structuralism. Of course, Frank by no means suggests that his essay influenced the course of French Structuralism or that there was any effort on the part of specific French critics to come to terms with it. (Indeed, "Spatial Form in Modern Literature" was not translated into French until 1972.) Rather—and what is perhaps more telling for Frank's argument—he sees common purposes, though arising independently and within separate frames of reference, in his efforts and in those of the French Structuralists. As a complement to the Anglo-American tradition described in the first part of his essay, he here describes briefly the pertinent high spots in the development of French Structuralism, pointing out along the way the parallel between the Structuralists' goals and assumptions and his own. He begins with the linguistics of Saussure and Jakobson, which comprises the foundation of literary Structuralism, and goes on to the Russian Formalists, who deal more directly with narrative technique. French Structuralism—in the form that most interests Frank—arrives at its fullest development in the work of Todorov and Genette, and Frank describes in some detail the latter's studies involving narrative form and space. Like Foust, Curtis, and others in this volume, Frank sees spatial form as part of a wide literary horizon: "The theories of this critical movement [French Structuralism] have shown not only that spatial form is a concept relevant to a particular phenomenon of avant-garde writing, but also that it plays a role, even if only a subordinate one, throughout the entire history of literature." In a variety of ways, the previous essays in this collection corroborate this view.

On the basis of this collection of essays, then, one should be able to understand why spatial form has exercised such attraction—and why it has aroused such hostility—over the last several decades. One source of its appeal is its utility in describing narrative technique. Although it is true, as Eric Rabkin has said, that Occam's razor should make us dispense with spatial form, the theory nonetheless continues to appeal to us as critics and readers in spite of this logical objection. And, as the essays in the language, structure, and reader perception sections all suggest, the comprehensiveness of spatial form—its ability to draw together under a single rubric different aspects of and approaches to narrative technique—accounts for its continuing vitality. No other theory of narrative form has such inclusiveness. Moreover, as the essays in the theoretical section show, the attractiveness of spatial form also stems from its important role as a theory. It not only has practical application to narratives, but it also lies at the heart of modern critical theory, having points of contact with major critical, intellectual, and cultural developments in Europe and America since the turn of the century. In sum, the essays in this volume amply testify to the fact that spatial form is one of the most seminal critical theories of this century.

I

Spatial Form and Language in Narrative

I

The Novel as Artifact:
Spatial Form in
Contemporary Fiction

Jerome Klinkowitz

Is complete realization of spatial form in the novel possible? There is a suspicion voiced by Joseph Frank that the perfection of such form in fiction is more of an ideal than a practical reality, that one is forever fighting the narrative, sequential tendencies of the novel which by their very definition argue against space as a key structural element. "To be properly understood," Frank admits, "these word-groups must be juxtaposed with one another and perceived simultaneously,"[1] a physically impossible act. Again, Frank notes the plea of modern poetry for "its readers to suspend the process of individual reference temporarily until the entire pattern of internal references can be apprehended as a unity"[2]—a feat that is possible in an art form where the reader confronts the physical expanse of a page or two or three, but that seems an unfair request when the reader is faced with the three or four hundred pages of writing that are likely to make a novel. Finally, there is the novel's habitual insistence upon *story*, which by definition depends upon sequence for effect. Although spatial fictions have always existed,

1. Frank, "Spatial Form in Modern Literature," in his *The Widening Gyre: Crisis and Mastery in Modern Literature* (New Brunswick: Rutgers University Press, 1963), p. 12.
2. Ibid., p. 13.

the very terms of Frank's arguments show that these forms are the exception rather than the rule, and that to champion a spatially organized fiction would throw one against the deepest traditions of the novel, at least as it has been written through modern times.

"Pure spatiality is a condition toward which literature aspires, but which it never achieves," Cary Nelson argues in his *The Incarnate Word: Literature as Verbal Space*. "The desire to overcome time," he insists, "competes with the temporal succession of words."[3] Moreover, since the material of literature is words, and since the specific words of a text precede our individual reading, all sorts of associations and references outside the text are inevitable, even as we read it for the first time. Frank's strongest argument for the existence of spatial form in conventional fiction is that it happens occasionally, as a set piece within the ongoing narrative structure of the novel at hand. For the duration of a scene in *Madame Bovary*, he argues, "the time-flow of the narrative is halted; attention is fixed on the interplay of relationships within the immobilized time-area. These relationships are juxtaposed independently of the progress of the narrative, and the full significance of the scene is given only by the reflexive relationships among the units of meaning."[4] Here spatial form seems freed from the limits of its previously negative definition, for its effect is possible within the sequence of words, even within the action described by the author. The reason for success is that the action is represented not in narrative movement, but rather as a tableau, an artifact in itself. The fiction is seeking not to imitate an action that has taken place in an observed world, but instead to create the very elements of action, which then develop into a story within the reader's imagination—not on the page of recorded history, with its dependence upon time and sequence, cause and effect.

Frank has described a scene that stands independent of time, with no antecedents or consequences in the narrative. The ideal spatial fiction, then, would be an entire novel that conformed to this pattern. Such a work would have to be absolved of the responsibility of representing some action in the world; even more so, it should not have to represent some other, secondhand reality at all, but rather be

3. Nelson, *The Incarnate Word: Literature as Verbal Space* (Urbana: University of Illinois Press, 1973), p. 3.
4. Frank, "Spatial Form in Modern Literature," p. 15.

its own reality, where the pleasure of the reader is not to recognize the artful depiction of a familiar world, but to appreciate its elements of composition, which just as in a painting would be a spatial affair. The work as self-conscious artifact becomes fully self-reflexive, which is the key Frank saw to making spatial form possible in literature. As Cary Nelson notes about Jorge Luis Borges, who writes fiction of this type, "the reader is made aware that a work creates itself before his eyes."[5] Narrative succession is not the culprit in debasing spatial form; the true problem is the illusion of predisposed narrative succession, which forces the reader to absorb a work in only one way, with attention to the sequence of developments distracting from compositional act. "The collapse of illusionary time in realistic fiction," says Ronald Sukenick, "parallels the collapse of illusionary space in perspective painting and serves a parallel function: the assertion of the validity of the work of art in its own right rather than as an imitation of something else."[6]

Since the publication of Frank's three-part essay on spatial form in 1945, and even since its republication in 1963, an entirely new form of fiction has developed that is primarily spatial in form. Its popular works include Kurt Vonnegut, Jr.'s *Slaughterhouse-Five* (1969), Donald Barthelme's *Snow White* (1967), and Jerzy Kosinski's *Steps* (1968). Its depth is shown by the dozens of novels written by such emerging talents as Ronald Sukenick, Gilbert Sorrentino, Clarence Major, Steve Katz, and Walter Abish, whose style of work has come to dominate the literary quarterlies, academic journals, and experimental magazines that have historically been the best indicator of dominant trends to come.[7] The most striking feature of this new work is that it discards conventional notions of character, action, thematic development, narrative sequence, and ultimately illusion itself ("suspension of disbelief") in favor of a fully self-conscious form of writing. Authors like Sukenick and Sorrentino show no interest in fabricating stories which the reader may easily identify with history. Instead, they destroy all illusion by making

5. Nelson, *The Incarnate Word*, p. 9.
6. Sukenick, "Twelve Digressions toward a Study of Composition," *New Literary History*, 6 (1974–75), 433.
7. For a full discussion of this phenomenon in recent literary history, see Jerome Klinkowitz, *Literary Disruptions: The Making of a Post-Contemporary American Fiction*, rev. ed. (Urbana: University of Illinois Press, 1980), and *The Life of Fiction* (Urbana: University of Illinois Press, 1977).

themselves their own central characters, talking about the actual writing of their books, and depending upon the reader's sense of comedy and play for the work to succeed. Their works cancel themselves, make fun of their continuing creation, refuse interpretation (in the hermeneutic sense of "why something happens"), and engage both author and reader in self-reflexive game-playing. The very disruptions of conventional technique, though practiced for the effect of reestablishing the truly *fictional* (and not historical) basis of fiction, has made this new writing dominantly spatial in form. Replacing the illusion of narrative with the self-conscious artifice of compositional order, then, is all that has been needed to end time's tyranny over space.

The new fiction of Sukenick, Sorrentino, and their colleagues develops along lines suggested by Frank. The impetus for their anti-illusionistic writing is the same as for spatial-form fiction. Frank reminds us of Wilhelm Worringer's thesis that Realism and Naturalism, expressing the triumph of temporal-form fiction, have tended to be created by cultures anxious to demonstrate man's ability to "dominate and control" the world. In the novels of Sukenick and Sorrentino, there is no intention of controlling the world. As Sukenick says, "The fairy tale of the 'realistic' novel whispers assurance that the world is not mysterious, that it is predictable—if not to the characters then to the author, that it is available to manipulation by the individual, that it is not only under control but that one can profit from this control." The key to this impulse is verisimilitude, which is inevitably based upon time rather than space, since the novelist's aim is usually to demonstrate the "realistic" qualities of life in action—in sequence, in causality, in time. By asking the reader to suspend disbelief, Sukenick asserts, "one can make an image of the real thing which, though not real, is such a persuasive likeness that it can represent our control over reality."[8] The new fictionists value their own art above what the world has made; indeed, one of their themes has been to show that what passes for "reality" is just arbitrary convention given the appearance of permanence and validity through time and habit, and that what we accept as "real" in our world is often distressingly insane, once questioned by the self-conscious artist. Instead, the writer is called upon to create his own

8. Sukenick, "Twelve Digressions toward a Study of Composition," p. 429.

reality; even then, the emphasis is upon his act of creation and not upon the final product.

The Modern period made some progress beyond Realism and Naturalism, but looking back at Frank's critique of the period we can see why it was unable to produce a spatial-form fiction unfettered by the claims of time. "If there is one theme that dominates the history of modern culture since the last quarter of the nineteenth century," Frank suggests, "it is precisely that of insecurity, instability, the feeling of loss of control over the meaning and purpose of life amidst the continuing triumphs of science and technics."[9] Cultures at ease with the external world produced Naturalism; those at odds with the environment tend toward abstraction and nonrealistic forms. But the Modern period, as Frank shows, was in its very rebellion against external reality quite conscious of its own alienation from it. There seems little doubt that the center of meaning, informing the value of all aesthetics, whether conformist or rebellious, is found in the empirical, documentary world. Even as the Modernists describe their alienation from it, the basis of their art remains the sequential time as exhibited by that world in process. Of Pound's *Cantos* and the other "peculiarly modern" works that Frank sees as having spatial form, he remarks that "all maintain a continual juxtaposition between aspects of the past and the present so that both [past and present] are fused in one comprehensive view."[10] Only by moving so elusively within the bounds of historical time does spatial-form fiction have the chance to slip away from time's grasp.

But the new fiction disavows historical time entirely, depending upon no reference whatsoever to the temporal world. The Modernists transformed experience into myth—for which, as Frank says, historical time does not exist. Yet myth is the deepest Reality underlying the historically real, an Absolute of absolutes, which limits the spatial freedom of fiction even more strictly than occasional temporal necessity. Myth is, after all, an arbitrarily constructed order superimposed upon existence with the purpose of giving that existence meaning. But as meaning is achieved, the conventional nature of myth is replaced by an absolute dependency upon it to enforce that meaning. Art becomes less an artificial act of composition and more an imitation of a preexisting realm. Whether Real or Ideal, the

9. Frank, "Spatial Form in Modern Literature," p. 55.
10. Ibid., p. 59.

result is the same—for in terms of representation, which both demand, *eternal* is no less tyrannizing than *temporal.* The point of art becomes not itself but something else. An idea, which is just as dependent upon temporal representation as any action, becomes the point of art. "Component kernels of thought or impression," as Edward Marcotte describes them,[11] are as much the stuff of linear fiction as the depiction of panoramic events. Myth is simply the end point of representational fiction. As Marcotte describes it, "the character in turn is appropriated to fulfill some *action,* all of which incorporates itself into a *plot,* which in its turn is illustrative of some general truth, or *idea.*"[12] When literature is about something else, when there is an explicit idea or meaning behind the work, what results is the dramatization of that idea through story. And once that happens, the possibilities for space are limited. Marcotte contrasts traditional and innovative art: "For Michelangelo the form is essential and in a sense eternal; for [John] Cage form is an inhibiting construct of the human ego."[13]

Pure self-reflexiveness is what distinguishes the success of spatial form in contemporary fiction, over and against the limitations of more conventional works that shared the same intention of space. Nathaniel Hawthorne's *The House of the Seven Gables* is distinguished among other nineteenth-century American novels for its insistence upon setting over action, which is one of the key ingredients in spatial-form fiction. Hawthorne's use of time is ironic, using it almost as the servant of space, for the whole drama is played out within the bounds of the house itself. Characterization is secondary to the house's pervasive influence, and action is seen as recurrent within the pattern of ancestral sin and guilt; time when so patterned becomes a spatial fact. The action itself takes place within such strictly limited bounds that the effect is spatial, as characters and themes move back and forth across the stage set of shop window, balcony, and front door.

But Hawthorne's attempt to spatialize his scene—to have pure atmosphere do the work of narrative action—is sold short by his manner of characterizing the house. Because of the author's insis-

11. Marcotte, "Intersticed Prose," *Chicago Review,* 26, No. 4 (1975), 36.
12. Marcotte, "The Space of the Novel," *Partisan Review,* 41 (1974), 266.
13. Marcotte, "Michaelangelo, Cage and Others," *Chicago Review,* 26, No. 3 (1975), 94.

tence upon idea, the house is not allowed to maintain itself as pure spatial setting, but instead becomes a representation of Hawthorne's self-admitted moral, that to inherit a great fortune is indeed to bring down upon one's self a great misfortune. The house is depicted with anthropomorphic qualities, such as its brooding exterior and expressive melancholy nature. By humanizing his setting, Hawthorne asks it finally to perform as a character, taking an active role in the coursings of history which the bare structure of the novel does not need. A spatial element is thereby temporalized, simply by the fact that it is made to perform representational duties.

A transition to self-reflexive fiction may be found in the frame-story. Robert Coover's *The Universal Baseball Association, J. Henry Waugh, Proprietor* (1968) uses the device of a card-table baseball game to show how one element (the temporally "real" world of the game-player) can be effectively counterpointed with the other (the spatially artificial world of the table-top game itself). Coover solves Hawthorne's problem by locating the *idea* in the first realm, where it more properly belongs, leaving the story of the game as pure artifice, representing nothing other than itself. Other fictions use deliberately temporal elements, such as a journey, to emphasize the structural properties of space. Gilbert Sorrentino's *The Sky Changes* (1966) adopts the form of a cross-country journey as the vehicle for a protagonist to piece together why his marriage has disintegrated; but the succession of times and places is absolutely meaningless, and in fact is deliberately thrown out of order to emphasize the absolute stasis of his mind. Sorrentino's novel about a Brooklyn neighborhood, *Steelwork* (1970), again mixes vignettes of many different times and places so that the reader may construct an imaginative picture of the neighborhood, a picture that is independent of the vicissitudes of time and of the ravages of history over space: a dozen different street corners and a dozen different years come together to form a single picture, which in itself—independent of all the changes—constitutes an imaginative realization of this place.

Successful spatial-form fiction must create its own meaning out of the artifice of fiction, having compositional elements do the work otherwise assigned to externally imposed meaning. "As artifice," writes Ronald Sukenick, "the work of art is a conscious tautology in which there is always an implicit (and sometimes explicit) reference to its own nature as artifact—self-reflexive, not self-reflective. It is not an imitation but a new thing in its own right, an invention."[14] The artist must believe absolutely in the reality of his own work; otherwise it dissolves into irony and self-parody, the literature of exhaustion written by John Barth and Thomas Pynchon, who are caught in the dilemma of realizing how futile it is to represent something in their literature, but lacking the confidence in their own works as real. The poetic truth of fiction is, according to Sukenick, "a statement of a particular rapport with reality sufficiently persuasive that we may for a time share it. This kind of 'truth' does not depend upon an accurate description of 'reality,'" he emphasizes, "but rather itself generates what we call reality, reordering our perceptions and sustaining a vital connection with the world."[15] It is noteworthy that Jean-Paul Sartre shared this same notion of fiction's generative role, since Joseph Frank has speculated that Existentialist philosophy may have been responsible for the increased interest in spatial form. Distinguishing the fictive act from simple perception, Sartre argued that "All fictions would be active syntheses, products of our free spontaneity, and all perceptions, on the contrary, would be purely passive syntheses. The difference between fictional images and perceptions would therefore spring from the fundamental structure of intentional syntheses."[16]

Although spatial form is a creation of various literal elements, fictional space exists in the mind alone. When Edward Marcotte contrasts Michaelangelo's belief that his sculpture already existed in the raw block of marble, waiting only the sculptor's hammer and chisel to remove the extraneous material, with the more aleatory and random theory of composition expressed by John Cage, he is noting one of the axioms of the new fiction that makes spatiality finally realizable. In our times, Marcotte argues, "the locus of competition has been shifted: the *work* is no longer the sculpture chiseled out of rock, nor the poem hammered from the resources of language, but an organization actuated within the observer's mind, under the badge of an occasion."[17] What was physically impossible for space

14. Sukenick, "Thirteen Digressions," *Partisan Review,* 43 (1976), 99.
15. Ibid., p. 100.
16. Sartre, *Imagination: A Psychological Critique,* trans. Forrest Williams (Ann Arbor: University of Michigan Press, 1962), p. 142.
17. Marcotte, "Michaelangelo, Cage and Others," p. 97.

in Modernist (and earlier) literature suddenly becomes an easy possibility.

From the compositional elements offered by the spatial artist, the reader composes in his own mind the fiction to be made; the reader is no longer chained to the temporal succession of events noted on the page but rather is invited to make his own sequential conclusion from the objects of the work itself. Marcotte makes an instructive comparison of random passages from Joyce and Robbe-Grillet, noting "the predominance of images and ideas having to do with action and process in the example from Joyce, as opposed to an equal fixation in spatial forms and relationships in the Robbe-Grillet."[18] Although lacking the exuberance and creative play of more recent fiction, the French New Novel establishes both itself as object and its primary function as the uninhibited notation of objects, in defiant protest against the idea that fiction should represent a conceptualization recorded for the reader's passive appreciation. The result is "a fiction that is hermetic and self-sufficient, having relinquished its metaphorical connections as well as its metaphysical claims. In the author's own words, it does not even aspire to be conventionally realistic. . . . Thus we end up with a form of fiction that has succumbed entirely to its fictionality."[19] "Humanizing metaphors," as Jerzy Peterkiewicz describes them, lead to the same restrictions of time and story as did Hawthorne's tendency to anthropomorphize his spatial setting; this aspect of the French New Novel looks backward to the spatial promise anticipated by Ezra Pound and forward to the realization of the novel as its own being. It is the eclipse of Modernism, for, according to Peterkiewicz, "Above all, Robbe-Grillet is against the pathetic fallacy which, in our time, has slowly brought about the 'tragification of the universe,' either in the form of despair at the discovery that the external world does not after all contain the human meaningfulness with which it has been invested, or in the form of a cynical acceptance that this world is meaningless and therefore absurd."[20]

From Roland Barthes we learn how the efforts of later New

18. Marcotte, "The Space of the Novel," p. 270.
19. Ibid., p. 271.
20. Peterkiewicz, *The Other Side of Silence: The Poet at the Limits of Language* (London: Oxford University Press, 1970), p. 66.

Novelists, primarily Michel Butor, extend the range of fiction toward pure spatiality. Butor's *Mobile* makes no attempt to dramatize theme (a temporal affair) but instead chooses a purely combinatory variety. "The units of discourse," Barthes observes, "are . . . essentially defined by their function (in the mathematical sense of the term), not by their rhetorical nature: a metaphor exists in itself; a structural unit exists only by distribution, i.e., by relation to other units." The resulting work of fiction, then, is distinguished by a movement "of perpetual transmission, not of internal 'growth.'"[21] Plot, that servant of time, recedes under the weight of spatially described objects, which are energized not by their enforced movement on the page, but by their actualization in the reader's mind as it breaks the code of composition. Barthes makes his point in *Writing Degree Zero*: "it is now writing which absorbs the whole identity of a literary work."[22]

Writers of this new style of fiction have discovered ways to actualize concrete language as the substance of their work. Ronald Sukenick's *Out* (1973) uses a highly syncopated prose style, with deliberately run-on sentences impelling the reader forward through his words, with one sentence tumbling into the next. All the while, characterization and plot are purposely confused, so that the only home for sustained attention is the writing itself. The book is given a forward rush by Sukenick's technique of dropping one line of type and adding one line of space respectively for each chapter, so that ten lines of type make way for nine lines of type and one line of space, followed by eight lines of type and two lines of space, then seven-three, six-four, and so forth, until the second from last chapter reads one line of type to nine of space, and the very end is pure space. Walter Abish's *Alphabetical Africa* (1974) uses a similar expansion-contraction technique, but here with the words themselves. Fifty-two chapters are titled according to the ascending and descending alphabet. In Chapter A, only words beginning with the letter "a" are used; in the next chapter, "b" words are added, until by Chapter Z the full alphabet is in use. Then the book contracts backward through the alphabet, each chapter losing a letter. Although

21. Barthes, "Literature and Discontinuity," in *Critical Essays,* trans. Richard Howard (Evanston: Northwestern University Press, 1972), p. 181.
22. Barthes, *Writing Degree Zero,* trans. Annette Lavers and Colin Smith (Boston: Beacon Press, 1970), p. 85.

there are characters and plot, they are successively added and lost as the book proceeds. Attention is riveted not upon their action in the story, but upon their concrete action within the spatial confines of the book. All the prerequisites for spatial-form literature are present: self-conscious construction, a book that creates its own reality rather than representing another one, and the use of objective factors rather than illusions to structure the fiction.

Sukenick's and Abish's works display the generative quality of this new fiction, which stands in direct opposition to the representational mode of the conventional novel. "It seems to me that the real difference in question," says Sukenick, "is simply that between an imposed order and the one that develops as it goes along—'occurs as it occurs,' as Stevens would say, 'by digression' as Laurence Sterne would put it, or, in terms of jazz, by improvisation."[23] To evaluate such fiction, one must know that "the art field is a nexus of various kinds of energy, image, and experience. What they are, and how they interact, may in the long run be the most profitable area for criticism: the study of composition."[24] The art of this new fiction is generated by spatial elements in the prose; and unlike conventional fiction, which generally uses space as a relief from the ongoing action of time, these newer works are consistently spatial in their organization and purpose. If the anticipatory works of Robbe-Grillet and the fuller realizations by Sorrentino, Sukenick, and Abish are sometimes received as difficult to understand, their total reliance on spatial form may be the reason. Their language is almost childishly simple; they offer no complexities of plot or characterization; there are no profound or elusive ideas to confuse the reader. But the new fiction does abandon time as an organizing element, and time has been the mainstay of narrative art since the novel took that turn— toward Fielding and Austen, away from Sterne and Rabelais—two centuries ago.

23. Sukenick, "Thirteen Digressions," p. 93.
24. Sukenick, "Twelve Digressions toward a Study of Composition," p. 435.

2

Romantic Irony, Spatial Form, and Joyce's *Ulysses*

Ann Daghistany and J. J. Johnson

I

Joseph Frank's "Spatial Form in Modern Literature" connects the spatial emphasis of modern art with the attitudes behind artistic style found in Wilhelm Worringer's *Abstraction and Empathy*.[1] Frank believes that Worringer's notions, if understood in light of T. E. Hulme's prophecies of a new age of nonorganic, nonpersonal, and thus non-naturalistic art, have "laid bare . . . the 'psychological' roots of spatial form in modern literature."[2] These roots lie in the attempt to abandon "the very condition of that flux and change from which . . . man wishes to escape" with the result that "the inherent spatiality of the plastic arts is accentuated by the effort to remove all traces of time-value" (pp. 56–57). The key phrase in this statement for our discussion of the connection between spatial form and

1. Worringer, *Abstraction and Empathy: A Contribution to the Psychology of Style* (New York: International University Press, 1953). Worringer's primary point is that when man feels secure in his relationships in the universe, his art is human in orientation and depicts man in nature; thus it is naturalistic. But when anxiety about man's position in the world becomes dominant, art reflects a preference for abstract forms that purify the artistic object of its flux and uncertainty; in short, art becomes non-naturalistic.

2. Frank, "Spatial Form in Modern Literature," in his *The Widening Gyre: Crisis and Mastery in Modern Literature* (New Brunswick: Rutgers University Press, 1963), p. 57.

48

romantic irony is "the effort to remove all traces of time-value." According to Frank, modern literature that is non-naturalistic seeks a timeless unity, resulting in literary works having, as we shall show, a fixed, a static, quality. This closed state is developed through intricate systems of "reflexive reference" of elements that cross-refer to one another in the text and receive their meaning simultaneously in spatial juxtaposition. The typical example is *Ulysses,* which, Frank declares, can "only be reread. A knowledge of the whole is essential to an understanding of any part; but unless one is a Dubliner such knowledge can be obtained only after the book has been read, when all the references are fitted into their proper places and grasped as a unity" (p. 19).

But spatial form in narrative need not give rise solely to a *closed* system in the sense of a finished or completed system. It can involve systems of relationships that are open-ended, even infinite. The best example of this type of spatiality is the use of romantic irony, or the deliberate destruction of the illusion that the art work is a self-contained reality system. We propose to exhibit the two types of spatial unity—closed and open—as they interact in *Ulysses.*

Worringer's analysis of the process of abstraction contains the notion of closedness, as in a closed shape with boundaries, from which he draws the following implications. Abstraction has its psychological root in "an immense spiritual dread of space." For the primitive artist, space is the element linking all things together in the flux of temporality and phenomenalism. Since the phenomenal world is a source of fear because of its uncontrollable qualities, the primitive artist desires to represent things in their absoluteness. Thus in primitive art the aim of the artist

> was not to perceive the natural model in its material individuality, which could have been made possible in practice by walking round it and touching it, but to reproduce it, that is, from fragments of structure and the temporal succession of perceptual moments and their amalgamation, as represented by the purely optical process, to form a whole for the imagination. It is a question of imagination, not of perception. For only in the reproduction of this closed whole of the imagination could man find an approximate substitute for the absolute material individuality of the thing, which is forever beyond his reach.[3]

3. Worringer, *Abstraction and Empathy,* p. 40.

For Worringer abstraction depends on closedness: all facets of the individual object are represented in a closed planimetric whole. Frank draws an analogy between what Worringer says about individual objects and about narrative structure in modern literature. As in primitive art, the modern writer presents his subject as a whole whose unity lies not in temporal relationships but in a closed system of spatial relationships. Dread of space has been replaced by dread of time; the aim of each artist is to reduce the world of objects to a closed temporal whole.

The burdens that spatial form in narrative place on the reader are, of course, very great. James M. Curtis has aptly described the complexity of reflexive references by using an analogy with linguistics.[4] Structural linguists make a distinction between *langue* and *parole,* the one referring to the system of linguistic usage and the other to any given instance of usage. In order to understand any one instance of linguistic usage, the hearer must have the system at his command. Analogously, in narrative literature, the particular *langue* of the narrative, as it were, must be learned by the reader before he can adequately interpret any particular event in the narrative. That is, he must be able to see any event in the context of the narrative as a whole. It would be easy to see the placing of these great burdens on the reader's memory as a kind of dehumanization of narrative art, by requiring an abstract attitude alien to the flow of human life. Narrative events are seen no longer in their temporal, dramatic character but as parts of a total, static pattern. Indeed, a sort of pride on the part of the reader and author may be involved, since this view of narrative events seems to imply their godlike aesthetic distance. This is the position taken recently by William Spanos:

> the critical act begins for the formalist not at the beginning . . . but only after the reading or perceptual process terminates; at the vantage point, that is, from which, like an omniscient god—which, it is worth reminding ourselves, man cannot be, no matter how good his memory is—one sees all its temporal parts at once as a whole, the many and particular as one, thus radically minimizing the sequential dimension and reducing the existential experience.[5]

4. Curtis, "Spatial Form as the Intrinsic Genre of Dostoevsky's Novels," *Modern Fiction Studies,* 18 (1972), 139. See also below, pp. 176–177.

5. Spanos, "Modern Literary Criticism and the Spatialization of Time: An Existential Critique," *Journal of Aesthetics and Art Criticism,* 29 (1970), 89.

Spanos confuses omniscience, which would be a simultaneous grasping of all possible perspectives on something, with the capacity to grasp form and to perceive and organize particulars through and with that form. Perhaps this is godlike, but it is a human capacity also. Moreover, Spanos seems to suppose that the form becomes identical with the particulars it organizes, and this in such a way that the latter not only lose all other properties except the single property of participating in that form, but also somehow cease to be particulars altogether. But the function of the perception of form is not to *replace* particulars but to enrich their significance by revealing *additional* properties, which in the particular case of spatial form means an integrative property. Still, one might sympathize with Spanos's sense of "reduction" and "minimization" for other persons if spatial form were necessarily closed in the sense of *complete* or *finished*. But that is not an essential part of the concept.

Frank feels that the work of James Joyce is saturated with the non-naturalistic impulse. For example, in *Ulysses* the reader identifies with Stephen Dedalus, who impatiently follows William Blake's historical "Daughters of Inspiration" in his quest for truth, rather than Mr. Deasy, Stephen's teaching colleague, who follows his own decaying, sequentially oriented memory in his error-filled recounting of fact. The static universe sought by Stephen is revealed also when he meditates: "I hear the ruin of all space, shattered glass and toppling masonry, and time one livid final flame. What's left us then?"[6] If Stephen is the final judge, the answer seems clear; in Frank's words we have the "linear-geometric" and "cyclical" styles of Joyce, which appear in his later works, the "collideor-scapes" of *Ulysses* and *Finnegans Wake*.

On the other hand, these two works, both replete with specific references to and structural use of the mandala—*nacheinander* (one after another) and *nebeneinander* (one next to another) encircled—demonstrates specifically and effectively what José and Miriam Arguelles call the "mandalic attitude":

> The mandalic attitude is neither egocentric nor necessarily anthropomorphic. Nothing is excluded: everything finds its place and is understood as an integral aspect of the whole process. And because everything is interrelated and derives meaning only through rela-

6. Joyce, *Ulysses* (New York: Vintage, 1961), p. 24.

tionship, things in themselves are seen to be void of any self-nature. The openness is the basis of all things and is at the very center of the Mandala.[7]

Frank and Worringer would presumably call this the non-naturalistic attitude. Yet what is this openness, as described above, if not the realization that a particular is really constituted by its infinitely inexhaustible relationships?

Other bases for openness *within* form also exist. One of them has been described by Sharon Spencer in *Space, Time and Structure in the Modern Novel* in her discussion of open forms.[8] Here a narrative assumes an infinite extension through the use of such techniques as the interior duplication and infinite regression of layers of narrative action which Philip Quarles describes in *Point Counter Point*. These narratives seem, according to Spencer, to spill out into life.

Openness within form can also be achieved by the technique of romantic irony. In his *Critical Miscellanies,* Coleridge, acknowledging his debt to Jean Paul Richter, states that "when we contemplate a finite in reference to the infinite, consciously or unconsciously, humor arises. In humor the little is great, and the great is little, in order to destroy both, because all is equal in contrast with the infinite."[9] Such humorous reduction of finitude, the artist's work included, is called romantic irony; and, while this particular ironic technique has been practiced in Western art from the time of Aristophanes, as well as during Sterne's eighteenth century, the result is the same as the type of modern non-naturalistic art described by Frank and the primitive art analyzed by Worringer: a stasis is achieved.

The reader of a spatial-form narrative cannot perceive the characters or their actions as he does in a traditional narrative—that is, he does not perceive separate, individual characters developing and interacting in a linear time frame, because this linear temporal development is largely missing. Instead, as he grasps the relationships between the parts through reflexive reference, the attentive reader of spatial form begins to perceive a pattern or whole form. The percep-

7. Arguelles, *Mandala* (Berkeley: Shambala Publications, 1972), p. 127.

8. Spencer, *Space, Time and Structure in the Modern Novel* (New York: New York University Press, 1971), chapter 3.

9. Quoted in Arthur Hill Cash, *Sterne's Comedy of Moral Sentiments: The Ethical Dimension of the "Journey"* (Pittsburgh: Duquesne University Press, 1966), p. 20.

tion of spatial form demands that the reader maintain an aesthetic distance from the particulars of the work, so that he may see the whole. Accordingly, spatial form is greatly enhanced by the presence of romantic irony, which enforces this aesthetic distance.

The reader's comprehension of a work of spatial form takes place not on the level of particulars but on the more abstract level of the form itself. That is, the reader is encouraged to identify not as a particular human being with particular characters but as a human mind experiencing a form, such as a square or labyrinth, created by the interaction of fictional beings with one another and with their environment. Furthermore, when romantic irony is employed, the reader is forced, as we shall see, to experience this form as it has been created by another human mind, that of the author.

The technique of romantic irony, traditionally defined as the deliberate destruction of the art work's illusion, involves the reader in a process which, although occurring so swiftly as to be experienced instantaneously, actually consists of three stages. In the first stage of romantic irony, the reader is brought against the presence of the artifice itself when, through the craft of the author, he is forced to face the work as a purely mental creation, a merely fictive entity. Stage two proceeds naturally from stage one as the author, who has mocked himself as a creator by destroying the illusion of his "creation," requires the reader to ponder the absurdity of the artist as a creator-god figure. This stage is a threshold for the third step, the disturbing perception of the coalescence of illusion-reality levels within all existence, the reader's life included. Through the enforced distance from the work achieved in stage one, the reader has confronted the illusion of the work's "reality" in his own mind; in stage three he doubts the boundaries of his own existence as a separate entity, much as he questioned the hitherto hermetic "zone" within which the art work had its "life."

There is a fourth stage, although it does not occur when romantic irony alone is used. This stage relies upon the reader's recalling previously developed leitmotifs. When the fiction within the text is resumed, the reader is drawn back into its illusory "self-containment," although the quality of the experienced text may again be "contained" only momentarily. The flux generated by the seemingly infinite regression of illusion and reality levels becomes unified after a temporary and mystical self-transcendence.

The technique of romantic irony offers attitudes and assumptions that prepare for the appreciation of spatial form. The self-mockery characteristic of works using romantic irony has a philosophical basis, since it is used to place the work in relationship with the universe. "The admission of constant inadequacy . . . is the first proof that humanity does not persist in vain self-reflection but is lifted by means of its spirit beyond the shortcomings of its understanding."[10] Any effort at literary creation is inherently, in this view, an effort limited by the imperfections of the creator. But admission of these limitations frees the work through self-awareness. The goal of romantic irony, therefore, is to enable "humanity to hover free and unfettered over all things in the universe."[11]

The experience romantic irony produces in the reader also clearly reflects the foundation upon which the perception of spatial form itself is based: the comprehension of the whole, in which the unit derives meaning and identity only *through* relationship of other units. In order for the form to be grasped, each unit *must* be seen by the reader in relation to the whole. Through such devices as the mirror effect and the use of autonomous characters who escape the frame of the novel, the romantic ironist forces the reader to question his own divisions between fiction and reality and perhaps his own life as a fictive separate entity. In this case the relationship between reader and work is uppermost. At other times the author addresses the reader directly about the fictional work, a procedure that deflates the work itself as an organic, self-contained "imitation of reality." Whenever the serious nature of the artwork as a separate entity dissolves—or, in terms of the mandalic attitude, when the self-nature of the artwork is denied—the relationship between the author and the reader sharpens through admonitions, "cajoling . . . announcements of what the reader is to expect . . . seemingly angry exhortations about his impatience and bad manners."[12]

A key element of romantic irony is the humor or atmosphere of jest that surfaces in the context of the artwork deflated as a serious self-entity precisely because the relationship has shifted to that of author-reader rather than that of character in context of an illusory

10. Oskar Walzel, *German Romanticism* (New York: Capricorn Books, 1966), p. 43.

11. Ibid., p. 44.

12. Oskar Seidlin, "Laurence Sterne's *Tristram Shandy* and Thomas Mann's *Joseph the Provider*," *Modern Language Quarterly*, 8 (1947), 113.

"world." The pretensions of the finite become visibly incongruous and worthy of mockery. In the act of self-mockery, however, these pretensions are transcended through the obvious humility of the vehicle. It is for this reason that the romantic ironist achieves perhaps the wisest perspective of himself in relationship to the infinite, and through his perspective the reader is brought short, forced to face his own pretensions squarely, only to share, through his perception, in the author's transcendence of individual limitations. Thus the ultimate tranquility achieved by the reader of romantic irony, the ultimate stasis of illumination,[13] is similar to that obtained through the mandalic attitude: the consciousness of book, self, or indeed any individual part or unit, no longer as an enclosed entity but deriving value primarily through relationships with other animate and inanimate inhabitants of the universe. The romantic ironists were clearly pointing beyond the espousal of Romantic individualism or the glorification of the solitary ego. Indeed, the idea in the twentieth century toward which they point is modern ecological consciousness, the sanctity of systems as *wholes*.

II

In *Ulysses* we discover perhaps the finest example of spatial form complemented by romantic irony. Joyce's proposition that we "collide [Mr. Deasy's method] or [e]scape [Stephen's method]" is not final, as these two characters would have us believe. Instead, we too must "pare our fingernails" in our full understanding of art as illusion and art as object. Joyce's use of romantic irony allows us to reach that transcendent position from which we can view the existential buffoonery of Mr. Deasy, the essential foolishness of Stephen Dedalus, and perhaps the equal finitude of our own individuality in relationships with all other temporal and spatial forms, static and dynamic. In "Proteus," the episode following this either/or confrontation, Joyce joins the static concept of closed spatial form and the explosive use of romantic irony. In "Proteus" he first provides an initial closed stasis, then destroys this stasis in an admission of its inadequacy, thus providing a second, open stasis of illumination:

13. The phrase is borrowed from Robert Scholes and Robert Kellogg, *The Nature of Narrative* (New York: Oxford University Press, 1969), p. 235.

His shadow lay over the rocks as he bent, ending. Why not endless till the farthest star? Darkly they are there behind this light, darkness shining in the brightness, delta of Cassiopeia, worlds. He sits there with his augur's rod of ash, in borrowed sandals, by day beside a livid sea, unbeheld, in violet night walking beneath a reign of uncouth stars. I throw this ended shadow from me, manshape ineluctable, call it back. Endless, would it be mine, form of my form? Who watches me here? Who ever anywhere will read these written words? Signs on a white field. Somewhere to someone in your flutiest voice. The good bishop of Cloyne took the veil of the temple out of his shovel hat: veil of space with coloured emblems hatched on its field. Hold hard. Coloured on a flat: yes, that's right. Flat I see, then think distance, near, far, flat I see, east, back. Ah, see now. Falls back suddenly, frozen in stereoscope. Click does the trick. You find my words dark. Darkness is in our souls, do you not think? Flutier. Our souls, shame-wounded by our sins, cling to us yet more, a woman to her lover clinging, the more the more. [p. 48]

As Stephen Dedalus walks along the strand in "Proteus," contemplating the forms of substance, he asks, "Who watches me here?" This initial question, which possibly involves the reader in a direct and immediate perception of himself drawn into the text, is amplified by Stephen's next question: "Who ever anywhere will read these written words? Signs on a white field." Although Stephen refers to words he has written on a table of rock, the full statement awakens the reader to the *fact* of the words on the page before him, also a white field. It isolates these words from the establishment of illusion and by admitting them into an immediate reality admits the contextual inadequacy of the words. The reader suddenly hovers over the situation, freed from the novel's web of fictional and linguistic circumstance.

If this liberated perception moves outward, beyond the one statement, over the entire surface of the novel to the extent that the *fact* of the whole is perceived, the reader is able to isolate the entire work in the fabric of his own circumstance of external reality. The fictional movement is thus halted and a stasis is achieved, a stasis of illumination whereby the reader extends the concept of romantic irony to his own inadequacy. In the same manner that the words have been admitted into the reader's immediate reality and the work as a whole opened to this larger context of external reality, so also is the reader's former integrity as an individual, bound-by-the-skin, now a part of a larger whole.

In this Proteus episode and elsewhere in *Ulysses,* Joyce fractures the illusory movement of his work of art and forces the reader to distance himself. If the ideal or ultimate distance is achieved, the resulting stasis of illumination fulfills Karl W. G. Kumm's notion that spatiality in fiction is essentially religious.[14] In Eugene Timpe's words, the achieved space has "gone off the map."[15] This is the final result when romantic irony is combined with spatial form, and the importance of this larger understanding in relation to general theories of aesthetics and epistemology is without question. But perhaps equally important in the preparation for this ultimate stasis, certainly in relation to the more specific concepts of spatial structures in fiction, are the preliminary means enabling the achievement of the ultimate end by both Joyce and his readers.

First, Joyce firmly establishes in this Proteus scene a fictional frame, much like one cinematic frame in a strip of film. Second, he uses a "sliding perspective"[16] of pronominal shifts from third to first person in order to decrease distance and increase focus, much like the film technique of "zooming" toward an object. These two processes, discussed in more detail below, are the preliminary means by which Joyce freezes his fictional object, and then, through increasing detail and narrowing focus, he suddenly shatters the surface of the work of art; the *fact* emerges and a new ultimate space is achieved.

The initial preliminary product, the frozen frame occupying psychological space outside the flow of narrative, is established through several techniques of spatial structuring. The most obvious and necessary is the fixation of chronology; time and sequence must be halted on all levels to enable minute focus and prevent any possible blurring of this newly erected antithesis to the previously illusory narrative movement. Place must be without ambiguity and must have absolute constancy. Stephen's "shadow lay over the rocks as he bent, ending. Why not endless till the farthest star?" On Sandymount Strand, Stephen moves increasingly within the Platonic

---

14. Kumm, "Michel Butor: A Spatial Imagination" (unpublished Ph.D. diss., University of Washington, 1970).

15. Timpe, "The Spatial Dimension: A Stylistic Typology," in *Patterns of Literary Style,* ed. Joseph Strelka (University Park: Pennsylvania State University Press, 1971), p. 194.

16. Kumm, "Michel Butor," chapter 3.

world of forms, attempting to discover the timeless form of forms, inaccessible to memory and sequential orientation. In Structuralist terminology he is, of course, attempting to dispense with the diachronic or sequential movement of phenomena and to move along the synchronic axis, both simultaneous and vertical, of perception.

The second technique of framing used by Joyce in this scene is that of leitmotif, a spatial device not only giving significance to any event but also clarifying the vertical dimensions or meaning levels of it. Joyce establishes relationships aiding both our awareness of the particularities of the scene and the preparation for the ultimate stasis. As Clive Hart states, leitmotif "functions primarily at the surface level, within the verbal texture. [The reader is] constantly impelled to shift . . . attention from the subject matter . . . to the words themselves."[17]

On the fictional level, with the mind of the particular character occupying the frame, Joyce uses a third spatial technique: a fictional stasis of illumination occurs. Stephen realizes that he, too, as a fictional being and as a character, is formally subject to transformation. As many previous events and thoughts are suddenly drawn together in Stephen's mind and he turns his back to the sun, a halting or frozen effect is achieved; the epiphany, as this technique is conventionally termed, is both genuine and static. Stephen realizes the eternality of form and transformation: "Darkly they are there behind this light, darkness shining in the brightness. . . . I throw this ended shadow from me, manshape ineluctable, call it back" (p. 48).

A fourth technique used by Joyce to establish this preliminary stasis is related to leitmotif but differs from the previous techniques in its philosophical implications. Giordano Bruno's mystical notion of ultimate coincidence can be used in a structural manner to dispel not only ironies but also symbols that might have entered the reader's private response. If the frame is successfully frozen, all things must come together in an absolute manner; the scene must have its own independent integrity. Fictional opposites must coincide, contradictions and ambiguities must disappear, and the scene must begin to assume its own meaning, without any possibility of exotericism. On the preliminary fictional level, it is obvious that Joyce, in this Proteus-based scene, would have provided such a coincidence;

17. Hart, *Structure and Motif in "Finnegans Wake"* (Evanston: Northwestern University Press, 1962), pp. 62, 67.

we will discuss below the idea that authorial destruction of art is of equal necessity in the achievement of ultimate integrity in this scene.

Once Joyce has separated, outlined, and detailed this scene in the reader's mind, the second phase of his spatial presentation begins: the zooming, or use of "sliding perspective." This technique is one of point of view, and it is achieved through a pronominal shift from the third person point of view of the first sentence of the paragraph. "His shadow lay . . ." is an objective depiction of the character of the scene that disappears in the remainder of the paragraph as the presentation shifts to first person, a subjective consideration of the scene by the character. In other words, Joyce moves into Stephen's mind and the attentive reader follows, identifying with the character as the focus on particular internal aspects is intensified. Ironically, however, as the reader loses his own subjectivity in this shift from the objective to the subjective, the reader's perception of particular internal aspects is objectified. If the process is successful—that is, if it is successfully achieved *and* perceived—the reader attains a liberation from former subjective illusions and the author attains a liberation from aesthetic restrictions, created by naturalistic demands imposed by external reality. Both reader and author become free to destroy their own creations.

The preliminary stasis has been established. The character has taken on a life of his own and now becomes complete through the initial framing:

> His shadow lay over the rocks as he bent, ending. Why not endless till the farthest star? Darkly they are there behind this light, darkness shining in the brightness, delta of Cassiopeia, worlds. He sits there with his augur's rod of ash, in borrowed sandals, by day beside a livid sea, unbeheld, in violet night walking beneath a reign of uncouth stars. I throw this ended shadow from me, manshape ineluctable, call it back. Endless, would it be mine, form of my form? Who watches me here? Who ever anywhere will read these written words? Signs on a white field. [p. 48]

He is intensely real because of the use of the first-person point of view; his concerns have become both those of the author and those of the reader. He is the synthesis of artistic achievement and critical perception. This meeting ground, the character, becomes finitude itself, a world complete but inadequate because it remains ultimately an illusion. Yet an antithesis to the illusion exists, and it is the character who must present this opposite. In the Proteus scene, Stephen does this by reminding us of ourselves when he merely admits his own transitoriness and inadequacy. The increasingly detailed and narrowed focus of his fictional world is suddenly shattered by his admission that this firmly established world of his is nothing but illusion; its surface is its all—ink, on a page, "signs on a white field," a fictional closed system, which has as its only basis the fact that its illusory depth is its substance and that its surface is its form.

Joyce's use of romantic irony aids in the creation of a work of absolute integrity. Not only is Mr. Deasy's method of narrative sequence utilized in the creation of chronological verisimilitude, but also Stephen's simultaneous perceptions are carefully outlined to increase the reader's sense of involvement. Both directions, horizontal and vertical, contribute to the firm establishment of illusion so necessary before the full illuminating impact of romantic irony can be felt.

Joyce has committed an act of self-destruction in his Proteus episode. His ultimate transformation of the *Ulysses* world of articulation to the antithetical world of silence beyond has openly engaged his art in the real world of Protean transformation. If the god of transformation, Proteus, is to rule this episode, and if Joyce is truly attempting to create an aesthetic revelation of Protean transformation, then Joyce's direct addressing of the reader through the character is necessary to provide a distanced position outside that fictional world of change from which the reader may view not only the "form" but also the relationship of that "form" to other "forms." In fact, since leitmotif as the prevailing spatial device of *Ulysses* is a technique of Protean transformation, and since similar larger and smaller units of reflexive reference follow the paradigm of Proteus, in no way other than through willful self-destruction could this spatially structured and organically valid work of art achieve ultimate integrity.

II

Spatial Form and Narrative Structure

3

Types of Spatial Structure
in Narrative

David Mickelsen

Although Joseph Frank's term "spatial form" helped focus attention on a previously neglected type of fiction, his 1945 essay and the retrospects here published are only initial statements, lacking the precision required of critical tools. Indeed, he himself calls for critics to begin filling in the details of a theory of literary structures for which he and others have provided only the outline.[1] This chapter proposes to continue the elaboration of varieties of spatial form by examining its structure, thematic focus, verbal texture, pace, and epistemology.

Perhaps because of its imprecision, the term "spatial form" has been used both too much and too little: some critics apply the term in inappropriate contexts, while others ignore it in appropriate ones. Ricardo Gullón, for example, mentions Frank in a 1975 essay otherwise concerned with fictional renderings of physical space and its connotations, even though Frank's generic, structural focus has little in common with space as discussed by Gilbert Durand, Poulet, Bachelard, and others cited by Gullón.[2] By contrast a great many critics have been legitimately talking about (or around) spatial form

1. Frank, "Spatial Form: An Answer to Critics," *Critical Inquiry,* 4 (1977), 251. See below, p. 227.
2. Gullón, "On Space in the Novel," *Critical Inquiry,* 2 (1975), 11–28.

without actually using that label. Unfortunately, this convergence has been obscured by the lack of a common terminology. The following essay will draw upon a spectrum of these critics, most of them writing after Frank in apparent ignorance of his term, to show that some common terminology is necessary.[3]

References to a variety of critics (as well as a variety of primary works) may also help validate the concept of spatial form for critics like Philip Freund, whose judgments are narrowly based on neoclassical concepts of plot. Freund offers this critique of Camus's *The Fall*: "Very short, the narrative is also slow-moving. Our attention is held only by a promise that something interesting will be told us, but that never does occur. Clamence's self-characterizing monologue is repetitive: he makes the same point over and over in variations, some of them clever, but none advancing the action."[4] As I will argue, all the traits Freund criticizes—the replacement of action by characterization, the slow pace, the lack of resolution, even the repetition—are justifiable hallmarks of spatial form.

I

We can begin by looking at the connections between parts of the work. Although episodes are not connected chronologically in spatial form, their order is not unimportant. The early appearance of the goodnight kiss in *Remembrance of Things Past* is qualitatively important in determining the reader's expectations and values. But the tendency in spatial form is for totality as an aggregate of parts to predominate over totality as an ordered, sequential whole. In speaking of his *Roman des Phänotyp* (1949), Gottfried Benn uses an image that aptly describes structures from which chronological sequence

3. Three critical pieces have been particularly useful—one preceding Frank and two others following him: Edwin Muir, *The Structure of the Novel* (London: Hogarth, 1928); Roger Shattuck, *The Banquet Years: The Origins of the Avant Garde in France, 1885 to World War I*, rev. ed. (New York: Random House, 1968): and Reimer Bull, *Bauformen des Erzählens bei Arno Schmidt* (Bonn: Bouvier, 1969). So as not to encumber the text with citations, I have neglected the Structuralist and Post-Structuralist critics already amply covered in other essays, although they, too, are much concerned with synchronic structures. See, for example, Gérard Genette's excellent "Discours du récit," in his *Figures III* (Paris: Seuil, 1972), pp. 67–273. English version: *Narrative Discourse: An Essay in Method*, trans. Jane E. Lewin (Ithaca: Cornell University Press, 1980).

4. Freund, *The Art of Reading the Novel* (New York: Collier, 1965), p. 402.

has been eliminated: "The novel is . . . built like an orange. An orange consists of numerous segments, the individual pieces of fruit, the slices, all alike, all next to one another [*nebeneinander*—Lessing's term], of equal value . . . but they all tend not outward, into space, they tend toward the middle, toward the white, tough stem. . . . This tough stem is the Phenotype, the existential—nothing but it, only it; there is no other relationship between parts."[5] This metaphor—that novels may be orange-structured—correlates fruitfully with spatial form. Spatial-form novels are not carrots, growing cumulatively and without interruption toward a climatic green effusion; rather, they are oranges with a number of similar segments, going nowhere or in circles focused on a single subject (the core).

The orange metaphor implies a lack of development. In this sense, the spatial-form novel is an alternative to the *Bildungsroman*. It offers a *Bild*, a picture; it portrays someone who has *already* developed, who is largely past change. Without development, the narrative's "and then" has atrophied to simply "and." Aristotle insisted on a beginning, middle, and end, but as Roger Shattuck observes, "without causal progression, everything is middle" (p. 347)—the beginning almost random and the conclusion arbitrary. The progress of the narrative, then, involves uncovering a more or less static picture. Reimer Bull uses the idea of particles forming a "field": "The representation of a field replaces a linear, phased sequence with a compound of a number of factors acting simultaneously and contiguously. From the sequence of one after another [*nacheinander*, another of Lessing's terms] comes the reference system of one next to another [*nebeneinander*]" (p. 63).[6] In this light, sequence is of minor importance; a puzzle assembled in various orders still forms the same image.

A very pure example of a novel without appreciable development is Huysmans's *A rebours* (*Against the Grain*, 1884). This novel is built around a single character, des Esseintes. Time is unimportant within segments: little occurs in the actual present, and the narrative oscillates from the eternal present of essays (a timeless world of assertion and speculation), to the unreal present of dreams, to the remembered present of recollection. Nor is there any real plot pro-

5. My translation. The original is quoted by Reinhold Grimm in "Romane des Phänotyp," *Akzente*, 9 (1962), 468.
6. My translation.

gression in des Esseintes's departure from Paris, his worsening illness, and finally his return to Paris. Des Esseintes's decline is certainly a cumulative matter, the result of sensory aggravations, but Huysmans shows his disdain for sustained, causal development by managing the decline in three sudden jumps. Moreover, the decline would happen regardless of the sequence of these aggravations, which are purely additive. Transitions are perfunctory or entirely ignored, and the arrangement of episodes is apparently not governed by a developmental principle. The chapters are blocks that might have been arranged virtually at random without significantly altering the outcome—either for the protagonist or for the reader. The chapters have no *necessary* interrelation; their sole point of tangency is des Esseintes himself.

The result is a kind of "roman à tiroirs," each chapter-*tiroir* of which embodies the inversion and hyperbolic eccentricity of the protagonist. This underlying congruence of episode imaged by the orange conforms to Shattuck's principle of "homogeneous juxtaposition," which stresses the near-identity, not the opposition (as in "heterogeneous juxtaposition"), of parts (Shattuck, p. 338). Erich Auerbach claims that modern writers—and readers, one assumes—are confident "that in any random fragment plucked from the course of a life at any time the totality of its fate is contained and can be portrayed."[7] Although this view may be extreme, it at least acknowledges that in this type of spatial form both the selection of incidents and their distribution tend to be arbitrary: what matters is the composite whole, not the process of arriving at it.

Against the Grain, then, exemplifies in a concrete way all that Benn's orange implies. Although Huysmans takes a single individual as his subject, he does not tell us the story of that individual's life; rather, he tells *about* des Esseintes—moves about him, contributes fragments from his life, especially his mental life. Congruent chapters, each having equivalent importance, result in a portrait, with all the atemporal, static, spatial qualities that "portrait" connotes. *Against the Grain* is an early example of spatial form, and it admirably epitomizes the shift away from the "classic" novel of Balzac and Trollope.

7. Auerbach, *Mimesis: The Representation of Reality in Western Literature,* trans. Willard Trask (Garden City: Doubleday, 1957), p. 484.

II

Maurice Z. Schroder has argued that the *Bildungsroman* offers the quintessential model for the novel;[8] I counter that it is but one subgenre coexisting with several others governed in varying degrees by spatial form. In fact, the *Bildungsroman* and the spatial form novel can be viewed as polar opposites, in that they represent structural extremes: spatial form minimizes the temporal dimension, the *Bildungsroman* (exemplifying all "classic" novels predicated on causality) maximizes it. While reading a novel of education, one may well recall earlier parts of the narrative (to help clarify a character's action, for example); nevertheless, the main impetus is forward, toward the *consequences* of that action, and the concluding maturation, the entry into the world of experience, is paramount. In spatial form, by contrast, forward momentum is minimal; the reader's main task is to project not so much forward ("what happens next") as backward or sideways.

The detective story, even though it retains a strong causal/chronological thread, exhibits the beginnings of spatiality. With every clue the reader must resort to reflexive reference—an attempt to piece together fact and conjecture. Identification of the criminal forces a last, thorough review of the clues and a retrospective reassessment of those who had been suspects. A similar effect operates with the reappearance of Henry Sutpen at the end of *Absalom, Absalom!* in Faulkner's much more complex work and in the trick endings of "Mr. Arcularis" (Aiken), "Occurrence at Owl Creek Bridge" (Bierce), and *Pincher Martin* (Golding).

Spatiality can also be seen in picaresque novels, which are only superficially temporal and linear. Lazarillo's "progress" in time is preeminently a change of place. No alteration is registered in his rudimentary personality (indeed, a *pícaro*—a rogue who succeeds through cunning—by definition does not change), and the events he recounts are crudely juxtaposed rather than knit into a flowing (much less building) narrative. These episodes might even be rearranged without appreciably altering the meaning and effect of the work, for they merely reiterate Lazarillo's cunning while portraying

8. Schroder, "The Novel as Genre," in *The Theory of the Novel,* ed. Philip Stevick (New York: Free Press, 1967), pp. 13–29.

various segments of society. In either case, a static portrait is the result. (This iterative, interchangeable structure also appears in the rhythm of continual defeat which informs Kafka's *The Trial* and *The Castle,* and the lack of temporal referents plants his work even more firmly in the sphere of spatial form.)

A degree of spatiality may be achieved through leitmotifs or extended webs of interrelated images. Like flashbacks, recurring images arrest the reader's forward progress, and they also direct his attention to other, earlier sections of the work.[9] James Curtis has attempted to restrict spatial form to this kind of novel in his articles on *Crime and Punishment* and *War and Peace* (see below, Bibliography). But these works are clearly governed by a strong movement through time—a progression important for the meaning of the works, even if nothing "happens" in them. Although a system of images does establish connections among disparate passages, it largely corroborates the meanings that arise from a sequential reading and certainly does not override that sequence. (A more interesting—and more spatial—case occurs when the image pattern *contradicts* the surface, sequential meaning, as in the counterpoint between the elevated religious imagery in *Story of O* and the increasing debasement of the protagonist.) Again, the effects of this spatializing technique are still relatively minor, even when they are as fully developed as in, say, Mann's "Tonio Kröger." Furthermore, this technique appears—perhaps in subdued form—in nearly any well-written novel from *Don Quixote* on.

Another means of approximating spatial form is the multiple story—for example, *Vanity Fair, War and Peace, Man's Fate, Mrs. Dalloway.*[10] Although these novels retain a linear plot, several juxtaposed story lines (compare Shattuck's "art of juxtaposition," p. 335) force the reader to cope with simultaneous actions, thus eroding temporal progress and replacing it with a more static entity.

9. Genette's "Discours du récit" thoroughly analyzes the effects of "anachronies" and repetitions; see especially the sections "Ordre" (pp. 77–121) and "Fréquence" (pp. 145–182).

10. Muir's description of *Vanity Fair* as a "novel of character" strikingly anticipates Frank's spatial form: it "has no 'hero', no figure who exists to precipitate the action, no very salient plot, no definite action to which everything contributes, no end towards which all things move. The characters are not conceived as parts of the plot; on the contrary they exist independently, and the action is subservient to them. . . . The situations are typical or general, and designed primarily to tell us more about the characters, or to introduce new characters" (pp. 23–24).

Finally, true spatial form appears when chronology is eliminated or at least severely attenuated. For example, the interval of narrated time may be quite short (as in Böll's *The Clown*—two hours), so that change is improbable.[11] A similar case occurs in the internalized and subjective or the speculative and metaphysical narratives (as in Borges's stories) where clock time—or linear time of any kind—is not a factor. Or narrated time may be relatively long (as in *Against the Grain*—two months) but uneventful, without significant change. This unlikely situation, however, is rarely used.

If change and development in time are present, they may be obscured in order to approximate spatial form. The narrative may contain no reference to passing time (perhaps abstracting into a mythical realm of nontime, as in Kafka). In this variety, no system of guideposts orders the narrative, and the reader becomes disoriented. A more common procedure, though, is simply to scramble the time scheme. When Frank says the time flow is halted and spatialized in the county fair scene of *Madame Bovary* (p. 15), he means that the time sequence has been disrupted and, in a modest fashion, concealed. It may be possible to disentangle the time levels (as in *The Death of Artemio Cruz* by Carlos Fuentes), but it would do violence to the work itself—the disorder, after all, is deliberate and has specific effects. Finally, the time scheme can be so refined, so fragmented into discrete particles, that although a linear time frame is retained, the reader loses track of it in the dense, slow, close-up attention to detail. In all these cases, the passage of time from one point to the next is unimportant; the relevant dimension is spatial.

III

Unity was traditionally achieved by unity of action and by a causal (hence chronological) structure, implied, for example, in Aristotle's insistence on necessary connections between episodes. For Shattuck, this kind of organization typifies the "arts of transition": "those works that rely upon clear articulation of the relations be-

---

11. The term "narrated time" (the time covered by the narrative) and its companion, "narrating time" (the time taken to narrate), to be used below, derive from Günther Müller's essay, "Erzählzeit und erzählte Zeit," in *Festschrift für Paul Kluckhohn und Heinrich Schneider* (Tübingen: Mohr, 1948), pp. 195–212. See also A. A. Mendilow, *Time and the Novel* (1952; rpt. New York: Humanities Press, 1965).

tween parts at the places they join: connection at the edges (though
other, inner connections may exist as well). It means one event, one
sensation, one thing at a time . . ." (p. 332). But picaresque novels
virtually discard causal structure, multistrand novels discard unity of
action, and spatial form discards even chronological structure, moving toward what Shattuck calls "simultanism." Then what unifies?
This question is posed by such seemingly chaotic works as "In the
Heart of the Heart of the Country" by William Gass. To establish the
organizing framework, we need to elaborate Frank's claim that in
spatial form "syntactical sequence is given up for a structure depending on the perception of relationships between disconnected word-
groups" (p. 12). He does not mention what *kind* of relationship
provides a connection, but in the shift from the diachronic to the
synchronic outlined above, the major unifier left is thematic.

This thematic coherence resulting from related motifs crystallizes
into two kinds of spatial form: portraits of individuals and tableaux
of societies. "The importance of plot," observes Ian Watt, "is in
inverse proportion to that of character."[12] Modern fiction certainly
supports this thesis: the teeming world of nineteenth-century narrative is in the twentieth often narrowed to an individual, and the
world becomes an adjunct to or function of that character. To allow
a full and undistracted exploration of the protagonist, other characters (hence "action") are eliminated or greatly reduced in importance; action moves inward. The goal is to expose an individual's
complexities, especially the multiple factors resulting in any given
decision or state of mind. Benn's orange image is again strikingly
apt: the narrative moves *around* the protagonist, adding fragments of
information, piecing in the portrait. In the words of Jean Pouillon,
writing at the same time as Frank, "many novels are static in the
sense that the characters don't change; however, their initial presentation is incomplete, and the unfolding role of the narrative is
precisely to complete it."[13] Robert Scholes and Robert Kellogg
agree: "plots began to be developed which were based on rearranging time so that the resolution became not so much a stasis of
concluded action as a stasis of illumination, when the missing pieces

12. Watt, *The Rise of the Novel: Studies in Defoe, Richardson, and Fielding*
(Berkeley and Los Angeles: University of California Press, 1957), p. 279.
13. Pouillon, *Temps et roman* (Paris: Gallimard, 1946), p. 26; my translation. The
following quote is from Scholes and Kellogg, *The Nature of Narrative* (New York:
Oxford University Press, 1966), p. 235.

of the temporal jigsaw puzzle were all finally in place and the *picture* [my emphasis] therefore complete." In these latter-day novels of education, the *reader* is the one being educated. It is not the characters who change, but our knowledge of them (cf. Muir, p. 24).

Exclusive focus on a single individual almost requires extended attention to his thoughts. In effect, spatial-form works of this type become depictions of a state of mind. Robbe-Grillet, for example, has written novels about the experience of jealousy (in *Jealousy*) and confusion (in *The Labyrinth*). Both works encourage an identification of reader with protagonist in such a way that the former *also* feels jealous or confused (again, the reader is "learning"). Robbe-Grillet emphasizes his subjective, internalized bias in relating the work of Alain Resnais to his own: "I saw Resnais' work as an attempt to construct a purely mental space and time—those of dreams, perhaps, or of memory, those of any affective life—without worrying too much about the traditional relations of cause and effect, or about an absolute time sequence in the narrative."[14] A similar subjectivization is manifest in the claustrophobic or undefined settings so common in modern literature (Kafka, Beckett, Borges, and Hedayat, as well as Robbe-Grillet) when we recognize them as externalizations of states of mind. Finally, we can recall the "essay-chapters" of *Against the Grain* on flowers, modern literature, art, which are justified because they describe des Esseintes's preoccupations.

But individual portrait is just one pole of spatial form. It may also offer a picture of a society. Once again, Muir anticipates subsequent theory by marking the genre's boundaries: "The plot of the character novel is expansive . . . the action . . . begins with a single figure, as in *Roderick Random,* or with a nucleus, as in *Vanity Fair,* and expands towards an ideal circumference, which is an image of society" (pp. 59–60). Now *Vanity Fair* is not truly a spatial-form novel, but the expansion identified by Muir is an important one. This broader, social focus seems to reverse Benn's orange image, for he rules out structures that "tend . . . outward, into space."[15] *Manhattan Transfer,* for example, does indeed open outward, en-

14. Robbe-Grillet, "Introduction," *Last Year at Marienbad,* trans. Richard Howard (New York: Grove, 1962), p. 8.
15. This contrast of focus parallels similar polarities advanced by Shattuck (homogeneous and heterogeneous juxtaposition, pp. 337 ff.) and Sharon Spencer

compassing a diverse nucleus of elements. But the orange metaphor
can still serve if we view the core, in these broader schemes, as a
society rather than an individual. Whether the subject is an individual or a group, the procedure is the same: a large number of
congruent segments make up a static whole.

An even more radical retreat from "story" can shift the primary
focus of a narrative beyond portrait or tableau to style—a third
means of unification in spatial form. Unlike the plain style often
associated with the realistic novel, the style of spatial form often
drifts away from closely representational, denotative language. The
exigencies of "story" no longer constrain the author to streamline his
prose; he can indulge in extended imagery, syntactic complication,
word-play, attention to the aural rather than semantic aspects of
language. In Proust's work or in that of Cuban Guillermo Cabrera-
Infante stylistic artistry becomes an attraction in itself.

If style is not the subject of spatial form, it can at least be a means
of spatializing the narrative, a means of dwelling on or in the present
moment by retarding the pace of the novel. Complicated syntax, an
unusual vocabulary, or elaborate imagery all slow the reader's progress. As Dorrit Cohn puts it, "the enlargement through similes of
each minute inner event is the main stylistic feature that imbues the
text with an anti-narrative, nearly stationary quality, making it 'un-
readable' in the ordinary sense of the word."[16] The pace of forward
energy of a work can be gauged by what I shall call the "time ratio,"
that is, the ratio of narrating time (the time taken to narrate) to
narrated time (the time covered by the narrative). Obviously the
ratio will be high if narrated time is low (little happens) or if narrating time is high (what happens is told in great detail). Both cases
occur in spatial form to allow exploration of what Muir calls a
"continuously widening present" (p. 24). The novel is the first genre
with a time mesh fine enough to record everyday life in its moment-
to-moment particularity (Watt, p. 22; see also pp. 191–192). But if
this interest in detail is carried far enough, the pace slows to a crawl

(open and closed forms, pp. 2–3 of *Space, Time and Structure in the Modern Novel*,
New York: New York University Press, 1971).
    16. Cohn, "Psycho-Analogies: A Means for Rendering Consciousness in Fiction,"
in *Probleme des Ezrählens in der Weltliteratur*, ed. Fritz Martini (Stuttgart: Klett,
1971), p. 293. For a discussion of the retarding function of style, see Stephen Ullman,
Style in the French Novel (Cambridge: Cambridge University Press, 1957), and
Jacques Dubois, *Romanciers français de l'instantané au XIXe siècle* (Brussels: Palais
des Académies, 1963).

while the reader is buried in a mass of particulars, seemingly frozen in time. A related means of manipulating narrative to approximate a static present is by fragmenting the narrative. Bull identifies a technique of discontinuity which he calls "the *isolation* of all situations and the *renunciation of narrative formulas of connection* between one situation and another. This renunciation leads to . . . severed momentum [*koupierten Einsatz*]" (p. 31). As a consequence, "the reader becomes disoriented and is forced to concentrate on the identification of new aspects of situation" (p. 32).[17] That is, through discontinuity (juxtaposition), the reader experiences the continuing presentness of events. In this jumbled realm of no-change, the author turns to repetition for coherence, emphasis, and—once again—presentness. Bruce Kawin notes that when a work "begins again," its manifest tense is the present.[18] Repetition, of course, is implicit in Benn's orange image. The same images (in *The Death of Artemio Cruz*), the same ideas (in *The Fall*), or even the same episodes (in Robbe-Grillet) keep returning, building a sense of unity among the fragments while at the same time suggesting that time is not progressing or that it is going in circles. Because of this circularity, spatial-form narratives are only ended, not concluded, since possible increments are infinite. Indeed, a conclusion is unnecessary, since the subject is fixed from the start: in *The Castle*, for example, K.'s story is over the moment he enters the village.

In another sense, though, spatial-form novels are far from resolved. Kafka can again serve as an example. The very fact that K. does not progress means that the questions raised by his situation, especially the implied metaphysical ones, are not solved. The juxtaposition found in spatial form typically involves mutually conflicting elements; especially in "heterogeneous juxtaposition . . . we are surrounded with conflict and contrast and cannot expect to reach a point of rest or understanding in the conventional sense" (Shattuck, p. 337).[19] Nor is a point of rest appropriate, at least within the novel

17. My translation.
18. Kawin, *Telling It Again and Again: Repetition in Literature and Film* (Ithaca: Cornell University Press, 1972), p. 113. See chapter 4 of Robert Humphrey's *Stream of Consciousness in the Modern Novel* (Berkeley and Los Angeles: University of California Press, 1954) for a fuller discussion of unifying devices.
19. In terms of film theory, spatial form can embody either Eisenstein's conception of montage, with discontinuities and conflicts between elements, or Pudovkin's, based on smooth linkages.

proper. Sharon Spencer (and, before her, Robert Adams) holds that closed-form works characteristically present an assertion of belief, whereas those with open form are *explorations* (p. 52).[20] The more open vision of spatial form, it should be evident, imposes added burdens on the reader. The world portrayed is in a sense unfinished (unorganized), requiring the reader's collaboration and involvement, his interpretation. If "exploration" is to be winnowed to "assertion," the reader must do it. Thus the "implied reader," in Wolfgang Iser's phrase, in spatial form is more active, perhaps even more sophisticated, than that implied by most traditional fiction.[21]

IV

The preceding taxonomy can be focused and clarified by applying it to a specific work. For this purpose I have chosen Apuleius's second-century novel, *The Golden Ass.* Although not an absolutely pure example, it shows nevertheless that the subgenre identified in Frank's "Spatial Form in Modern Literature" can be extended to ancient literature as well.[22]

The variety of ways mustered by Apuleius to undercut his ostensible story of man become ass may not be obvious. In fact, the author goes to great lengths to avoid the forward momentum that typifies so many novels. Instead, he utilizes a protatic coherence based on thematic variations: *fortuna,* curiosity, deception, sex, and death.

Interpolated tales are perhaps the most obvious way that Apuleius undermines his story. Lucius's life as an ass is interrupted by more than a dozen stories, varying from brief anecdotes to the elaborate and mannered tale of Cupid and Psyche, which extends over two and a half books. These tales make no pretense of advancing the narrative, of moving us closer to Lucius's return to human form. Even when the stories concern characters who figure directly in the action, their impetus is centrifugal. The stories of Aristomenes, Thely-

20. Adams's work is *Strains of Discord: Studies in Literary Openness* (Ithaca: Cornell University Press, 1958). See also Volker Klotz, *Geschlossene und offene Form im Drama* (Munich: Hanser, 1969).

21. See Iser's *Der Implizite Leser* (Munich: Wilhelm Fink, 1972), translated as *The Implied Reader* (Baltimore: The Johns Hopkins University Press, 1972). See also John Preston, *The Created Self* (New York: Harper and Row, 1970).

22. This analysis of *The Golden Ass* was prepared in collaboration with my colleague James T. Svendsen of the Department of Languages, University of Utah.

phron, and the thieves all originate in the main sequence, but all move rapidly away from it, establishing their own independent sphere of interest and expectation. Like the interpolated tales, a related device retarding temporal progression is stylistic complexity. Apuleius's diverse diction and convoluted rhetoric (especially ekphrasis) constantly delight and bewilder the reader and retard his progress through the narrative.

While diversionary material and complex style certainly undermine the momentum of the narrative, Apuleius blurs the sequence in other, less obvious ways as well. Although the narrative is ostensibly a retrospective account, the reader is confined almost exclusively to the perspective of the experiencing self. The functional moment is "now," not "then," and this gain in immediacy is necessarily accompanied by a loss in coherence: the narrator and the reader are too immersed in particulars to grasp their organization and direction. The account is less controlled and organized than a truly retrospective narrative, which benefits from the selectivity and clearer judgment of hindsight.

Minimal control is manifest in the casual way episodes are connected. The core episodes in *The Golden Ass* form a relatively unbroken series, but the causal links between them are not emphasized, and the transfer from one to another is neither carefully anticipated nor extensively detailed. Thus when the soldier sells Lucius to the two brothers, the exchange is accomplished in a single sentence. The focus quickly settles into these new circumstances, and we never look back. More significantly, Lucius's condition at any moment is rarely dependent on previous states. Transitions between the adventures of Books VII–X are perfunctory or completely ignored, and the arrangement of episodes is structured more by juxtaposition or parataxis than by temporal progression. The wanderings of the transformed Lucius, like those of his picaresque analogues, are only superficially temporal and linear; his "progress" is little more than a change of place. The concluding reversion to human form is fittingly arbitrary, a sudden halt in the succession of episodic adventures rather than their culmination.

Since Apuleius has foregone the traditional attraction of a continuing story, one must look elsewhere for the primary interest in this work, its main unifying device. Although works of spatial form often present an intensive, atemporal picture of a single character,

Lucius's personality remains superficially presented. Nor is the novel primarily a portrait of society, even though the variety of Lucius's associates and masters ultimately covers a wide spectrum of society. That spectrum is thinly developed, with little depth or detail.

Not a portrait, not a tableau of society, not a linear story, *The Golden Ass* is most meaningfully envisioned as thematically related episodes governed by several dominant foci, especially metamorphosis and curiosity, agglomerated *around* a central situation (a man become an ass ruled by various masters). The paradigmatic pattern centers on a sexual relationship (*voluptas* frequently appearing and denoting several kinds of "delight" or "pleasure") between an older woman and a younger man that often ends in revenge, violence, and death. As with most generalizations, this schema blurs and falsifies, but it does offer an entrée into the novel's submerged coherence.

The concept of spatial form can also help us grasp the literary logic of the problematic abrupt conclusion of *The Golden Ass*. The conclusion of spatial-form novels is very often an arbitrary stopping rather than a true summing up; fatigue, rather than structural fulfillment, imposes an end. The ending is typically "open" (in Robert Adams's sense). Novels with no more than tendencies toward spatial form may be closed, but this closure is abrupt, unprepared. Such is the case with *The Golden Ass*. Lucius's initiation into the rites of Isis provides a sudden, definitive, almost arbitrary break in the potentially endless cycle evident in the preceding ten books. The disparity between the last book of *The Golden Ass* and the preceding ten forces a rereading ("reflexive reference") of the earlier material; the reader is thrust back into the story once more to correlate the work's seemingly discontinuous sections.

The Golden Ass has always proved elusive when subjected to the question of genre. Yet the problem posed by its inclusiveness seems less problematic to readers of the modern novel, especially novels of spatial form, for the concept of spatial form provides a useful framework for the exploration of the novel's narrative structure. Doubtless its contemporary aura results from the modernity of its form as well as its themes.

V

In conclusion, we touch briefly on the epistemological implications of spatial form. Although Frank suggests a retreat from everyday reality ("modern literature has been engaged in transmuting the time world of history into the timeless world of myth," p. 60), in a sense spatial form embodies a more rigorous attachment to that reality. In the schema developed by Scholes and Kellogg, spatial form belongs to the mimetic subcategory of empirical narrative—that is, requiring allegiance to reality. This variety aims for "truth of sensation and environment" and depends on "observation of the present rather than investigation of the past. . . . Its ultimate form is the 'slice of life' " (p. 13). If literature is life structured by organizing selective perspectives, spatial form resorts to a minimum of these organizers in order to render a given "space" with maximum accuracy. Watt notes that "the poverty of the novel's formal conventions seems to be the price it must pay for its realism" (p. 13), but novels of spatial form discard even the minimal conventions of causality and chronology in their quest for realism. Even in real life, clock and calendar time are arbitrary; their regular markings rarely correspond to the variable dynamics of life's values. Refusing this kind of distortion, spatial structures acknowledge that we are not linear in our being. Existence is a complex, multiform totality in which any given element is tangential to countless others. Discarding a causal, linear organization at least moves *toward* an organic conception of life, a life in which events are not so much discernible points on a line as they are random (and often simultaneous) occurrences in a seamless web of experience. In short, spatial form conveys a sense of the scope of life rather than its magnificence or its "length."

It becomes clear, however, that spatial form avoids the distortions arising from linearity only to lapse inevitably into another kind of distortion, also arbitrary and artificial, since linearity is still a vital component of human experience. We see here a literary corollary to Heisenberg's Uncertainty Principle: an author can delineate with precision either the velocity (time) or the position (space) of a subject, but not both. The accuracy of their measurement is inversely proportional, since any gain in one dimension is matched by a loss in the other. The writers I have mentioned in this essay sacrifice the temporal dimension in order to convey an organic, holistic vision of reality.

The twentieth-century ascendance of this vision of the world is paralleled by shifts of interest within that world. Reproducing the empirical dimensions of a physical and social reality became less interesting, less important, than portraying the subjective workings of individual minds. This new focus, in turn, required other fictional forms. As Robbe-Grillet argues in *For a New Novel,* the novel of Balzac is an inadequate, even irrelevant vehicle for representing post-Freudian reality (see "A Future for the Novel" and "On Several Obsolete Notions"). Its linear structure, external point of view, and empirical orientation all impede an exploration of a state of mind. This problem, plus the post-Romantic demand for originality, led to a departure from the realistic novel: spatial form.[23]

This generalized, theoretical overview has dealt with tendencies. An absolutely pure example of spatial form—from which time is completely absent and whose order is totally arbitrary—probably exists only as a gleam in a critic's eye. Most works mentioned here are "spatial-ish"—exhibiting a tendency toward spatial form. Although the roots of spatial form extend back to the Roman period, most of my examples have been drawn from the twentieth century. Not that spatial tendencies are manifest in all of the best works of this century (cf. Solzhenitsyn, Achebe, Carpentier), but the concept certainly does help us appreciate what is new in modern fiction. Stendhal's formula, "The novel: a mirror carried along a road," images the structure and content of the nineteenth-century novel.[24] That kind of novel mirrors the physical details of environment within a continuous, progressive, linear structure. But with the advent of Proust, Kafka, Joyce, and Woolf, the mirror stops moving and turns inward. A discrete subgenre of fiction gains prominence after 1910, one that has an identifiable structure and subject matter. It focuses closely on a single individual or an aspect of society and does so by dwelling statically on the present. The nonchronological juxtaposition of elements is not ultimately resolved, perhaps because no absolute conclusion is possible. Instead, the reader is confronted with an open-ended array of thematically interrelated factors he must weld into a picture— into a "spatial form."[25]

23. A fuller treatment of the broad cultural analogies to literary modes has been developed by William Holtz in "Spatial Form in Modern Literature: A Reconsideration," *Critical Inquiry,* 4 (1977), 271–283.

24. Stendhal, *Le rouge et le noir* (Paris: Garnier, 1960), p. 76; my translation.

25. My thanks to colleagues who read earlier versions of this essay: John Nelson, Michael Rudick, Gerhard Knapp, and, especially, Vicki Mickelsen.

4

Spatial Form and Plot

Eric S. Rabkin

To speak of the "spatial form" of a plot is to speak metaphorically. A plot, as actualized, must occur through time in the mind of a reader. H. G. Wells's Time Traveller justifies his invention of a time machine by asserting that "There is no difference between Time and any of the three dimensions of Space except that our consciousness moves along it."[1] This difference, however, is crucial for understanding the perception of narrative precisely because that perception involves the movement of our consciousness. In one sense of the term "plot," this movement is definitive. Joseph Frank's justly famous essay "Spatial Form in Modern Literature" importantly pointed out that many modern narrative techniques *tend to spatialize* our understanding of narrative; we perceive *Ulysses* much more structurally than we perceive a typical romance. But "structure" need not be thought of as spatial only. When Sharon Spencer[2] creates the category of "architectonic novel," which achieves purely spatial form by virtue of the strange yet stable perspective of a narrative character, she reduces the progress and playfulness of *The Tin Drum* to a

---

1. Wells, *The Time Machine*, chapter 1.
2. Spencer, *Space, Time and Structure in the Modern Novel* (New York: New York University Press, 1971).

sculptural exploration of Oskar's unique ontology. This reduction flows from the acceptance of a critical metaphor as literal description and ignores the temporal—diachronic—experience of the text. I would like to argue that all reading of narrative is both diachronic and synchronic, and that all narratives have always played on both perceptual modes. To do this, I would like to recall the Russian Formalist definition of plot and show how it can be reinterpreted to elucidate both the diachronic and synchronic aspects of our oldest forms of narrative (using the fairy tale and the romance as examples), and then show how this reinterpretation of plot can be expanded first to discuss modern plots and then, more closely, modern rhetorical and narrative strategies. This will, I hope, recall the metaphorical nature of the "tendency to spatialize" and simultaneously expand the power of this metaphor to offer us insights into the development of narrative and the structure of particular narratives.

In his excellent essay "Art as Technique," Victor Shklovsky argued that "art exists that one may recover the sensation of life; it exists to make one feel things, to make the stone *stony*."[3] He assumes—and this assumption is not valid in all cases—that objects, emotions, events become "familiar" and in so doing disappear as individuals, existing only as schemata to which we respond automatically. We stop at red lights, but do we notice whether the device itself is orange or green or black? We may be able to walk safely through our studies blindfolded, but do we feel the spring of the carpet or note the habitual smell of the air? If, in a narrative, one reads that a character picks up a stone, we are not aware of the weight and solidity of that stone. But by writing "weight and solidity" we not only highlight certain properties that a stone may have but also force the reader to spend three more words' worth of reading time in his perception of the stone. The simple word "stone" is *familiar*; the expression "makes the stone *stony*" *defamiliarizes* the stone and heightens our perceptions of it. Shklovsky goes on to argue that all "artfulness" resides in the techniques of defamiliarization and that "art is a way of experiencing the artfulness of an object." We should note, as Shklovsky does not, that the particular device he

3. Shklovsky, "Art as Technique," in *Russian Formalist Criticism: Four Essays,* trans. Lee T. Lemon and Marion J. Reis (Lincoln: University of Nebraska Press, 1965), p. 12.

exemplifies for defamiliarization prevents in one sense the forward diachronic progress of the narrative; the stone is made stony here by a synchronic accretion of reading time and reported qualities. Novels in general use three different modes of report: narration, dialogue, and description. Understanding that even with a given mode, such as the description of a stone, the relation between the diachronic flow of language and the synchronic focus of attention can be manipulated, we can still note that in general narration reports occurrences in a reading time considerably less than actual time ("He ran all the way home."), dialogue reports occurrences in a reading time roughly congruent with actual time ("How are you?" "Fine."), and description reports occurrences in a reading time considerably greater than actual time ("The stone weighed heavily in his hand, clammy yet deeply textured, the solidity of its feel somehow incompatible with the delicacy of its silver veining."). Thus with the interweaving of narration, dialogue, and description a narrative not only defamiliarizes what it reports but guides the reader's consciousness through rhythms of correspondence between reading time and actual time. As long as we do not stay *entirely* in one mode—and we never do—these rhythms adjust the movement of our consciousness so that unconsciously at least we more or less approach synchronicity, depending on the particular techniques—but we never achieve it. Spatial form may be thought of as a tendency, but in ordinary languages it is never fully achieved.

Considering plot specifically, Shklovsky begins by postulating "story" as the chronological/causal sequence of events that underlies a narration.[4] "Plot" is defamiliarized "story." He is here concerned with events per se, and he notes cogently that plot in a given narrative may well present them in some order other than those of story. Let us construct a typical romance which will be useful to us here and later in this discussion: A: boy meets girl in the spring; B: boy and girl are in love in the summer; C: an obstacle prevents the consummation of this love in the fall; D: boy undergoes tests/trials/penance in the winter; E: boy and girl consummate their love in the spring. We can easily imagine a narrative, told from the point of view of the boy suffering in the winter in which he first establishes his temporal locale (D1), then bemoans the nature of the obstacle

4. Shklovsky, "Sterne's *Tristram Shandy*: Stylistic Commentary," ibid., pp. 27–34.

(C), but reminds himself of the girl (A) and how much her love means to him (B) so that he in effect steels himself to complete his trial (D2), hence wins her in the end (E). This "plot" (D1-C-A-B-D2-E) is a clear defamiliarization of the normal "story" (A-B-C-D-E). All of us have undergone the structure of the "story" involved here: something (or someone) attracts our interest, it becomes important to us, we consider possessing it with a combination of hope and fear, and finally our desires succeed (or fail). The progress of Eros (which underlies the oldest romances, such as Greek New Comedy) is a familiar diachronic structure; hence, by *defamiliarizing* the familiar structure (story), plot makes us "feel things."

A number of points need to be made here. First, as soon as the boy begins to narrate his situation in the plot, we begin to hypothesize the story that underlies that plot. Frank Kermode has treated this constructive process quite generally, beginning with an analysis of eschatological thought, as a universal need for *The Sense of an Ending*. More specifically for narrative, E. D. Hirsch, Jr.,[5] has described the way in which the reading process begins with an attempt by the reader to fit what he reads into a genre; this attempt is corrected (often merely refined) as the text proceeds. Both these formulations reveal the reader's effort—diachronically—to construct a synchronic context within which to make sense of the words he is reading diachronically. Thus the apprehension of plot always has a synchronic component, and synchronic phenomena, of course, can always be metaphorically represented by spatial constructs. These constructs, however, represent not the plot, which is actual only in the diachronic reading, but the (changing) constructs of underlying story, the familiar which the text defamiliarizes.

Second, the plot need not itself change the temporal sequence of story in order to defamiliarize story. In *Daphnis and Chloe,* for example, Longus uses the device of alternating chapters. Daphnis is discovered as an abandoned infant with royal tokens in the first chapter; Chloe is similarly discovered in the second. It is obvious from the convention of royal tokens that these characters will grow up to be beautiful, fall in love, meet some obstacles, and finally marry. The text ultimately confirms this. But along the way, atten-

5. Hirsch, *Validity in Interpretation* (New Haven: Yale University Press, 1967), chapter 3.

tion shifts back and forth from chapter to chapter, first to Daphnis and then to Chloe, thus forcing the reader to suspend—make unchanging, hence synchronic—his reading from one character's point of view while he attends to the parallel development from the other character's point of view. This suspension is a technique of defamiliarization quite as important as the reordering of the events themselves. In Longus, indeed, the only event out of sequence is the penultimate confirmation of the infants' royal births. Thus Shklovsky's notion of plot as defamiliarized story needs to be extended from the mere (though common) reordering of sequence to *any* technique of defamiliarization.

This brings us to a third point. Shklovsky's discussion rests on the notion of the familiar story as a causally ordered sequence of events. Events, however, are susceptible to two important considerations: they are ill-defined and they are finally inseparable from the rest of the text. Consider the definition of an event. When did World War II end? From the standpoint of many Americans, it ended with the signing of the Armistice with Japan; but from the standpoint of the occupied Japanese, and from the standpoint of the occupying soldiers, perhaps it didn't end until the end of occupation years later. From the standpoint of the Koreans, the current state of national division might well be seen as an extension of World War II, hence Viet Nam was only another battle in an extended global conflict. Our courts continue to trouble over the definition of death. And soap operas make it clear that love affairs may have no boundaries whatsoever. An event is a separable item for attention only after we characterize the point of view of the attending individual.

To see events as defined only in terms of point of view shows how inextricably plot is bound up with all the features of a narration. In *A Death in the Family,* James Agee gives us the "death" of the father quite early; but the "plot" of this meditative novel really involves the developing reactions of the family members, especially the son, to the possibility and actuality of that death. "Plot," then, is a term which we must always remember reflects a reader's *focus* of attention, not some objectively definable series of isolatable events. This realization is a radical extension of the Formalist notion of plot into a means for considering the general effects of defamiliarizing techniques.

A simple example may help make this point about focus clearer. The Eskimo folktale "How Crane Got His Blue Eyes"[6] is apparently a bare-bones narrative, in this case an explanatory myth. Crane flies from the tundra to a place he knows of where berries grow. He leaves his eyes on a stump, instructing them to be watchful, and goes to eat some berries.

> Crane: "Eyes, you watch for me. If you see anything coming, call me. I will not go far away." Eyes: "Yes, Master, I will watch for you." Crane went fast to get to the berries. He ate some of the sweet, juicy berries. Then Crane's eyes began calling him. Eyes: "Master, Master, I see something coming this way. Please hurry, Master, before it gets me."

Crane returns, inserts his eyes, sees nothing and chides Eyes for calling him. Three times this sequence occurs, and on the last when Crane returns the Eyes have gone. He then tries to find substitutes. Blackberries and cranberries are unsuitable, but blueberries made "everything . . . so very pretty." "That is how Crane got his blue eyes." End of tale. What are the plot events here? If one considers that the notion "explanatory myth" exhausts the tale, then the events are the taking out of Eyes, the thrice repeated sequence of eating berries and return to Eyes, the thrice repeated attempts to replace Eyes. I would argue, however, that this is a moral tale. Notice that Crane's gluttony is part of his minimal characterization: "Crane went *fast* to get to the berries." The berries are not merely berries, but are made berry-ish: "He ate some of the *sweet, juicy* berries." Just as a shift in temporal rhythm makes the stone stony, the arrest of actual time to dwell on the succulence of the berries defamiliarizes them and makes us more clearly perceive their attraction. This attraction—in nature—has motivated Crane's unnatural act, the removal of his eyes. Similarly, the tripled exposition causes an accretion of synchronic weight for the events of the moral tale that might better be read as "Crane unnaturally removes his eyes to indulge in nature's gifts gluttonously; he loses his eyes; nature supplies him with new eyes, but eyes that mark him forever." Moral: live in a moderate harmony with nature. The sight of a blue-eyed Crane should remind the child listener of this unspoken moral.

6. Gladys Fancher as told by Maggie Lind, in *Tales of Eskimo Alaska*, ed. O. W. Frost (Anchorage: Alaska Methodist University Press, 1971), pp. 23–26.

In the reading of this tale, then, we see that the definition of events depends on the point of view of the moralist teller, not the more usually described events seen by some hypothetical disinterested observer. The events of this folktale constitute a plot—which is sequenced in precisely the same way as its underlying story—because narrative point of view has operated. The repetition of occurrences and the attenuation of description combine to give synchronic weight to certain features which the diachronic story might—or might not—display. Thus we see that plot is useful as a critical abstraction, but to see it as a truly separable element of a text is to misapprehend how texts affect us.

To pursue folktale a bit further, Propp has shown in *Morphology of the Folktale* a truly amazing phenomenon: "all fairy tales are of one type in regard to their structure."[7] (His translator notes that the Russian term includes both folktales and fairy tales without distinction.) This conclusion is based on a notion of "function"—that is, what someone or something does, regardless of who does it. For example, "absentation" is an obligatory function (it always occurs), and it occurs whether the hero leaves home or his family abandons him or his mother dies; in all cases, from the hero's point of view, "absentation" has occurred. Propp shows that there are precisely thirty-one functions in folktales and that these may be numbered. Some are obligatory, some may or may not occur, some may be freely trebled, but whichever do occur, they always occur in their numerical order. Propp, in working with oral tales, has thus demonstrated the existence of a highly defined and rather extended familiar diachronic structure. His conclusions have since been tested against tales from non-Russian cultures, and they seem to hold up. (There are minor discrepancies, for example functions that treble in European folktales quadruple in tales of American Indians. This is insignificant for our purposes, since the matter of trebling versus quadrupling does not invalidate the thesis of fixed sequence and since any normal listener to a tale would have access to the narrative assumptions of his own culture.) We can return to plot as more commonly understood by using Propp's conclusions as a starting point.

In the Grimm brothers' version of "The Table, the Ass, and the

---

7. Vladimir Propp, *Morphology of the Folktale*, trans. Laurence Scott (Austin: University of Texas Press, 1968), p. 23.

Stick,"[8] a tailor has three sons and a goat. On succeeding days he sends each son out to graze the goat. Each time the goat asserts to the son that he has had his fill, but each time reports to the tailor that he ate nothing. Each time the tailor thereupon drives out his son. On the fourth day, the tailor has the same experience, shaves the goat's head and drives her out, lamenting the unwise loss of his sons. Each son has a magical adventure through which he wins a magical token: a table that provides unlimited food, an ass that spits gold, and a stick that beats people on command. First the tale turns to the eldest son and reports how he won the table. Thinking that the possession of the table might redeem him with his father, he turns toward home. He stops at an inn, where the landlord sees the value of the table and exchanges it for an ordinary table while the young man sleeps. The son carries this table home, announces its properties, and the father convenes the neighbors for a feast in which, of course, they are disappointed. The second son then has his adventure reported; he, too, has his token exchanged by the landlord, and he, too, disappoints the neighbors. The youngest son then has his adventure, but he realizes that the landlord is not to be trusted, returns home, hears the tales of the other brothers, returns to the inn and has his stick beat the landlord until he returns the other tokens. The neighbors are feasted and enriched, and the family rejoined. "But what became of the goat?" the tale asks. "She felt so ashamed of her bald head that she ran into a fox's hole." The fox returns and is frightened by her glowing eyes so he runs away. He meets a bear, tells him his story, and the bear investigates but is also frightened away. Together they meet a bee who flies in, stings the goat viciously on the head, and the goat runs off. The last line of the tale: "and to this hour no one knows where she ran to."

Although this is a rich tale worthy of much discussion, let us concentrate on its plot as that term would normally be understood. We have here a perfectly ordinary Proppian tale of a father and three sons; in addition, we have a second ordinary Proppian tale of a goat. The first tale begins and is manifested in a triple display. This is interrupted in order to get three linear Proppian stories of three brothers, each tale itself suspended just before reinstatement and all three reinstatements occurring simultaneously with the youngest

8. Jakob and Wilhelm Grimm, *Household Stories,* trans. Lucy Crane (New York: Dover, 1963), pp. 149–159.

son's success. Then the story of the goat, which had begun as a coda to the first tale, is completed with just retribution exacted through a three-part structure of fox, bear, and bee. The trebling of functions here is very interesting. According to an analysis such as we applied to the Eskimo folktale, the ultimate restitution devolving to the youngest brother reveals one use of the tale in confirming the child's own sense of worth, what Piaget calls "the illusion of central position." In addition, we could do a stylistic analysis, as we did with "sweet, juicy berries," to show how plot adjusts temporal rhythms in order to develop both character and theme. What is most obvious, however, is that trebling itself is not a "free" function, as Propp claims. By having one goat to be fed, rather than three separate tasks (as is so often the case), we find that more reading time is necessarily spent on the sons and less on the goat. Thus the repetition with the sons (one son would do as well, after all—as it does when one hero has three separate tests, succeeding only at the last)—the repetition makes that aspect of overall structure firmer and makes our synchronic hypotheses about the structure clearer than would be our hypotheses about the goat's story. Indeed, since that story has repetition only in its inception and conclusion, it is closer to the familiar Proppian linear structure, hence of less interest. Where the trebling has defamilizarized the sons' stories, we find the tale's emphasis. Thus at this obvious level we can see that techniques of defamiliarization allow us, during the diachronic progress of reading, to construct synchronic hypotheses that focus our attention and align it with a particular point of view. Plot is diachronic, but reading balances this diachronic process with the continual creation of synchronic hypotheses.

Less obviously, we can say firmly that "The Table, the Ass, and the Stick" is a literary tale—using that term as Shklovsky would. Since Propp has taught us that functions must occur in their numerical sequence, and since the embedding and interweaving of tales here clearly suspends (violates) that sequence, the Grimm brothers' version is not oral. And as we well know, Jakob collected transcriptions of tales from his country informants and collated them into an ur-text; then Wilhelm rewrote that text to make it widely readable. What is an event? How did Jakob decide which tales were part of or linked with others? How did Wilhelm decide which wordings would retain the original "essence" presumably captured as a least common denominator by an ur-text? We cannot now learn the answers to these questions, but, by examining plot we can see that the defamiliarizing techniques that make synchronic hypothesizing more important are changes from the familiar Proppian model. Thus structural analysis of plot shows even in these very simple tales that the construction of a spatial representation for the tale only partially explains how the plot shapes events, how the tale *means*. Similar conclusions would follow from a closer stylistic analysis of the particular words and rhetorical devices used, as was clear in the Eskimo case.

To return to romance, then, a spatial, synchronic representation of our boy-and-girl narrative would look like this:

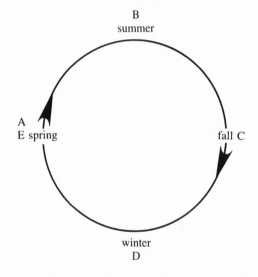

This kind of spatialization has a natural appeal because we are all used to thinking of the cycle of the seasons. It is for this very reason that texts follow such a seasonal variation as a correlate to character interaction, as Frye has pointed out so well.[9] This "representation," however, is in two important senses metaphorical. First, the seasons do not go in circles; we experience them one after the other. That we have all had this experience many times allows us to conceive of our

9. Frye, *Anatomy of Criticism* (Princeton: Princeton University Press, 1957); see "Third Essay: Archetypal Criticism: Theory of Myths."

experience as cyclic, hence allows a synchronic, spatial metaphor to
inform a plot; but that hardly means that seasons really do go in
circles or that books really do end where they began. In fact, quite
the opposite must be true: if a book ended where it began it would
not have accomplished anything, the progress (which might better
be thought of as a spiral) would be a static and uninteresting circle
only. Thus no matter how modern the literature, I would argue,
seeing its form as only spatial reduces the text and makes it impossible to learn how that form is achieved and what it achieves for a
reader.

Second, the diagram is metaphoric in its use of up and down. If
we are interested merely in a circle, we could put spring anywhere
and align the other seasons accordingly. However, if we view
springtime, procreation and warmth time, as good, and summer as
the height of passion, and fall as the falling into death, and winter as
the depth of despair, and spring again as a resurrection, then the
diagram represents not so much the structure of a tale as the structure
the tale validates for us about the meaning of natural phenomena.
That Daphnis and Chloe end in the spring with royal consummation
merely validates the rightness of a natural mating by class and destiny; the romance is not just a manifestation of the experience of
Eros but a confirmation of the possibility of order. Seen this way,
the "synchronic" diagram is not synchronic at all, but diachronic and
not at all indicative of Longus's text unless we know where to begin
the circle and in what direction to go. Those are diachronic facts.
Hence, the "spatial" representation might better be drawn thus:

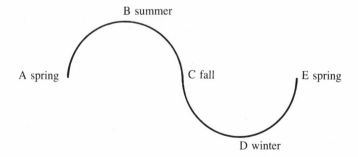

Allowing a sinusoidal curve to supplant the circle has the effect of
keeping the diachronicity of the text before us.

However, as I have argued, all reading is both diachronic and synchronic. Though it is wrong to see the circle diagram as spatial, it is equally wrong to rely on the accuracy of the representation of the curve diagram. Though the text has a plot that moves our consciousness along a curve (if one is willing to retain the height metaphors for judgments about the events of the plot), the circle diagram rightly represents our ongoing sense, as we read, of the circular—or at least spiral—story from which the plot is made. By this example we learn that reading—plot as actualized—is both synchronic and diachronic, and also underscore the weakness of the Formalist position: the defamiliarization of story into plot is a matter of *any* narrative technique (such as alternation of chapters) and not the mere reflex of reordering a sequence.

In a much later narrative, Gottfried's *Tristan*, we see how the dialectic between synchronic and diachronic can develop.[10] The tale opens with a lengthy chapter recounting the lives of Tristan's parents, Rivalin and Blancheflor. We see how they have fallen deeply in love and this love is compared at length to a limed bird. Then we see Rivalin, having served his friend King Mark, gravely wounded, and Blancheflor comes to his deathbed after four days of mourning. They are roused to passion and conceive Tristan. Blancheflor lives long enough to die in childbirth, Rivalin long enough to recover and die a glorious battlefield death, again in Mark's service. Tristan, as is well known, grows to take his father's lordship. In service of King Mark he abducts Ysolt, but they accidentally share a love potion. Nonetheless, the bride is delivered to Mark. Years later, having married another woman named Ysolt, Tristan is on his deathbed. He sends for his first love through an emissary instructed to raise a white sail on the returning vessel if Ysolt lives, a black one if she has died. He has his deathbed moved to a promontory overlooking the approach. On the fourth day the ship returns with a white sail flying, but the wife claims it is black and Tristan expires. Ysolt steps ashore, sees her dead lover, lies down with him as Blancheflor had with Rivalin, but instead of conception there follows her demise.

We can see from this summary two ways in which Gottfried balances the diachronic aspects of his text against the synchronic.

10. Gottfried von Strassburg, *Tristan*, trans. A. T. Hatto (Baltimore: Penguin, 1960). I have treated the suspense structure of this work at greater length in *Narrative Suspense: "When Slim Turned Sideways . . ."* (Ann Arbor: University of Michigan Press, 1973), pp. 121–125.

The first chapter (which itself could be analyzed as a traditional romantic circular/sinusoidal plot) gives us a synchronic hypothesis for the structure of the remainder of the book. However, since Tristan's love is one forbidden by his vassalage to Mark, this love must not result in union, resurrection, and birth. The synchronic structure with which we are left at the end of the first chapter is an exact inversion of the synchronic structure we are left with at the end of the whole book. Hence the plot of the book involves the hypothesizing of a story that reverses the story we have just been reminded of, and a diachronic dialectic between that developing inversion and the progress of events. In this development from Longus we see that the writer can expect his audience to have experience not only of the cycle of seasons but of literary texts. In an effort to create a text that will continue to make his audience "feel things," Gottfried has adopted a technique that plays against the familiar synchronic memory his readers would have of a traditional romance, a memory of which he reminds them in his first chapter. As early as the Middle Ages, then, we can see the effort to make art functional for a contemporary audience expressing itself in techniques that demonstrate the *tendency to spatialize*. This expression and the development of new techniques accelerates as the reading public grows and as individual readers have greater access to many texts, a phenomenon to which we will return in the discussion of twentieth-century literature.

The second way in which Gottfried creates a dialectic between the synchronic and diachronic is in his excursus on the limed bird. If love is like a limed bird, it can end only in domestication or death. Since it ended in domestication for Rivalin, it quickly becomes clear that it will end in death for Tristan. But this is not a simple statement. When we see *Romeo and Juliet* for a second or hundredth time, the play retains its power despite our foreknowledge that the lovers will not be able to marry and live. The text—the play—always enforces the hope-against-hope which gives that work its poignancy not only on a hundredth viewing but on a first. Thus the detailed analysis of the text, the plot as actualized, would have to reveal both the synchronic structure resulting in failure (running around the romantic circle backwards)[11] and the synchronic structure

11. That the romantic circle can be used flexibly enough that diverse texts can pick it up at diverse points and run it in either direction is what gives it such heuristic power. This accords well with Joseph Campbell's famous construction of

resulting in success. The diachronic plot is a supremely achieved structure that moves our consciousnesses back and forth between changing versions of these two possibilities, despite the fact that we know which possibility must prevail. In *Tristan* the central metaphor of the limed bird, with its possibility of domestication, and the avatar of that metaphor as a love potion, continually offers us a hope-against-hope that Tristan and Ysolt will marry. Of course, we recognize that a "happy ending" would hardly be happy from an aesthetic point of view and that the plot does not allow anything like free variation between the synchronic possibilities. Thus a full examination of the text would bring us back again to close analysis. But we have already said enough to conclude that the experience of reading *Tristan* cannot be accurately represented by a spatial, synchronic metaphor, notwithstanding the conclusion that *Tristan* exhibits the *tendency* to spatialize inherent in the synchronic focusing of attention enforced by the application and development of narrative technique. Using these conclusions, we can turn our attention to the techniques of more modern literature.

Shklovsky's own comments on "plot" and "style" arise in his discussion of Laurence Sterne's *Tristram Shandy*.[12] Shklovsky is primarily concerned with the famous interruptions of events, such as Uncle Toby's knocking out his pipe, which begins on page 63:

> striking the head of it two or three times upon the nail of his left thumb, as he began his sentence,——I think, says he:——But to enter rightly into my uncle *Toby's* sentiment . . .

and ends on page 99:

> ——What can they be doing, brother? said my father.——I think, replied my uncle *Toby*,——taking, as I told you, his pipe from his mouth, and striking the ashes out of it as he began his sentence;——I think, replied he,——it would not be amiss, brother, if we rung the bell.

Such interruptions, of course, allow Shklovsky to discuss how the insertion of one event within the normally contiguous report of

---

a monomyth underlying all narratives, which he schematizes as a circle (*Hero with a Thousand Faces*, New York: Pantheon Books, 1949, p. 245). A parallel demonstration of the power of prior structures in narrative is John Cawelti's discussion of the simple "formula" underlying Westerns (*Six-Gun Mystique*, Bowling Green: Bowling Green State University Popular Press, 1970).

12. Sterne, *Tristram Shandy*, ed. James A. Work (New York: Odyssey, 1940).

another event reorders the sequence of inferred story and thus creates plot. By our analysis it would have been enough to show the attenuation of the report of the pipe-knocking by devices much less drastic than a thirty-six page digression, to show the operation of point of view in shaping the events of plot. Nonetheless, in this case our conclusions agree with Shklovsky's. In three ways, however, our conclusions point beyond those of the Formalists.

First, we should note that one aspect of Sterne's text is an attempt to create new techniques (of reversal and stylistic insertion) to defamiliarize, hence revive for perception, the same phenomena reported in *Tristan,* an earlier namesake narrative. The famous misnaming of the eldest son Tristram, his circumcision or castration by the window sash, his uncle Toby's revival to love after his war wound by the Widow Wadman, and the flight from Death across Europe all recall and defamiliarize episodes from the medieval romance. Here again we see the historical effort to renew the vitality of literary conventions as a force behind the development of technique, and each new technique functions to adjust the balance between the synchronic (the memory of conventional romance) and the diachronic (reported events) in shaping plot.

Second, Sterne himself was clearly aware that his mode of report manifested the tendency to spatialize, as when Tristram provides his own line diagrams (pages 473–474) of the shape of his "autobiography," diagrams that double back on themselves to create a complex spatial parody of novelistic progress. He then promises to continue henceforward more "excellently" by

going on even thus;

---

which is a line drawn as straight as I could draw it, by a writing-master's ruler, (borrowed for that purpose) turning neither to the right hand or to the left.

We note here, of course, that the attenuation of the promise to draw a straight line by a digression about the "writing-master's ruler," the parenthetical insertion and the description of nondeviation all contribute diachronically to an attenuation that forces the reader to stop and focus on the promise; it is this promise that is the plot event; and thus the "story" of the life, interrupted by the "story" of the telling of the life, is further interrupted by the techniques by which the first interruption is actualized. The synchronic "life story" is heightened in intensity by the diachronic "writing story" that it includes, thus again balancing the synchronic and diachronic, the spatial and temporal, in the movement of the reader's consciousness. This is fitting in a work very much about time.

The third point this brings us to is a simple but important one: although we have been overtly discussing the "events" of "plot," we have covertly been discussing narrative technique, style itself. The first sentence of *Tristram Shandy*, like the first chapter of *Tristan*, offers an analogue for the structure of the whole book.

> I wish either my father or my mother, or indeed both of them, as they were in duty both equally bound to it, had minded what they were about when they begot me; had they duly consider'd how much depended upon what they were then doing;—that not only the production of a rational Being was concern'd in it, but that possibly the happy formation and temperature of his body, perhaps his genius and the very cast of his mind;—and, for aught they knew to the contrary, even the fortunes of his whole house might take their turn from the humours and dispositions which were then uppermost:——Had they duly weighed and considered all this, and proceeded accordingly,——I am verily persuaded I should have made a quite different figure in the world, from that, in which the reader is likely to see me.

This is a parody of a periodic sentence, but a parody retaining the effect of periodicity by holding each clause in suspension synchronically until the whole diachronic structure works its way out and comes crashing down on "me," as does the window sash, Walter's philosophizing, and life in general. Much of this sentence could be called a digression, certainly an attenuation, but the effect of slowing the flow is to strengthen the reader's sense of diachronic structure: a grammatically complete form that begins with "I" and ends with "me." This mirrors the thematic effort of the book, which throughout conjoins Tristram as subject and object. Viewed as a "speech act," as John Searle would, or analyzed according to Kenneth Burke's "dramatistic pentad," this first sentence *is* the first event of the plot, although the first event of the story—as we will learn—is Tristram's conception (which is under question here). The event is a wish by a present narrator and consequently occurs much later in the story than the conception of that narrator. Thus the grammatical structure itself, style, becomes inextricably involved in the way plot presented through time contributes to the development of a spatial sense of story.

In twentieth-century literature the structural device that seems most newly obtrusive is fragmentation. In considering works like Eliot's *The Waste Land,* critics have not only followed Frank's lead to see fragmentation as a spatializing (not spatial) technique but have also pointed out that the fragmentation of twentieth-century literature is an analogue for the felt fragmentation of twentieth-century culture. And this is often true. The term "fragmentation," however, at least in reference to the pipe-knocking episode, may be seen as equivalent to the term "attenuation," which we have used. Attenuation, much more pointedly than fragmentation, indicates the effect of narrative technique in creating diachronically a synchronic suspension. Fragmentation equally creates suspension, however, as we will see later in *The Sound and the Fury.*

Although fragmentation—which leads to so-called "spatial form"—has garnered most of the attention of critics, I would like to suggest that a more common and equally new device of twentieth-century literature is the trick of beginning the narration of an event with pronouns the antecedents of which are unknown to the reader. Consider the first sentence of Hemingway's *A Farewell to Arms*: "In the late summer of *that* year *we* lived in a house in a village that looked across *the* river and *the* plain to *the* mountains" (emphasis mine). Each of the five italicized words functions as a pronoun; however, the reader has no notion whatever of the antecedents of those pronouns. Which year? Who? Which river, plain, mountains? Since this sentence is primarily descriptive, the traditional notion of plot events suggests that no event has yet occurred. However, if we use our notion of event as bound to point of view, this sentence is indeed the first plot event of the novel. In part, for example, it reveals that the narrator's concern with his own problems and situation is so strong that he is careless of the needs of his auditor. This act of carelessness about others in the very first sentence already prepares us for the lonely despair of the novel's final sentence: "After a while I went out and left the hospital and walked back to the hotel in the rain." Thus the first event of the plot flows easily into the last, and we can hypothesize that the romance of Catherine Barkley and Frederick Henry is part of the historical tradition of romance.

However, in order to make romance defamiliar, Hemingway uses a number of devices foreign to Longus. The most obvious is that the romantic circle of the story is intercepted in the winter and runs to the winter with a consequent tragic instead of comic outcome. Less obviously, the device of antecedentless pronouns forces the reader to suspend—for lack of knowledge—any judgments about the description. Does the reader have an antipathy to Switzerland, a dislike for heterosexual relations, a lack of interest in World War I? It hardly matters, because at this point the reader has no way of knowing that he is involved with these things. He must suspend the activity of constructing a synchronic story until more information is supplied. Thus, unlike Gottfried, who reminded his readers of the familiar structure before inverting it, Hemingway takes a more radical approach. The effect of this is to force the reader tentatively to accept the narrator's point of view, at least for a while. The device thus helps foist a value system on the reader. Simultaneously, of course, it creates a new dialectic between story and plot, between the spatial and the temporal.

The notion of a narrator and a reader sharing values is worth elaboration. In *Mimesis* Erich Auerbach compares the styles of the *chansons de geste* and courtly romance (chapters 5 and 6).[13] The latter style he characterizes as "hypotactic." Hypotaxis is the rhetorical tactic of drawing connections between concepts ("Like all men, he did it for love"). Parataxis is the rhetorical tactic of juxtaposition ("He loved her. He killed him"). Without a value context we have great difficulty in ascertaining how we are to take a paratactic statement. Is it to be thought ironic that he killed for love? In the hypotactic situation, the answer is clear. Obviously parataxis is more economical than hypotaxis and thus might represent an aesthetic good. If the author believes that a paratactic statement will not be clear to his audience, however, he must resort to hypotaxis. From this Auerbach reasons that the *chansons,* which are paratactic, must have been thought by their singers to support a value system shared by the audience. Hence, they might well be, as has been surmised, energizing poems recited to embolden the troops on the eve of battle. Courtly romance, however, is hypotactic. From this, Auerbach reasons that these highly literary works present an ideal of behavior that was not fully operative in the value system of the audience. I would like to suggest that Hemingway's device of antecedentless pronouns attempts to foist a value system on the

13. Auerbach, *Mimesis,* trans. Willard R. Trask (Princeton: Princeton University Press, 1953).

reader and that it succeeds, as parataxis does, because that value system is available to the reader. After the Great War, culture may have been fragmented, but the reading public had access to each of those fragments, and Hemingway's failure to make logical connections forces his readers to actualize in their own minds the value system that sees loneliness as a justification for self-indulgence. Indeed, later in the novel the implicit value of the individual prevents any stigma from attaching itself to our view of Henry's military desertion, although in other value contexts we might well view desertion with opprobrium. Hemingway's stylistic trick, which has become a standard of our literature, is a paratactic device for enforcing the reader, despite the fragmentation of his own world, into accepting a coherent value system.

Just as we extended the term "parataxis" to deal with this new rhetorical device, we can extend the stylistic distinction between hypotaxis and parataxis to help us compare plots. Since we have seen the intimate connection between plot and style, this should not be surprising. I would like to suggest that a hypotactic plot is one in which all the causal relations are made clear. Now all stories, as we have been using that term, have clear causal relations by definition, but plots need not. Still, even such radical defamiliarizing techniques as Sterne's pipe-knocking do not obliterate the causal relations of plot. Similarly, simple flashback, devices of framing or story-within-a-story, parallel chapters, authorial intrusion—none of these obliterates causal connection in plot. But we can easily imagine a paratactic plot in which one event is juxtaposed to another without connections being drawn. Such plots most invite the label "spatial."

The Sound and the Fury can be considered in one sense as a four-part plot involving four separate and extended speech acts or plot events from particular points of view. These four events are merely juxtaposed; hence we have a paratactic plot. As with Hemingway, Faulkner foists a value system on us rhetorically, one system for each section; in addition, the parataxis among the parts foists on us a value system that incorporates the whole. In each of the first three sections we are forced to see through the eyes respectively of Benjy, a thirty-three-year-old idiot, of Quentin, an introspective and suicidal adolescent, and of Jason, a mean and self-centered failure at life. In the fourth section we adopt a third-person point of view for which Dilsey, an Earth Mother type, serves as ethical center. Although the events are presented paratactically, our unconscious minds quickly recognize that Caddy is the center of concern for each of the narrating brothers. Each has been moved by her, none has had her, not as mother (Benjy), not as sister/lover (Quentin), and not as dutiful daughter (Jason). Together, paratactically, these three sections force us to assume a value system that seems to exhaust the possibilities of male-female relationships and shows each possibility wanting. Caddy herself has no section; she is mute; we are forced to see from a male point of view. But in the third-person fourth section, Dilsey is very much present. She is regal, she has procreated, she protects and loves her son and has kind words for Caddy. Dilsey seems to represent an alternative to Caddy. But Dilsey does not represent such an alternative for the Compson brothers, because she is not truly a member of their family, because she is clearly not a member of their race, and—as the appendix makes clear—because the white man's sin of slavery has prevented him from every benefiting in a moral sense from blacks. Thus the first three sections, none complete alone, force us to suspend judgments, as did Hemingway's device, until all three come together instantaneously as a single synchronic structure; this structure is paratactically juxtaposed to the fourth section to show the contrast of successful womanly action, but a success inaccessible to the white man. Thus the overall value system foisted on us shows the downfall of the white man because of his sin against the black woman. It is a powerful structure and a powerful novel.

With *Absalom, Absalom!* we most easily fall prey to the seductive metaphor of spatial form. This work, with interracial incest at its ethical center, is told by a series of narrators who are successively farther removed from the evil fountain of this tale—Thomas Sutpen. The paratactic juxtaposition (fragmentation) of narrators has led many critics to suggest that the form of the novel is a series of concentric circles, each representing the totality of understanding of a different narrator, with Sutpen as the silent center (although Grandfather Compson reports some of Sutpen's words—how accurately we do not know). To see the plot of this work as a series of concentric circles, however, is to fall into the same error we discovered in considering the romantic circle. The plot, which concerns the uncovering of truth through layers of report, presents a progress, through the fragmented narrative, from vague legend to near confrontation with the source of evil; then, the evil glimpsed as well as it can be, the consequences of evil are actualized in the narrative world as the old Sutpen place burns down and the plot withdraws Quentin, the second most distant narrator, to his college dormitory room, in which the tale is completed imaginatively by his Canadian roommate, Shrevlin McCannon, the narrator most removed of all in terms of age, locale, and culture. Thus the plot is a progress into and out of evil; the story, which we keep trying to construct as the reading proceeds, is *finally* a series of concentric circles. But this, clearly, does not mean that *Absalom, Absalom!* has a spatial form. The form, which is the experience of the movement of the reader's consciousness, is a dialectic between spatial structures as they are created and more closely come to resemble that circle of stories, and the plot that moves rather more simply in and out.

I conclude, then, that spatial form is a useful metaphor for focusing our attention on the development of narrative techniques. If we understand plot events as observable only through some point of view, then the notion of spatial form directs our attention most specifically to works like Eliot's and Faulkner's in which the ultimate point of view must be foisted on the reader by the parataxis of the text. This parataxis, of which fragmentation is the most obtrusive but not the only manifestation, is common in twentieth-century literature because modern writers felt two needs that could be served by it: first, supporting the tendency to spatialize revitalizes familiar literary forms and, second, the particular spatializing techniques of parataxis (including fragmentation) use the necessary dialectic between the synchronic and diachronic aspects of reading to retrieve a coherent value system for a reader who may well feel himself to be in an incoherent world. The metaphor of spatial form, which arose in response to modern narrative experimentation, can thus help provide us with insights into technical problems throughout literary history.

5

Secondary Illusion:
The Novel and the
Spatial Arts

Joseph Kestner

I

Although the novel is inherently a temporal art form, it has crucial relations with the spatial arts of painting, sculpturing, and architecture. When Thomas Mann observed, in the initial pages of *The Magic Mountain,* "Space . . . possessed and wielded the powers we generally ascribe to time," he was noting a powerful dimension of the spatial form of the novel, its fundamental and pervasive secondary illusion. The foundation of this theory was well expressed by Marcel Proust in *Swann's Way:* "All these things made of the church for me something entirely different from the rest of the town; a building which occupied, so to speak, four dimensions of space— the name of the fourth being Time." If time is the fourth dimension of space, one must examine the relation of the temporal art of the novel to its spatial elements. The inherent temporality of the novel and its linguistic medium, as Gérard Genette observes in his essays "Proustian Palimpsest" and "Space and Language" (*Figures I*) and "Literature and Space" (*Figures II*), cannot suffice to explain completely its artistry: "Language, thought, contemporary art are *spatialized*"; "Language spaces itself so that space, in itself, becomes language, is spoken and written." Even the critical act, Paul de Man argues in *Blindness and Insight,* is spatial: "In describing literature, from the standpoint of the concept of modernity, as the steady fluctuation of an entity away from and toward its own mode of being, we have constantly stressed that this movement does not take place as an actual sequence in time; to represent it as such is merely a metaphor making a sequence out of what occurs in fact as a synchronic juxtaposition." Criticism must therefore consider the spatial elements of the object it seeks to explain. The necessity of accounting for spatial secondary illusion was well expressed by Marcel when he advised Albertine in *The Captive*:

> Do you remember the stone-masons in *Jude the Obscure,* in *The Well-Beloved,* the blocks of stone which the father hews out of the island coming in boats to be piled up in the son's studio where they are turned into statues; in *A Pair of Blue Eyes* the parallelism of the tombs, and also the parallel of the vessel, and the railway coaches containing the lovers and the dead woman; the parallelism between *The Well-Beloved,* where the man is in love with three women, and *A Pair of Blue Eyes* where the woman is in love with three men, and in short all those novels which can be laid one upon another like the vertically piled houses upon the rocky soil of the island.

Here is an early statement of spatial reading by superimposition.[1]

The relation of the temporal art of literature to the spatial arts was noted as early as Aristotle's *Poetics*: "The plot, then, is the first essential of tragedy . . . and character takes the second place. It is much the same in painting; for if an artist were to daub his canvas with the most beautiful colors laid on at random, he would not give the same pleasure as he would by drawing a recognizable portrait in

1. Mann, *The Magic Mountain,* trans. H. T. Lowe-Porter (New York: Modern Library, 1952), p. 4; Proust, *Remembrance of Things Past,* trans. C. K. Scott-Moncrieff, 2 vols. (New York: Random, 1932), I, 46; Genette, *Figures I* (Paris: Seuil, 1966), pp. 101, 108, translation mine; *Figures II* (Paris: Seuil, 1969); de Man, *Blindness and Insight* (New York: Oxford, 1971), p. 163; Proust, *Remembrance,* II, 644.

Concerning superimposition, one should note Tzvetan Todorov's method of finding the "primal plan" of Henry James's stories: "The search for such an invariant factor can only be carried out . . . by superimposing the different works one on the other . . . reading them as if they were a series of transparencies" (in *Structuralism: An Introduction,* ed. David Robey, Oxford: Clarendon, 1973, p. 74). See my reading by a palimpsestic transparency of Joyce in "Virtual Text/Virtual Reader: The Structural Signature Within, Behind, Beyond, Above," *James Joyce Quarterly,* 16 (1979), 27–42, and of Jane Austen in *Jane Austen: Spatial Structure of Thematic Variations* (New York: Humanities Press, 1974).

black and white." Horace in *Ars poetica* made several decisive remarks. In the opening passage of the treatise, Horace noted that both
painters and poets were entitled to liberty (curbed, however, by
discretion, probability, and congruity). Later in the poem occurs the
famous passage: "A poem is like a painting [*ut pictura poesis*]: the
closer you stand to this one the more it will impress you, whereas
you have to stand a good distance from that one; this one demands a
rather dark corner, but that one needs to be seen in full light, and
will stand up to the keen-eyed scrutiny of the art-critic." It is clear
from the complete quotation that in context, as Rensselaer Lee
observed in his *Ut Pictura Poesis,* such a passage is legitimate,
calling for critical flexibility and nondogmatism. In the hands of the
Renaissance critics, however, the phrase became the provocation for
specious theories as much as for serious aesthetic philosophy. In
1695 Dryden wrote his "A Parallel of Poetry and Painting" as a
preface to Du Fresnoy's *De arte graphica.* Calling poetry and painting "the sister arts," Dryden established this association on the basis
of their common objectives of unity, imitation, and controlling
idea.[2]

 The distinction between the temporal arts, like music, dance, and
the novel, and the spatial arts, like painting, sculpture, and
architecture, received elucidation by Lessing. In *Laocoön* (1766),
explicitly in chapter four, he examined the contrast of the bodily
pain expressed by the sculptor and the cry represented by Vergil in
the poetry of the *Aeneid,* concluding: "A review of the reasons here
alleged for the moderation observed by the sculptor of the Laocoon
in the expression of bodily pain, shows them to lie wholly in the
peculiar object of his art and its necessary limitations. Scarce one of
them would be applicable to poetry." In the words of A. A. Mendilow in *Time and the Novel,* Lessing distinguished "between two
categories of art: those based on co-existence in space, and those
based on consecutiveness in time." The essential attribute of the
spatial art is its simultaneity; of the temporal art, its succession. A
further distinction exists in that the temporal arts are irreversible in
essence, while the spatial arts are not inherently irreversible. Thus

 2. Aristotle, *The Poetics,* in *Classical Literary Criticism,* trans. T. S. Dorsch
(Baltimore: Penguin, 1965), p. 40; Horace, *Ars poetica,* ibid., p. 91; Lee, *Ut
Pictura Poesis* (New York: Norton, 1967), p. 5; Dryden, *Essays,* ed. W. P. Ker
(New York: Russell and Russell, 1961), II, 117.

literature in its varied forms—cinema, dance, and especially
music—is temporal, that is, essentially consecutive and irreversible.
Painting, sculpture, and architecture are spatial, in essence simultaneous and reversible: at any one moment, Keats's entire Grecian
urn is present; his nightingale's song or Beethoven's Fifth Sym-
phony, however, are the images of temporality.

As Mendilow indicates, however, Lessing's limitation as an aes-
thetician rests in his acceptance of the logical limitations of the two
forms of art, his belief that the arts achieve their respective best
results by remaining within the confines of their spatial or temporal
essences. Lessing states, for example: "Since painting, because its
signs or means of imitation can be combined only in space, must
relinquish all representations of time, therefore progressive actions,
as such, cannot come within its range." Lessing does not consider
the extra-medial effects by which the spatial arts convey the illusion
of succession, the temporal arts the illusion of simultaneity. Walter
Pater in *The Renaissance,* discussing the School of Giorgione, observes, about limitation: "But although each art has thus its own
specific order of impressions, and an untranslatable charm, while a
just apprehension of the ultimate difference of the arts is the beginning of aesthetic criticism; yet it is noticeable that, in its special
mode of handling its given material, each art may be observed to
pass into the condition of some other art, by what German critics
term an *Anders-streben*—a partial alienation from its own limitations, through which the arts are able, not indeed to supply the place
of each other, but reciprocally to lend each other new forces." Thus
the simultaneity of the spatial arts implies a temporal relation; the
succession of the temporal arts implies a spatial relation. In the
spatial arts, therefore, time is the secondary illusion; in the temporal
arts, like the novel, space is the secondary illusion. The operative
secondary illusion of one art is the primary illusion of the other art.
Spatial form in the novel, in consequence, involves not only structures like figures but also the relation of the novel to the pictorial,
sculptural, and architectural arts that constitute its secondary illusion. The church at Combray, "four dimensions of space—the name
of the fourth being Time," is obviously paradigmatic of the spatiality
of the novel *Remembrance of Things Past.* In his seminal essay
"Spatial Form in Modern Literature," Joseph Frank recognized that
images and word groups, for example, need not rely for meaning on

"temporal relationships" but may use reflexiveness and spatial simultaneity "not . . . in unison with the laws of language"—that is, with the fundamental temporal medium.[3] The principle of secondary illusion may be precisely illustrated. The temporal secondary illusion of pictorial and sculptural art, for instance, is evident in the chronological history recounted on narrative sculptures like the Parthenon frieze, the Arch of Titus, or the Column of Trajan. Rodin's *Burghers of Calais,* by the simultaneous grouping of the six men, contains in reality the successive stages of conviction of each man; Courbet's *Interior of My Studio* presents in simultaneous form the temporal sequences of his life; Donatello's *David* stands on Goliath's head while still holding the stone; Rude's *Marshal Ney* has the hand placed on the scabbard to draw a sword already drawn; Boccioni's *Unique Forms of Continuity in Space* indicates by its name that its subject *is* temporal secondary illusion in sculpture.

In the temporal arts, artists have constantly noticed the spatial illusion and exploited it. Opera composers bring into spatial simultaneity what are in fact sequential compositions: Mozart in *Don Giovanni* quotes "Non più andrai" from *Le Nozze di Figaro;* Wagner echoes *Tristan und Isolde* in *Die Meistersinger.* Puccini in *Il Tabarro* quotes several phrases from *La Bohème.* (The corresponding situation in painting is Manet's Zola, which has his Olympia in it.) Frequently, the composition of musical works has been spatially in reverse: Wagner conceived *Der Ring des Neibelungen* backward, writing the text for *Siegfrieds Tod* (the basis of *Götterdämmerung*) in 1848; the text of *Siegfried* in 1851; for *Die Walküre* and *Das Rheingold* in 1852. The composition of *Lohengrin* was begun with "In fernem Land" from Act III. Wagner's system of motifs in both *Lohengrin* and the *Ring* is the direct result of this conception in reverse. The listener must perceive these works not only as temporal structures but also as spatial musical transparencies, since a motif may be altered from major to minor or may anticipate or recall a

---

3. Lessing, *Laocoön,* trans. Ellen Frothingham (New York: Noonday, 1969), pp. 20, 90; Mendilow, *Time and the Novel* (New York: 1952; rpt. Humanities Press, 1965), pp. 23, 26–28; Pater, *The Renaissance* (Chicago: Academy Press, 1977), pp. 133–134; Frank, "Spatial Form in Modern Literature," *The Widening Gyre: Crisis and Mastery in Modern Literature* (New Brunswick: Rutgers University Press, 1963), pp. 9, 13.

previous theme. Wagner's operas are therefore not only successive but also simultaneous, as motifs not only succeed but also sound through each other. The spatial illusion is made overt in *Der fliegende Holländer* when Senta, after contemplating the Dutchman's portrait, sees this temporal, legendary figure in the flesh. In dance the attitude was inspired by Bologna's *Mercury*, while the basic pattern of the pas de deux, pas, variations, coda, demonstrates spatial reversibility and return. More recently, in Glen Tetley's *Arena* a Rodinesque "Thinker" figure is attacked and destroyed by men who confront one another like the nudes of the Sistine ceiling. The cinema has exploited spatial elements since the time Lumière's films of card players directly suggested Cézanne. The revolutionary cutting of *The Great Train Robbery* for simultaneous effects has yielded to the use of dual projections of separate events on a single screen and to the actual painting in motion of Duchamp and Ray's *Anemic Cinema*.

Like the temporal arts of music, dance, and cinema, the novel has a tradition recognizing its spatial secondary illusion, extending as far back as the ekphrastic painting that generates the tale of *Daphnis and Chloe*. Each of the spatial arts has lent its peculiar properties to the spatial secondary illusion of the novel. Scene, characterization, and functional form derive from the pictorial, sculptural, and architectural spatial arts respectively. From the pictorial art, the novel derives setting and scene, which constitute the third location necessary for any perspective view, as in Balzac's houses, Jane Austen's Sotherton, or Robbe-Grillet's actual map in *Jealousy*. The idea of character embodies sculptural elements against this third location; the novel is the genre of Deucalion's stones. When Donatello steps from behind the *Faun* of Praxiteles in Hawthorne's *The Marble Faun*, he symbolizes the importance of sculptural illusion, particularly vis-à-vis volume and distance, to characterization. The fundamental property of architecture, that it be the form of its function, enters the novel in its attention to rhythm, scale, sequence, and proportion in arranging constituent units of word, sentence, paragraph, volume, and part. For this reason Victor Shklovsky argues that the architecture of chapters in *Little Dorrit* is itself the device of mystery, much more so than the events of the story. Novelists have always acknowledged the importance to their work of the spatial secondary illusion. Henry James, who wrote *The Por-*

trait of a Lady, was a critic of the "house" of fiction; Virginia Woolf records in *A Writer's Diary* her attempt to write "so that one had the sense of reading the two things at the same time"; Joseph Conrad declared his intention was "before all, to make you *see.*" For William Faulkner, "the aim of every artist is to arrest motion," a nontemporal objective compelling exploitation of spatial secondary illusion.[4]

II

The validity of spatial form in the novel becomes apparent when one investigates its pictorial secondary illusion, the function of painting in the novel. In his essay "The Space of the Novel," Michel Butor has observed: "With regard to space, the novel's interest is no less great, its relation to the arts which explore it—to painting in particular—is just as close. At certain moments it not only can but must include them." This inclusion of the pictorial is demonstrated in an early text from the history of the novel, Petronius's *Satyricon*: "I notice you can't pull yourself away from that painting of the Fall of Troy. Well, I'll try and interpret its subject in verse." Susanne

4. Shklovsky, "The Mystery Novel: Dickens's *Little Dorrit,*" in *Readings in Russian Poetics,* ed. Ladislav Matejka and Krystyna Pomorska (Cambridge: MIT Press, 1971), pp. 222–223; James, "Preface" to *The Portrait of a Lady,* in *The Art of the Novel,* ed. R. P. Blackmur (New York: Scribner's, 1962), p. 46; Woolf, *A Writer's Diary* (New York: New American Library, 1953), p. 101; Conrad, "Preface" to *The Nigger of the "Narcissus"* (New York: New American Library, 1962), p. 21; Faulkner, interview with Jean Stein, in *Three Decades of Criticism,* ed. Frederick Hoffman and Olga Vickery (New York: Harcourt, Brace and World, 1960), p. 80.

Important essays on the comparative methodology used in studying literature and the spatial arts include the cautionary essay of René Wellek, "The Parallelism between Literature and the Arts," *English Institute Annual* (New York: Columbia, 1942), pp. 29–63; Mary Gaither, "Literature and the Arts," *Comparative Literature: Method and Perspective,* ed. Newton Stallknecht and Horst Frenz (Carbondale: Southern Illinois University Press, 1971), pp. 183–200; and Ulrich Weisstein, "The Mutual Illumination of the Arts," *Comparative Literature and Literary Theory* (Bloomington: Indiana University Press, 1973), pp. 150–166. Recent studies using such methods include Jean Hagstrum, *The Sister Arts* (Chicago: University of Chicago Press, 1958); Wylie Sypher, *Four Stages of Renaissance Style* (Garden City: Doubleday, 1955), and *Rococo to Cubism in Art and Literature* (New York: Random, 1960); Helmut Hatzfeld, *Literature through Art* (Chapel Hill: University of North Carolina Press, 1969); and Ellen Eve Frank, *Literary Architecture* (Berkeley and Los Angeles: University of California Press, 1979).

Langer states in *Feeling and Form* that scene is the essential quality of painting, "a space opposite the eye and related directly and essentially to the eye." Thus, as signaled by Petronius and implied by Langer, the concept "scene" is a pictorial idea in the theory of the novel. Furthermore, Butor, in his crucial essay "The Book as Object," argues that the book itself is a diptych: "The first characteristic of today's Western book in this respect is its presentation as a diptych: we always see two pages at once, one opposite the other." All books in their physical appearance constitute paintings: "The simultaneous presentation of these two panels makes it possible for the material portrayed on them to spread out, to overflow from one to the next, to fill the entire open surface of the book, so that the lines on one side can correspond to those on the other." Sterne in *Tristram Shandy* employs the book as a diptych in the juxtaposed translation he uses in "Slawkenbergius's Tale." In approaching scene, all narrators are similar to the narrator in *Adam Bede* who notes: "The dairy was certainly worth looking at."[5]

In the theory of the novel, scene may be defined in two ways; first, as setting or place; second, as a moment dramatized in a specific time/place location. Dialogue, which is temporal, therefore is relevant only "in location"—for example, Isabel Archer on the staircase or Natasha Rostóv at the ball or Andrey Bolkonsky at the window. Extending Victor Shklovsky's essay on *Tristram Shandy*, Boris Tomashevsky in his "Thematics" evolved the concept of motifs, which is helpful in appraising the pictorial quality of scene. Tomashevsky distinguishes "bound" and "free" motifs. Bound motifs are those "which cannot be omitted," while "those which may be omitted without disturbing the whole causal-chronological course of events are *free motifs*," he observes. The distinction between story (*histoire*) and plot (*discours*), action and the construction of that action, is quite relevant to the idea of motifs. Bound motifs are crucial to "the actual chronological and causal order of events," which is the story; free motifs "sometimes dominate and determine the construction of the plot." A second dichotomy exists

5. Butor, *Inventory*, ed. Richard Howard, various translators (New York: Simon and Schuster, 1969), pp. 31, 55; Petronius, *The Satyricon*, trans. John Sullivan (Baltimore: Penguin, 1965), p. 97; Langer, *Feeling and Form* (New York: Scribner's, 1953), p. 86; Eliot, *Adam Bede* (New York: Holt, Rinehart and Winston, 1964), p. 82.

between dynamic and static motifs. Free motifs are usually static, including "descriptions of nature, local color, furnishings, the characters, their personalities. . . . The actions and behavior of the main characters are typically dynamic motifs." For Tomashevsky, "dynamic motifs are . . . central to the story and . . . keep it moving; in the plot, on the other hand, static motifs may predominate." Locations or places in a novel, therefore, although they are "descriptive," are a part of the pictorial spatial illusion that may be "bound." For instance, in any text where a title is a place, like *Petersburg, Mansfield Park, The Heart of Midlothian,* or *Howards End,* the scene as a place is bound and dynamic. For this reason, Lubomír Doležel in "Towards a Structural Theory of Content in Prose Fiction" declares: "Scene is an aggregate of dynamic motifs presenting certain constituent features. These features can be of various kinds, such as a certain place of action (setting), a certain time-span of action." The pictorial illusion of scene is evident, since in each of the four motifs involved there is an overtly spatial term: *static* and *free*, *dynamic* and *bound*.[6]

Boris Tomashevsky's theory of motifs has an interesting correlation with the system developed by Heinrich Wölfflin in *Principles of Art History*. Wölfflin saw the progress of painting moving from the linear to the painterly. A linear painting, like a work by Dürer, emphasizes line, with individual objects isolated from one another; the work is closed in that it does not extend beyond the picture space, with a unity based on a multiplicity of individual objects, emphasizing tactile values and representing being. On the other hand, a painterly work, like a Rembrandt canvas, emphasizes the merging of individual objects, emphasizing depth recession rather than the plane; its surface is open, ending beyond the picture space; its unity is composite, with an appeal to the visual rather than tactile, an image of becoming rather than of being. Wölfflin's concepts of "closed" and "open" correspond to Tomashevsky's "bound" and "free," while "being" and "becoming" correspond to "static" and "dynamic." These correspondences reveal the pictorial elements in the Formalists' theory about scene, and this connection between

6. Tomashevsky, "Thematics," in *Russian Formalist Criticism*, trans. Lee Lemon and Marion Reis (Lincoln: University of Nebraska, 1965), pp. 68, 67, 70; Doležel in *Literary Style: A Symposium*, ed. Seymour Chatman (New York: Oxford, 1971), p. 99.

scene and painting has a clear spatial consequence. In his "Boundaries of Narrative," Gérard Genette has observed: "Description, because it lingers over objects and beings considered in their simultaneity and because it envisages the actions themselves as scenes,
seems to suspend the flow of time and to contribute to spreading out
the narrative in space."[7]

The painterly quality of a free and static scene is apparent when the
reader is encouraged to recognize the characters as existing beyond
the canvas or to feel he has entered a picture. In *The Mayor of
Casterbridge,* for example, Henchard and Farfrae "sat stiffly side
by side at the darkening table, like some Tuscan painting of the two
disciples supping at Emmaus; Elizabeth-Jane, being out of the frame
and out of the group, could observe all from afar." Frequently a
character is nearly an embodiment of the pictorial secondary illusion. For example, in Constant's *Adolphe,* the doctor receives a
manuscript chest containing "the portrait of a woman and a notebook
containing the . . . account we are about to read." Both manuscript
and portrait are designated as "documents." A similar instance exists
in *Felix Holt, the Radical,* where both Mrs. Transome and her son
Harold are frequently associated with portraits. Harold is like a
painting by Thomas Lawrence. Mrs. Transome, confronting Jer-
myn, appears thus: "The brilliant smiling young woman above the
mantelpiece seemed to be appearing at the doorway withered and
frosted by many winters."[8] Such a motif is extreme in the ninth
chapter of *Henry Esmond* entitled "The original of the portrait comes
to England." In painterly fashion, static and free conceptions evoke
a space beyond the book/diptych of Michel Butor.

Some elements of the book/diptych, however, are static and
bound, indispensable to the story or actions, like the portrait in *The
Picture of Dorian Gray.* In that text the portrait of Dorian Gray,

---

7. Wölfflin, *Principles of Art History,* trans. M.D. Hottinger (New York: Dover,
1950), pp. 14–16; Genette, "Boundaries of Narrative," trans. Ann Levonas, *New
Literary History,* 8 (1976), 7. It is compelling that V. N. Volosinov in *Marxism and
the Philosophy of Language,* trans. Ladislav Matejka and I. R. Titunik (London:
Seminar Press, 1973), p. 120, uses Wölfflin's "linear" category to discuss reported
speech in the novel.

8. Hardy, *The Mayor of Casterbridge* (New York: Holt, Rinehart and Winston,
1964), p. 183; Benjamin Constant, *Adolphe,* trans. Carl Wildman (New York: New
American Library, 1959), p. 32; George Eliot, *Felix Holt, the Radical* (New York:
Dutton, 1966), pp. 411, 367.

although a descriptive element, is nevertheless bound, for the dé-
nouement could not occur without it; similar to this is Colonel
Pyncheon's picture in *The House of Seven Gables*. In *The Sentimental Education,* Flaubert uses static but bound motifs when, for
example, the narrator surveys a soirée. Genette notes that these
"interruptions" are specifically spatial, for they become part of "the
extra-temporal character" of Flaubert's novels. The depiction of the
mob in the throne room during the 1848 Revolution is a literal
canvas by Delacroix, The Death of Sardanapalus. In addition, a
static but bound scene may also achieve a different painterly effect,
locating every object in the totality of the scenic surface. George
Eliot in *Adam Bede,* for instance, uses this technique extensively.
When she writes, "Evidently that gate is never opened," one is
decidedly in a scene of recessed depth, indicated above all by "that"
and the sentences following: "It would be easy enough, by the aid of
nicks in the stone pillars, to climb over the brick wall with its
smooth stone coping; but by putting our eyes close to the rusty bars
of the gate, we can see the house well enough, and all but the very
corners of the grassy enclosure." There is a shift to a constant
present tense: "It is a very fine old place." Because of its ethical
emphasis, however, the scene is bound: "The house must be inhabited, and we will see by whom; for imagination is a licensed trespasser: it has no fear of dogs, but may climb over walls and peep in
at windows with impunity. Put your face to one of the glasspanes in
the righthand window: what do you see?"[9] There follows the ethical-
thematic description of Mrs. Poyser's kitchen. Here the function of
scene as pictorial secondary illusion is preeminently to accommo-
date the "licensed trespasser."

There is a highly specialized form of this pictorial illusion in the
frame narrative. Michel Butor in "The Space of the Novel" recog-
nizes this aspect of the pictorial secondary illusion. "Planting his
easel or his camera at one of the points of the space evoked, the
novelist will discover all the problems of framing, of composition,
and of perspective encountered by the painter," he observes. In *The
Theory of Prose,* Victor Shklovsky probed the importance of *encadrement* or framing. This framing not only emphasizes the spatial-
pictorial quality of the plot (in Tomashevsky's sense) but also func-

9. Genette, "The Silences of Flaubert," *Figures II,* p. 238, translation mine;
Eliot, *Adam Bede,* pp. 69–70.

tions in another spatial manner, as a "delay." Framing is a specific device of retardation of the narrative, a spatial practice opposing the temporal movement of the narrative. Shklovsky declares that in the *Decameron* this framing constitutes the delay, which serves two purposes: first, it eclipses the time during the plague; second, it is the catalyst of the narrative itself, simultaneously producing and retarding. Pursuing Shklovsky's idea, Tzvetan Todorov in "The Categories of Literary Narrative," calling this *enchâssement*, discusses one method of structuring the *discours* of a novel, by the enclosure of one story within another, a motif both bound and dynamic. "The inclusion of one story inside another" becomes not so much an element of narrative as of narration.[10] In its origin, such as in the tale of "Cupid and Psyche" from *The Golden Ass* or the digressive tales of *Joseph Andrews* or *Tom Jones,* these narratives remain free, but the bound function emerges in a work like Prévost's *Manon Lescaut,* where the narrator recounts the circumstances of the narration before Des Grieux speaks.

Spatial *encadrement* by the recessed narrative is often crucial to the *discours* by producing delay or *ralentissement.* An example of "delay" for the purpose of mystery exists in Maturin's *Melmoth the Wanderer* (Figure 1).

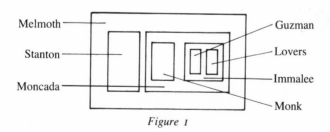

Melmoth — Guzman
Stanton — Lovers
— Immalee
Moncada — Monk

Figure 1

In this example, the enclosed structure serves several purposes. The extreme recession of the stories of Guzman, the Lovers, or of Im-

10. Butor, *Inventory,* p. 34; Shklovsky, *The Theory of Prose,* trans. Guy Verret (Lausanne: L'Age d'Homme, 1973), pp. 53–72, 101; Todorov, "The Categories of Literary Narrative," trans. Joseph Kestner, *Papers on Language and Literature,* 16 (1980), 22. On the nature of narrative enclosure, one should note Jean Ricardou's "L'histoire dans l'histoire" from *Problèmes du nouveau roman* (Paris: Seuil, 1967), pp. 171–190, where he develops the idea of the *mise en abyme;* my translation of this essay is forthcoming in the *James Joyce Quarterly.*

malee is a device delaying the accounts of Melmoth or Moncada while at the same time exposing Moncada. This structural claustrophobia creates terror because of the delayed certainty of the protagonists to be involved in the horrors: they are incapable of escape.

A striking instance of narrative retardation through pictorial framing serving specific thematic ends exists in Mary Shelley's *Frankenstein*, a text about the Narcissus complex. Victor Frankenstein's evident longing for another, despite his close friendship with Henry Clerval and his betrothal to Elizabeth, leads to the creation of a being who becomes the narcissistic Inadequate Other that is in reality Victor himself. Gérard Genette argues in his "The Narcissus Complex": "In itself, the reflection is an equivocal theme: the reflection is a double, that is to say at the same time an *other* and a *same*." In narcissism, he continues, "the Self is confirmed, but under the species of the Other: the mirror image is a perfect symbol of alienation."[11] The structural equivalent for this double, this mirrored narcissistic Other, is the framed narrative *Frankenstein* (Figure 2).

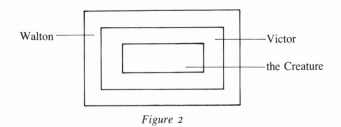

Figure 2

Many purposes are served by the spatial pictorial illusion. Mary Shelley finds a structural corollary for her narcissistic tale in the use of three embedded narratives. The first, which serves as the "outer frame," is a series of four letters from the Arctic explorer Robert Walton to his sister Margaret Saville in England. When Frankenstein strays to Walton's ice-bound ship, he recounts to Walton, chapters one through ten, his story of the invention of the Creature. Within his tale, chapters eleven through sixteen, the Creature recounts his story to Frankenstein, who recounts it to Walton. With

11. Genette, "The Narcissus Complex," *Figures I,* pp. 21–22, translation mine.

the seventeenth chapter, the narrative becomes once again Frankenstein's to chapter twenty-four, when Walton returns to his letters and concludes the narrative. Here through spatial *encadrement* the narcissistic theme is served perfectly. The device achieves, as well, the additional ends of suspense and credibility, postponing the Creature's tale until the reader has been thoroughly led into the narrative. Without its spatial frame, *Frankenstein* would not exist and could not be narrated in its complete significance.

The pictorial spatial illusion exists in several other texts for specific narrative purposes. In Emily Brontë's *Wuthering Heights,* the pictorial frame, by delaying the account of Heathcliff and Catherine I, lends it both credibility and an atemporal status vindicated by the apparition at the novel's conclusion (Figure 3).

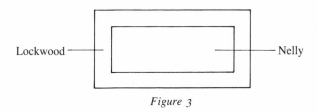

Figure 3

In this instance the painterly recessed narrative produces a paradoxical effect: it is the image of "becoming" in the sense that it is the device of narration, but also it is spatial in its tendency to *develop the narration by retardation.* This effect is especially evident in considering the calendar structure of the text. Lockwood's narrative concerns 1801–03, chapters one to four and thirty-one to thirty-four. Nelly's narrative, chapters five through thirty, concerns summer 1771 through October 1801. Thus events chronologically first are learned *later* than events chronologically later. A further intricate repudiation of chronology occurs in Lermontov's framed *A Hero of Our Time,* whose complexity exceeds the device in Brontë (Figure 4). Here there are three narrators: Narrator I is a Lermontov persona; Narrator II is Maksim Maksimich; Narrator III is Pechorin, who speaks through his journal. In the first story in the novel, "Bela," Narrator I meets Narrator II, who recounts events from June 1832 to December 1833. In the second story, "Maksim Maksimich," Narra-

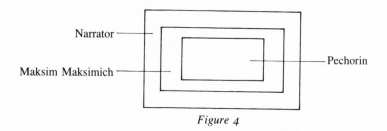

Figure 4

tor I tells how he and Narrator II met Narrator III, Pechorin, recounting events of autumn 1837. Finally, in the most enclosed of the three accounts, Pechorin, Narrator III, recounts "Taman" (dealing with 1830), "Princess Mary" (dealing with May 1832), and "The Fatalist" (dealing with December 1832). The repudiation of chronology and the delay lending Pechorin credibility and mythical status are served by the spatial pictorial illusion: through the exploitation of the spatiality of the text, Pechorin is made the archetypal estranged individualist. In his discussion of "the frame of an artistic text," Boris Uspensky notes an element of framing significant to both *Wuthering Heights* and *A Hero of Our Time*: "The cessation of time is indeed part of the function of the frame." Thus if Heathcliff and Pechorin assume atemporal, timeless dimensions, it is partially due to the spatial framing of the text.[12]

The extreme form of this pictorial illusion in the novel exists at the origin of the form, in Longus's *Daphnis and Chloe*. The novel begins with an actual ekphrasis:

> When I was hunting in Lesbos, I saw, in a wood sacred to the Nymphs, the most beautiful thing that I have ever seen—a painting that told a love-story.
> I was seized by a longing to write a verbal equivalent to the painting. So I found someone to explain the picture to me, and composed a work in four volumes as an offering to Love.[13]

12. Uspensky, *A Poetics of Composition*, trans. Valentina Zavarin and Susan Wittig (Berkeley and Los Angeles: University of California Press, 1973), p. 149. The concept of spatial secondary illusion would have reinforced several of Uspensky's valuable observations.

13. Longus, *Daphnis and Chloe*, trans. Paul Turner (Baltimore: Penguin, 1968), p. 17.

The result, early in the novel's development, was exceptional (Figure 5).

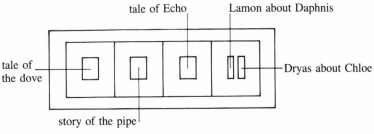

Figure 5

The crucial phrase *antigrapsai te graphe* ("to write in answer to that picture") is a summation of the pictorial secondary illusion: the root *graph* appears in both "picture" and "to write."

III

The sculptural secondary illusion of the novel is stated by D. H. Lawrence in *Women in Love* when Rupert Birkin observes, "You have to be like Rodin, Michael Angelo." The young Marcel in *Swann* remembers: "Another Combray person whom I could discern also potential and typified, in the gothic sculptures of Saint-André-des Champs was young Theodore, the assistant in Camus's shop." The tradition of the connection between sculpture and characterization is extensive; Jean Hagstrum in *The Sister Arts* notes that in the ancient world "the mute statue was given a voice and the silent form endowed with the power of speech." Ancient biography correlated sculpture with characterization; for instance, Varro called his biographies *Imagines*. In the history of fiction, a crucial example of this recognition of the sculptural secondary illusion occurs in Thomas's *Tristran*. Tristran recreates all the characters in *imagines*:

> The following day Tristran commanded him . . . to make a hall in a cavern and to fashion lifelike statues of Queen Ysolt and Brengvein.
> Whenever Tristran visits the image of Ysolt he kisses it and clasps it in his arms, as if it were alive.
> By means of the image, Tristan recalls the delights of their great

loves, their troubles and their griefs, their pains and their torments
. . . He made this image so that he might tell it what is in his heart.

The business of the novelist in characterization is that of Pygmalion.
Balzac writes in *Cousin Bette*: "One can copy a model and the work
is done; but to impart a soul to it, in the representing of a man or
woman to create a type, is to snatch fire from heaven like Pro-
metheus. . . . One statue is enough to make a man immortal, just
as it took only Figaro, Lovelace, and Manon Lescaut to immor-
talize Beaumarchais, Richardson, and the Abbé Prévost." From this
perspective, Mary Shelley's *Frankenstein*, "The Modern Prome-
theus," is a myth of the sculptural secondary illusion in the novel.[14]

Sainte-Beuve observed of Charles in *Madame Bovary*: "At certain
moments and situations in this book, the author could easily have
superimposed a coating of idealism over his implacable realism. By
so doing, he could have 'patched up' a character and rounded it
off—that of Charles Bovary, for example. A few more pats, and the
clay the novelist was molding could have turned out a noble and
touching figure instead of a vulgar one." Frequently, characters in
novels are overtly sculpted: in *Barchester Towers* Trollope entitles
an account of Mrs. Proudie "Mrs. Proudie Victrix," while in *The
Rainbow* Lawrence calls the chapter recounting Anna Lensky's giving birth to Ursula, a true Pygmalion situation, "Anna Victrix."
Certain settings reinforce the sculptural illusion. In *Great Expectations* Dickens locates Pip's origin and the origin of his characterization in the forge: meetings in museums, as in *The Marble Faun, The
American, The Age of Innocence*, or *Middlemarch*, symbolize the
quarry of character. For example, when Dorothea Brooke gets her
first view of Will Ladislaw, he is just turning from the Belvedere
torso. Hawthorne in *The Marble Faun*, in fact, argues that the story
must be viewed through the medium of sculpture. Referring to the
statues in the Capitoline Museum and their timelessness, he
observes: "The present moment is pressed down or crowded out, and
our individual affairs and interests are but half as real, here, as
elsewhere. *Viewed through this medium, our narrative . . .* may
seem not widely different from the texture of all our lives" (italics

14. Lawrence, *Women in Love* (New York: Viking, 1960), p. 349; Proust, *Re-
membrance*, I, 116; Hagstrum, *The Sister Arts*, p. 385; Thomas, *Tristran*, trans. A.
T. Hatto (Baltimore: Penguin, 1960), pp. 315–316; Balzac, *Cousin Bette*, trans.
Marion Crawford (Baltimore: Penguin, 1965), p. 219.

added).[15] This revolutionary statement causes one to recognize texts where statues indicate situations of character, as with the Apollo and Diana of *The Mayor of Casterbridge*, Apollo and Venus of *Jude the Obscure*, or the Sacrifice of Iphigenia group in *Vanity Fair*. By such techniques, the creation of character is related to the myth of Pygmalion. Characterization is the result of spatial sculptural secondary illusion in the novel.

The utility of sculpture for the novelist rests, above all, on its property of volume. Sculpture, as Susanne Langer claims in *Feeling and Form*, is a "virtual space," a created space whose purpose is "to make tactual space visible." As a creation, sculptural art is "not only a shape in space but a shaping of space," the property called volume, the power of a statue not only to occupy its own space but also to *in*fold into itself its surroundings. This coextensive volume is the core of all great sculpture, apparent in the approach to the *David* in the Academy, Florence. Elizabeth Bowen's remark, that it is impossible not to believe Elizabeth Bennet of *Pride and Prejudice* has just entered the room, illustrates this sculptural spatial illusion of characterization. Such coextensive volume is one method by which a novel exhibits what Butor in "The Book as Object" calls its *volumen*. E. M. Forster's statements about character in *Aspects of the Novel* likewise suggest the sculptural illusion: "We may divide characters into flat and round. Flat characters were called 'humorous' in the seventeenth century, and are sometimes called types." After analyzing Dickens's characters, Forster praises their opposite in the method of Jane Austen: "She is a miniaturist, but never two-dimensional. All her characters are round, or capable of rotundity. . . . All the Jane Austen characters are ready for an extended life," he observes. Forster's test of rotundity, however, is singularly inadequate: "The test of a round character is whether it is capable of surprising in a convincing way." Like W. J. Harvey in *Character and the Novel* after him, Forster only incompletely realizes the secondary illusion of sculptural coextensive volume involved in characterization.[16] The relationship of outer to inner, of the indi-

15. Sainte-Beuve, *Selected Essays,* trans. Francis Steegmuller and Norbert Guterman (Garden City, New York: Doubleday, 1963), p. 288; Hawthorne, *The Marble Faun* (Columbus: Ohio State University Press, 1968), p. 6.

16. Langer, pp. 71–72, 88–90; Bowen, "Jane Austen," in *The English Novelists,* ed. Derek Verschoyle (New York: Harcourt, Brace and World, 1936), p. 108;

vidual to his "surrounding space," of the distance between point of
view and these surroundings, are all posited on sculptural secondary
illusion.

The relationship in a novel of a protagonist to his milieu is sculptural, best indicated by Flaubert's reply to Sainte-Beuve's criticism
of *Salammbô*: "The pedestal is too big for the statue." This arresting
sentence is echoed by Joseph Conrad in *Lord Jim* about his protagonist: "He was like a figure set up on a pedestal, to represent in
his persistent youth the power . . . of races that never grow old"; for
this reason, to the virtual novelist Marlow, he is genuinely "symbolic." As Gogol observes in *Dead Souls,* characters are thrust into the
world, forced to be voluminous. Chichikov, when looking at
Sobakevich, realizes his is one of "many faces in the world over the
finish of which nature has taken no great pains, has used no fine
tools such as files, gimlets, and the like, having simply gone about it
in a rough and ready way: one stroke of the axe and there's a nose,
another and there are the lips, the eyes gouged out with a great drill,
and without smoothing it, nature thrusts it *into the world* saying: 'It
will do'" (italics added). That this situation of inner and outer space
is ethical is clear from Kate Chopin's *The Awakening*. Edna Pontel-
lier, whose body falls into "splendid poses," realizes "at the very
early period she had apprehended instinctively the dual life—the
outward existence which conforms, the inward life which questions." The relation between "outward life" and "inward existence"
is the duality both of character and of characterization. This duality
founded on the sculptural illusion of characterization was recognized
by George Eliot when she declared in the peroration of *Middlemarch,* "There is no creature whose inward being is so strong that it
is not greatly determined by what lies outside it" or when she noted
in *The Mill on the Floss,* "The tragedy of our lives is not created
entirely from within." The business of the novelist, as André Gide
declared in *The Counterfeiters,* is "to express the general by the
particular": "To arrive at this effect . . . I invent the character of a
novelist, whom I make my *central figure*; and the subject of the
book, if you must have one, is just that very struggle between what
reality offers him and what he himself desires to make of it" (italics

Forster, *Aspects of the Novel* (New York: Harcourt, Brace and World, 1954), pp.
74–75, 78; compare Harvey, *Character and the Novel* (Ithaca: Cornell University
Press, 1965), pp. 52–55.

added). Every novelist may say, then, *"je pose en figure centrale."*[17] A consideration of volume in characterization necessitates a reinvestigation of point of view, for any point occupies and is surrounded by space. One's comprehension of a center or filtering intelligence in a novel, in fact, can occur only by virtue of coextensive volume between protagonist and reader. Whether from the first or the third person, or from the ubiquitous implied author described in Wayne Booth's *The Rhetoric of Fiction,* point must have volume to exist at all. The central issue is one of "distance" between the "point of view" and the reader, a fact made clear in Ortega's essay "On Point of View in the Arts." While "Localization [point] of the sensible . . . is inevitable," he argues, vision may be proximate (convex) or distant (concave). Either form, nevertheless, involves volume. The significance of spatial sculptural volume is apparent in the opening of *Huckleberry Finn*: "You don't know about me, without you have read a book by the name of 'The Adventures of Tom Sawyer,' but that ain't no matter. That book was made by Mr. Mark Twain, and he told the truth, mainly. There was things which he stretched, but mainly he told the truth. That is nothing. I never seen anybody but lied, one time or another." Distance is made explicit by the existence of "you" and by the fact that the reader is supposed to know an actual person, Mr. Mark Twain. Quite obviously, without the operation of volume, a declaration about the first person narrator of *Huckleberry Finn* is insubstantial. At the end of the novel, Huck escapes the centripetal volume of other characters and, what is more important, the reader's own dangerous presence: "But I reckon I got to light out for the Territory ahead of the rest, because Aunt Sally she's going to adopt me and sivilize me and I can't stand it. I been there before." To escape is to no longer be a character in a novel; distance is destroyed only by disappearance.[18]

17. Flaubert, *Salammbô*, trans. J. C. Chartres (New York: Dutton, 1963), p. 318; Conrad, *Lord Jim* (New York: Bantam, 1963), p. 171; Gogol, *Dead Souls,* tr. David Magarshack (Baltimore: Penguin, 1961), p. 103; Chopin, *The Awakening* (New York: Holt, Rinehart and Winston, 1970), p. 215; Eliot, *Middlemarch* (Boston: Houghton Mifflin, 1956), p. 612; *The Mill on the Floss* (Boston: Houghton Mifflin, 1961), p. 351; Gide, *The Counterfeiters,* trans. Dorothy Bussy (New York: Modern Library, 1955), pp. 172, 173; *Les faux-monnayeurs* (Paris: Gallimard, 1925), p. 239.
18. Ortega y Gasset, "On Point of View in the Arts," trans. Paul Snodgrass and Joseph Frank, in *Aesthetics Today,* ed. Morris Philipson (New York: Meridian,

In the first person narrative, volume is centripetal. For example, after Michel's narrative in *The Immoralist*, the listening narrator declares: "We felt, alas, that by telling his story Michel had made his action more legitimate. Our not having known at what point to condemn it in the course of his long explanation seemed almost to make us his accomplices. We felt, as it were, involved." "Involved" has little to do with point or with watching but much to do with volume and absorption into it. Such statements as "Call me Ishmael" from *Moby Dick* or "Reader, I married him" from *Jane Eyre* demonstrate that the act of reading is always an act of becoming an accomplice, of being drawn into the spatial volume of character.

In the third person, volume becomes centrifugal because the reader is forced to experience the story in his own volume rather than in the character's. In Ortega's scheme, the first person is proximate, the third person is distant. Once one is no longer explicitly a reader ("Call me" or "you"), one is much more central, as Sartre observes: "Raskolnikov's waiting is *my* waiting, which I lend him." In the third person, reading becomes Sartre's act of "directed creation," as in the following from *Pride and Prejudice*: "Occupied in observing Mr. Bingley's attentions to her sister, Elizabeth was far from suspecting that she was herself becoming an object of some interest in the eyes of his friend. . . . Of this she was perfectly unaware." The third person coerces the reader to transcend itself, since the protagonist is a priori "unaware" to some extent. The distance between the protagonist and the reader is the important location necessary for any observation, and it is through sculptural coextension that the eclipse of distance may occur. The volume of sculptural secondary illusion, therefore, demonstrates the validity of a dynamic field theory of literature and reading, a "field of view," which is as essential to the novel as a "point of view." In *Anna Karenina*, when Leven meets Kitty, "He saw her, as one sees the sun, without looking."[19] Sculptural secondary illusion in the novel deals not with person but with presence.

1970), pp. 130–132; Twain, *Adventures of Huckleberry Finn* (Boston: Houghton Mifflin, 1958), pp. 3, 245. Shklovsky discusses *Huckleberry Finn* and devices of retardation in *Theory of Prose*, pp. 57–58.

19. Gide, *The Immoralist*, trans. Dorothy Bussy (New York: Vintage, 1958), p. 145; Jean-Paul Sartre, *What Is Literature?*, trans. Bernard Frechtman (New York: Harper and Row, 1965), p. 39; Jane Austen, *Pride and Prejudice* (Boston: Hough-

IV

In his essay "On Literary Evolution" in 1929, Jurij Tynianov emphasized the importance of the architectural secondary illusion of the novel:

> The evolutionary relationship of function and formal elements is a completely uninvestigated problem. . . . The evolution of forms results in a change of function.
> The relationship between form and function is not accidental. The variability of the functions of a given formal element, the rise of some new function of a formal element, and the attaching of a formal element to a function are all important problems of literary evolution. Investigation . . . must clarify the problem of the evolutionary interaction of function and form.

For Tynianov a function is "the interrelationship of each element with every other in a literary work and with the whole literary system as well." There are two types of functions, an auto-function, the interrelation of an element with similar elements in other works; and a syn-function, the relationship of an element with a different element in the same work. These ideas are closely connected with Susanne Langer's definition of architecture as functional form; for her, as for Tynianov, form does not follow function, nor does function follow form. The emphasis is on their interrelationship. The domain of architecture is "the sphere of influence of a function"; architecture "both excludes and forms the external world." This statement is close to Tynianov's concepts of auto-function, the connection with other works, and syn-function, the internal connection of elements in the same work. In his essay "Literature and Space," Gérard Genette observes that "the art of space, par excellence, architecture, does not speak of space: it would be truer to say that it makes space speak . . . in itself and . . . of itself." The importance of this concept is apparent, Michel Butor contends, in Balzac's *Human Comedy,* in which the reader himself becomes an architect: "Balzac's *Human Comedy* . . . provides the example of a work conceived

ton Mifflin, 1956), p. 16; Leo Tolstoy, *Anna Karenina,* trans. David Magarshack (New York: New American Library, 1961), p. 44. The concept of a field theory of literature is developed in the fourth chapter of my study *The Spatiality of the Novel* (Detroit: Wayne State University Press, 1978), pp. 134–177.

in distinct blocks which each reader, in fact, approaches in a different order." As Henry James noted in the "Preface" to *The Portrait of a Lady,* the "house" of fiction has a "number of possible windows." The extent to which a novel is an edifice, a "house," has been examined by Butor in his essay "The Book as Object." By virtue of its superimposed structure, a book becomes a volume, "the arrangement of the thread of speech in three-dimensional space according to a double module: length of line and depth of page." The book/diptych has the strongly spatial power of reversibility, of making "looking back easy." Furthermore, the design of the page lends itself to variable spatial arrangements: vertical, horizontal, oblique; with differences in body type, margins, and edges.[20]

Two essays, Todorov's "The Categories" and Shklovsky's "The Construction of the Short Story and of the Novel," contain considerable material detailing the architectural secondary illusion of the novel. Shklovsky discusses two methods of construction of a literary work, *en boucle* (circular) and *en paliers* (with stairs). These strategies employ three particular methods: repetition by superposition, parallelism (different characters in similar situations or the same character in different situations), and contradiction. The locations of these devices serve important goals, one of which, *ralentissement* or slowing the narrative, is particularly important to the spatial illusion of rhythm. In his essay, Todorov isolates three methods of repetition of actions in the *histoire* or story: (1) antithesis (as in the alternating letters of *Dangerous Liaisons*; (2) gradation, or development by increment; and (3) parallelism, of intrigues or of verbal elements. On the level of the *discours,* one may structure the *histoire* by three methods: (1) *enchaînement,* the juxtaposition of different actions; (2) *enchâssement,* with one story inside another; and (3) *alternance,* going back and forth between *histoires,* as in *Bleak House* or *The Old Wives' Tale.*[21] A brief survey of architectural principles indicates that repetition, parallelism, enclosure, gradation, and antithesis are among the oldest of architectural

20. Tynianov, in *Readings in Russian Poetics,* pp. 71–72, 68–69; Langer, *Feeling and Form,* pp. 94–95; Genette, *Figures II,* p. 44, translation mine; Butor, "Research on the Technique of the Novel," *Inventory,* p. 25; James, *Art of the Novel,* p. 46; Butor, *Inventory,* pp. 41, 42.

21. Shklovsky, "La construction de la nouvelle et du roman," in *Théorie de la littérature,* ed. Tzvetan Todorov (Paris: Seuil, 1965), pp. 179–180, 189–190; Todorov, "The Categories," trans. Kestner, pp. 6–7, 21–22.

practices, with the particular significance of unity, scale, rhythm, proportion, and sequence. Among these objectives, unity emphasizes not merely the integrity of the structure but also the importance of uniting with the observer's awareness; the observer must confront the structure's wholeness. Scale facilitates "the orientation of the observer with regard to the structure," by one of four types, natural, intimate, monumental, or "shock." As an element of architecture, rhythm is conceived as repetition, for example of columns, or "the repetition of elements whose *differences* progress uniformly." Rhythm may involve a major rhythm of columns with a secondary rhythm of windows, statues, or panels. Since rhythm is concerned with distances between elements, the speed (*vitesse*) of a building is rhythmic. Proportion, "the interplay of principal subordinating parts," is concerned with the composite result of function, materials, and scale, while sequence controls passage toward, into, through, and from the edifice. Sequence is especially concerned with progression and climax. The distinction between composition, the controlled pattern to a climax, and construction, the use of materials leading to the climax, constitute two aspects of the *discours* or narration of the novel, as Eichenbaum declared in his "The Theory of the 'Formal Method'": "Plot [*discours*] is a compositional element rather than a thematic element."

As a written object, the book involves several large elements, including chapter, part, and volume. In many novels the part or volume may be the major rhythm, with the chapter the secondary rhythm. In the preface to *Roderick Hudson,* Henry James noted that in the "house" of fiction "really, universally, relations stop nowhere, and the exquisite problem of the artist is eternally but to draw, by a geometry of his own, the circle within which they will happily appear to do so." The chapter is one primary dimension of this "geometry." In addition to its functions of rhythm and unity, the chapter, as Philip Stevick notes, is an important element of scale: "One responds to the form of a novel by responding to its chapter." Scale, Henry Hope Reed observes, is "the relation of the parts of a building to the human figure," permitting man "to measure a building, to find a place to rest." In *Joseph Andrews,* Fielding declared that "those little spaces between our chapters may be looked upon as an inn or resting-place . . . I would not advise him to travel through these pages too fast." Particularly important is Fielding's phrase "travel through," for the function of the chapter is architectural not only in providing a halting place but also in controlling sequence of passage through the novel. As Shklovsky has claimed, a chapter in *Joseph Andrews,* like one entitled "To Divert the Reader," is clearly a device of *ralentissement* or slowing, a function of rhythm.[22]

Several examples of *ralentissement* and *alternance* make this architectural illusion clear. In *Emma* chapter fifteen concludes with the heroine in turmoil after an unexpected proposal; chapter sixteen opens: "The hair was curled, and the maid sent away, and Emma sat down to think and be miserable.—It was a wretched business indeed!"[23] A stark *enchaînement* is found in chapters fifteen and sixteen of *Adam Bede,* where in "The Two Bed-Chambers" George Eliot presents simultaneously Hetty Sorrel and Dinah Morris. The next chapter, appropriately titled "Links," concerns Adam Bede and Arthur Donnithorne, the two men involved in the lives of the two women. The literal diptych of these two chapters is suitable for the end of the first part of the novel. *Alternance* is apparent in the awesome structure of *War and Peace,* where, in the first part, for instance, one advances from the soirée to the Rostóvs' home, from the public to the private, from talk of war to a celebration in peace. Parallelism and antithesis are used extensively by Virginia Woolf in *Mrs. Dalloway* and by William Faulkner in *As I Lay Dying.* Furthermore, Tolstoy, Faulkner, and Conrad use the arrangement of chapter, parallel or antithetical, to control the speed of revelation or development, as with the structure of *Anna Karenina.* Conrad in *Lord Jim* or Faulkner in *Absalom, Absalom!* conveys by this architectural illusion not only how one knows but also how rapidly a person knows information at all.

An important form of this speed of narration is the question of sequence and climax. Shklovsky examined the achieved and the illusory ending; in the former one has both action and reaction; in the latter, as in the tales of Maupassant, one has only action, with the

---

22. Eugene Raskin, *Architecturally Speaking* (New York: Bloch, 1966), pp. 42, 45–51, 61, 64, 95; Eichenbaum, in *Russian Formalist Criticism,* p. 116; James, *Art of the Novel,* p. 5; Stevick, "The Theory of Fictional Chapters," in *The Theory of the Novel,* ed. Stevick (New York: Free Press, 1967), p. 174; Reed, *The Golden City* (New York: Norton, 1970), p. 114; Fielding, *Joseph Andrews* (Boston: Houghton Mifflin, 1961), p. 73; Shklovsky, *Theory of Prose,* trans. Verret, p. 276.

23. Austen, *Emma* (Boston: Houghton Mifflin, 1957), p. 103.

reaction missing (*forme négative* or *désinence zéro*). An example of the extreme form of this *désinence* is the conclusion of *The Sentimental Education*, where the final episode is an action never achieved. Shklovsky distinguishes the *nouvelle* from the *roman* by the fact that in the short story the conclusion is the culmination of the narrative, while in the novel, frequently characterized by an epilogue (as in *War and Peace, Great Expectations,* or *The Return of the Native*), the culmination is not the conclusion. In its sequence, the novel must control the reader's progress to make the conclusion seem inevitable but never to make the culmination the completion. From this perspective the seemingly "hasty" conclusions of *Rob Roy, Jane Eyre,* or *Emma* are not defective but pursuant to the architectural norm of the novel. The chapters of *Little Dorrit,* Shklovsky argues, "retard the plot" and "undergo pressure from the plot" to achieve tense effects of *ralentissement* and *accélération,* the control of sequence, of passage through. The chapter, volume, or part may additionally express retrospection (analepsis) or anticipation (prolepsis), as Gérard Genette notes in *Figures III,* directly violating the linearity of the narrative for *ralentissement* and *accélération.*[24]

In this process, the smaller units of word, sentence, and paragraph constitute the minute blocks by which the "houses" of fiction are constructed. Genette emphasizes that not only the word but also its placement is crucial: "Each element is qualified by the position it occupies in the total picture." In "Space and Language" he indicates the distinction when the *signifiant,* the signifying sign, is the "spatial term" to the extent that its form remains constant, but what it signifies, the *signifié,* is the "variable object." Such a distinction has a startling prototype in the beginning of Vitruvius' *On Architecture*: "In all matters, but particularly in architecture, there are these two points;—the thing signified, and that which gives it its significance." Therefore, such a statement as "Reader, I married him" from *Jane Eyre* is significant both for word position and for the implications of the *signifiant* "Reader." "I married him, Reader" does not convey the sense of force that characterizes the protagonist, while the recognition of the narrative action is only one of the signified

24. Shklovsky, "The Construction," *Théorie de la littérature,* ed. Todorov, p. 117; *Readings in Russian Poetics,* p. 226; Gérard Genette, *Narrative Discourse,* trans. Jane Lewin (Ithaca: Cornell University Press, 1980), pp. 35–43.

intentions of "Reader." Devices such as juxtaposition, oxymoron, repetition, or zeugma are clearly architectural in their illusion. Types of sentences and of paragraphing serve important architectural functions of rhythm and sequence as well as of proportion. The lengths and types of sentences (or their absence, as in the opening of *Bleak House*) influence the speed of reception by the reader. In *Jane Eyre*, for instance, the opening, "There was no possibility of taking a walk that day," is abrupt and individual, an impression reinforced by the opening of the second paragraph, "I was glad of it."[25] The elaboration of each of these sentences in their respective paragraphs consists of a single longer sentence supplying a rhythm of fast, then slow. In each paragraph there is a great asymmetry between the short first and long second sentence, but between the two consecutive paragraphs, a fine balance. In her first paragraphs, Jane Austen gives an indication of the speed of the narration to follow. The short aphoristic single-sentence paragraphs of *Pride and Prejudice* and *Emma* contrast with the extended analysis of the first paragraph of *Mansfield Park*. From his first entrance the reader experiences the rhythm of narration.

One finds a particularly strong manifestation of the architecture of sentence, word, and paragraph in Flaubert's *The Sentimental Education*. In the following two consecutive paragraphs nearly all the possible architectural dimensions of these materials are exploited by careful position, interplay of proportions, balancing of complex and simple sentences, and progressive sequential movement to a climax:

> On remarquait en entrant chez lui deux grands tableaux, où les premiers tons, posés cà et là, faisaient sur la toile blanche des taches de brun, de rouge et de bleu. Un réseau de lignes à la craie s'étendait par-dessus, comme les mailles vingt fois reprises d'un filet; il était même impossible d'y rien comprendre. Pellerin expliqua le sujet de ces deux compositions en indiquant avec le pouce les parties qui manquaient. L'une devait représenter *la Démence de Nabuchodonosor*, l'autre *l'Incendie de Rome par Néron*. Frédéric les admira.
>
> Il admira des académies de femmes échevelées, des paysages où les troncs d'arbres tordus par la tempête foisonnaient, et surtout des caprices à la plume, souvenirs de Callot, de Rembrandt ou de Goya, dont il ne connaissait pas les modèles. Pellerin n'estimait plus ces

25. Genette, *Figures II*, p. 45, and *Figures I*, p. 103, translations mine; Vitruvius, *On Architecture*, trans. M. H. Morgan (New York: Dover, 1960), p. 5; Charlotte Brontë, *Jane Eyre* (Boston: Houghton Mifflin, 1959), pp. 426, 7.

travaux de sa jeunesse; maintenant, il était pour le grand style; il dogmatisa sur Phidias et Winckelmann, éloquemment. Les choses autour de lui renforçaient la puissance de sa parole: on voyait une tête de mort sur un prie-Dieu, des yatagans, une robe de moine; Frédéric l'endossa.

[As one entered his studio, one's eye was caught by two large pictures, in which the first tints, scattered here and there, formed patches of brown, red, and blue on the white canvas. Over them there stretched a tracery of chalk lines, like the meshes of a net which had been mended time and again; indeed it was absolutely impossible to make anything of it. Pellerin explained the subject of these two compositions by indicating the missing parts with his thumb. One was intended to represent "The Madness of Nebuchadnezzar," the other "The Burning of Rome by Nero." Frédéric admired them.

He admired some studies of nudes with disheveled hair, some landscapes abounding in storm-twisted tree trunks, and above all some pen-and-ink sketches, inspired by Callot, Rembrandt, or Goya, the originals of which were unknown to him. Pellerin thought very little of these early works of his; now he was for the grand manner; he pontificated eloquently on Phidias and Winckelmann. The objects around him gave added force to his argument; there was a skull on a prayer-stool, some scimitars, and a monk's frock, which Frédéric put on.]

Here there is an extraordinary arrangement of primary and secondary rhythms: the paragraphs open with long sentences, conclude with extremely short ones; they are linked by "admira" as if by the binding of a diptych. In the second paragraph, the sentences maintain the same falling rhythm as the paragraph: "éloquemment" or "Frédéric l'endossa." In each paragraph there is a terrifying lapse that becomes the very image of Flaubert's themes of despoliation, futility, and nullity. This proportion of *accélération* and *ralentissement* is apparent in the second and third parts of the entire novel, with the second significantly longer than the third, which therefore reproduces again the lapsing. The famous opening of part three, chapter six, is the signature of the power of architectural illusion in the novel:

Il voyagea.
   Il connut la mélancolie des paquebots, les froids réveils sous la tente, l'étourdissement des paysages et des ruines, l'amertume des sympathies interrompues.
   Il revint.

[He traveled.

He came to know the melancholy of the steamboat, the cold awakening in the tent, the tedium of landscape and ruins, the bitterness of interrupted friendships.

He returned.]

These architectural properties of rhythm and sequence, of proportion and scale, verify what Genette has called the province of architecture to make space speak of itself. In the novel, because "all our language is woven of space," the elements of word, sentence, and paragraph, chapter and part, comprise methods by which the novel may become its functional form. Thus Proust was justified in his desire for *Remembrance of Things Past*: "I had wanted to give each part of my book the title *Porch, Stained glass of the apse*."[26]

The pictorial, the sculptural, and the architectural spatial secondary illusions of the novel are crucial elements of its spatial form. The temporal art of the novel remains reliant on its spatial illusion. It is as Einstein proved and as Proust observed in *Contre Sainte-Beuve*: "Time has assumed a dimension of space."[27]

26. Flaubert, *L'éducation sentimentale* (Paris: Gallimard, 1965), pp. 57, 463; *The Sentimental Education*, trans. Robert Baldick (Baltimore: Penguin, 1964), pp. 48, 411; Genette, *Figures I*, p. 107, translation mine; Proust, in *Proust*, ed. René Girard (Englewood Cliffs, New Jersey: Prentice-Hall, 1962), p. 105.
27. Proust, *Contre Sainte-Beuve*, in *Marcel Proust on Art and Literature*, trans. Sylvia Townsend Warner (New York: Meridian, 1958), p. 249.

This essay was completed under a grant for a project to study the spatiality of the novel. The grant was from the Research Foundation of The City University of New York, which is hereby gratefully acknowledged.

III

Spatial Form and Reader Perception

6

Time Sequence
in Spatial Fiction

Ivo Vidan

In attacking pictorial poetry and allegorical painting, Lessing's *Laocoön*, says Joseph Frank, offered "a new approach to aesthetic form." Criticism, "instead of prescribing rules for art, was to explore the necessary laws by which art governs itself."[1] Frank's own seminal concept of spatial form in modern literature develops, paradoxically, from Lessing's polarization between the spatial and the temporal arts. To insist on simultaneity in the perception of a literary work—a poem or a novel—may seem once again to confuse the natural media of artistic expression. Yet the non-naturalistic tendency in modern art, Frank shows, reduces perspectives to surfaces, and motion to a moment of stasis, and transforms "the historical imagination into myth" (p. 60). Sequentiality, which is the chief intrinsic convention of literature, therefore loses its axiomatic status. The development of a story or indeed of any complex utterance in time may seem to be the arrangement that spontaneously follows the nature of things. Our age, however, has become aware that the quiddity of an art need not overlap with the mode of its natural presentation. In Russia the so-called Formalist school produced in the twenties the concept of literariness, the pur-

1. Frank, "Spatial Form in Modern Literature," in his *The Widening Gyre: Crisis and Mastery in Modern Literature* (New Brunswick: Rutgers University Press, 1963), pp. 7, 8.

pose of which was to create a focus for research into the means of
construction, the devices making up what is "literary" in a work of
literature.[2] If the "subject" and the "fable" of a novel or story do not
coincide,[3] this is because the author, in Henry James's phrase, did
the thing in the way "that shall make it undergo most doing"[4] or, in
Formalist terms, because a process of "defamiliarization" made the
work "literary."[5]

It has been shown that the masters of apparently traditional,
carelessly organized narration—Dostoevsky and Tolstoy—did not
produce "loose and baggy monsters," but carefully structured, highly patterned art constructs. It has even been argued that the concept
of spatial form fully applies to books like *Crime and Punishment*.
This certainly extends the notion to works that, apart from containing "reflexive reference" or "linkages"[6] on the level of words or
imagery, depend as large wholes primarily upon sinewy articulate
plots.

But can the plot itself, or simply the story, be considered a factor
of spatiality, of simultaneous perceptibility? Or is the plot rather the
guarantee of continuous sequential organization, making the story a
product primarily dominated by natural temporality irrespective of
chronological loopings, twists of perspective, or mechanical shuffling of time units?

2. Ewa M. Thompson, *Russian Formalism and Anglo-American New Criticism*
(The Hague: Mouton, 1971), p. 93.

3. "Tomashevsky creates an opposition between the sequence of events referred
to by the narrative and the way these events are presented in the story. 'The *fable*
would seem to consist of a collection of narrative motifs in their chronological
sequence, moving on from individual cause to effect, whereas the *subject* represents
the same collected motifs, but in the specific order of occurrence which they are
assigned to in the text. As for the fable, it is of little importance that the reader
should become aware of an event in any particular part of the story, or that this event
should be communicated to him directly by the author himself, inside the reported
story of one of the characters in the main story or by way of marginal references. On
the other hand, every narrative motif which is presented has an important role to play
in the subject.'" Tzvetan Todorov, "Some Approaches to Russian Formalism," in
Russian Formalism, ed. Stephen Bann and John E. Bowlt (Edinburgh: Scottish
Academic Press, 1973), p. 15. The same article quotes also different but related
definitions of the terms "fable" and "subject."

4. James, "The New Novel," in *Selected Literary Criticism,* ed. Morris Shapira
(New York: Horizon, 1964), p. 331.

5. Thompson, *Russian Formalism,* p. 26.

6. James M. Curtis, "Spatial Form as the Intrinsic Genre of Dostoevsky's
Novels," *Modern Fiction Studies,* 18 (1972), 140, 144.

Formalists such as Victor Shklovsky have often touched upon the distortions of the natural passage of time in narrative construction. Yet time as a medium of perception, a necessary medium for the apprehension of the work in its natural continuities (with all their digressions), remains outside their field of interest. Literary "science," as they understand it, deals with architectonics and texture, not with effects, with the subjective correlative of the construct in the perceiver's mind.

Spatial form in fiction is obviously a matter of effect. If certain requirements are met, it is produced in the process of reading that necessarily takes place in a segment of mechanical time. Frank himself, however, emphasized only the thematic organization and the function of reflexive references and juxtapositions, and did not discuss the relationship of time sequences in the inner organization of fiction. The idea of spatial form is usually associated with the novel as a poem or as a composition dominated by the recurrence and juxtaposition of verbal motifs, operative words, and key themes. There the recurrent elements produce spatiality in spite of all the variations, development, semantic shifts, whether we deal with the radiating "lighthouse" or a punning "throw away." But "verbal space acquires consistency as the stylistic rendering of the text becomes apparent: reiteration, allusion, parallelism, and contrast relate some parts of the narration to others, and the construction imposes itself on the reader through the action constituted by the reading."[7] What I will examine is whether the very handling of the sequential character of a story can also produce spatial form or be a dominant contributory factor to it. If so, then what are the requirements for such a form to appear? And what different models in the history of fiction can one adduce as evidence?

Having defined the aim of my inquiry, a further, basic question has to be put: can one in principle distinguish novels dominated by spatial form from those that are not? In order to understand later sections of any narrative, we must connect their content with that of the earlier sections, thereby establishing reflexive reference on the level of events, character features, etc. But the reflexive reference here is in the mind that constructs the story out of verbal signals, not necessarily in the reiteration of verbal signals. The sequential con-

7. Ricardo Gullón, "On Space in the Novel," trans. René de Costa, *Critical Inquiry*, 2 (1975), 12.

sistency makes the story easy to follow, and we are aware that here, too, we are dealing with a system of mutual relationships.

But there is a difference between traditional narrative wholes and more modern works, where on the one hand the story develops through chronological looping, and on the other the organization is not merely that of a story but of significant image patterns, of collocation and juxtaposition. In these latter ones a tendency is at work to expect the reader to construct a meaning out of seemingly loose elements. The story may still be comparatively simple or, again, it may be as difficult as it is in the most allusive works of the novel-as-poem type. In any case, we have encountered a tendency to rely on a subjective construction of meaning rather than on a fixed model opposed to that in traditional narrative.

The process by which a work of literature becomes knowledge is analyzed by the Polish philosopher Roman Ingarden in his *Vom Erkennen des literarischen Kunstwerks*.[8] This phenomenological thinker sees the work as a schematic construct to which its many cases of individual concretization have to be opposed. These concretizations are the result of each individual reading. The work is thus intersubjectively accessible and at the same time reproducible. These qualities relate it to the reading community, which means that the work allows itself to be surveyed from many individual angles: what remains in the mind is always a condensed Gestalt rather than the book or a complete part of the book that has been perused.

The very notion of spatial form may correspond to such a subjectively envisaged generalized shape. We may agree that there is no difference in principle between the way in which a traditional novel evolves into a Gestalt and that in which the more modern types create themselves in the reader's total perception. Yet there is something that distinguishes from the traditional model not only novels which grow on the principle of an organized system of imagery, but also those which have a distorted chronology. There is wider room for subjective interpretation, for deliberate construction.

Perhaps one can speak of spatial form in both cases, because consecutive narration has been broken up or distorted by the autho-

8. Ingarden, *Vom Erkennen des literarischen Kunstwerks* (Tubingen: M. Niemeyer, 1968); English version: *The Cognition of the Literary Work of Art*, trans. Ruth Ann Crowley and Kenneth R. Olson (Evanston: Northwestern University Press, 1973).

rial voice or a fictional narrator, or complicated by internal or external relationships between two or more voices. In any case, the inner time continuity does not proceed in its natural order and is instead problematized both by the order substituted for it and by the way the reader's consciousness experiences this problematization. This requires that the story should be felt as being not spontaneously related, but deliberately organized through the medium of an implied narrator, or several narrators, or one personalized narrator.

Joseph Frank sees spatial form as a twentieth-century mode, and it is therefore symbolic that *Lord Jim*, published in the year that divides the nineteenth century from the twentieth, should be such a characteristic case in point. We might understand Jim as a young man whose life takes the form of an adventure story. Yet what, then, is the meaning of Marlow's presence in the story? Marlow is in the story in order to undergo the process of achieving an understanding of Jim. Primarily the book presents not a story or the portraiture or delineation of character, but a partial, tentative, ambiguous *assessment* of a character, which opens a range of possible interpretations.

The interaction between narrator and protagonist creates three levels of narration: Marlow's story to his audience, Jim's encounters and indirect contacts with Marlow, and Jim's experiences before and between his meetings with Marlow. At the moment Marlow begins speaking about Jim, the narrative on the other two levels has not been finished. In addition, the ultimate authorial voice, which related the first four chapters, takes over briefly between the two long Marlovian sequences.

The time scheme to which these four levels simultaneously contribute is necessarily intricate, and more so since, apart from Marlow's encounters with Jim, there are tributary stories or informative observations by many episodic characters and witnesses. Thus on levels two and three the partial stories coming from various sources build up a complex unity. The structure of *Lord Jim* has often been described and analyzed, and though one could find occasion to add to the existing comments of details in the story and to the critical explanation of their function in the whole, we should here concentrate on one question: should *Lord Jim* be seen and evaluated in terms of spatial form?

If it is impossible to answer this question without hesitation, this may be due not only to scholarly scruples against making statements

about a work before it has been examined, but also to the fact that to
apply the very notion of spatial form to an individual work may
depend on our subjective evaluation of certain relevant elements in
the work. Thus spatial form cannot be objectively ascertained but
only felt as being intrinsically present or not. If this is so, what value
does the notion actually possess? But perhaps one should not hurry
with one's speculative conclusions. Let us instead look at the work
under scrutiny.

Lord Jim was started by Conrad as a short story that was not to
exceed 20 to 30 thousand words.[9] He thought of it more along the
lines of "Youth" than of Heart of Darkness.[10] But though it became
very long, it can still be considered as something short of a novel—a
story of a developing personality or of a relationship between persons. Arthur Symons saw it as a plotless study in temperament.[11]
This judgment can be compared with a statement by Conrad in a
letter to his publisher that the reader "is following the development
of one situation, only one really from beginning to end" so that the
work did not really have "chapters in the usual sense each carrying
the action a step further or embodying a whole episode." The divisions were meant to be no more than a device to enable the reader's
attention to rest.[12] Yet Conrad himself said in an earlier letter that the
story fell into two parts.[13] He also complained that its structure was
"a little loose"[14] and called it in the Author's Note "a free and
wandering tale." Despite the work's seemingly episodic composition, the modern reader can see it as a well-integrated whole: there
are Jim's three jumps, which define the story that is the external
concomitant of the psychological and moral issue; the parallel situa-

9. Letter to Edward Garnett, May 1898, in Letters from Conrad, 1895 to 1924,
ed. Edward Garnett (London: Nonesuch Press, 1928), p. 130. See also the letter to
David Meldrum, February 1899, in Joseph Conrad: Letters to William Blackwood
and David S. Meldrum, ed. William Blackburn (Durham: Duke University Press,
1958), p. 54.
10. Letter to William Blackwood, 22 August 1899, in Joseph Conrad, ed. Blackburn, p. 63.
11. Symons, Notes on Joseph Conrad (London: Myers, 1925), p. 34.
12. Letter to William Blackwood, 18 July 1900, in Joseph Conrad, ed. Blackburn, p. 106.
13. Letter to Edward Garnett, June 1899, in Letters from Conrad, ed. Garnett, p.
151.
14. Letter to William Blackwood, 22 August 1899, in Joseph Conrad, ed. Blackburn, p. 63.

tions, like Jim's failure and Brierly's suicide; Jim's analogies with Brown; the pattern of his behavior on the *Patna* and at Patusan; and the consistency with which he assumes the consequences of his actions.

What, then, is the function of the complex time scheme? Does it make for this situational unity or does it work toward its disintegration? As has been mentioned, the real complexity of the time scheme is vertical rather than horizontal. Through the greatest part of the book three strata of time seem to be involved at each particular moment: the time of Marlow's actual narration, the time of his experience or interview with Jim or some subordinate character, and the time to which Marlow and his partner refer in their conversation. The frequent general reflections and the associations that direct the transition from one set of circumstances involved in Jim's story to another belong to the nearest and highest time level: to Marlow's actual narration, which has a chronological continuity. On the lowest level, all single items form their own continuity together. Thus Jim's personal history and Marlow's narration both proceed evenly. The shuffling occurs only in the middle stratum through the backslidings and foreshortenings occasioned by the vagrancy of Marlow's mind as he is telling the story. An effect of the time looping is that an exact chronology of events is sometimes impossible to establish, although its general outline becomes clear once we start to sort out details. "The novel is made up of recurrences in which each part of the story has already happened repeatedly when the reader first encounters it, either in someone's mind, or in someone's telling, or in the way it repeats other similar events in the same person's life or in the lives of others."[15] The actual order in time has been suppressed through the actual juxtaposition of episodes, minor incidents, and analytical recallings: the effect is one of simultaneous relevance. Sequence is transposed into coexistence.

This unconventional composition is profoundly motivated in a mimetic sense: this is how an articulate sailor might actually spin a yarn. Yet, like one of Yeats's Byzantine nightingales—artifacts that imitate natural birds—this novel is a highly contrived narrative

15. J. Hillis Miller, "The Interpretation of *Lord Jim*," in *The Interpretation of Narrative: Theory and Practice*, ed. Morton W. Bloomfield (Cambridge: Harvard University Press, 1970), p. 223.

structure, one that uses a number of sophisticated narrative devices in order to imitate reality.

The temporal succession could be analyzed at every associative link in Marlow's narration, and it could be demonstrated that the association is produced on the basis of analogy or of contrast, or of progress in time with an elision of insignificant phases. The important fact is that the sequence of events can be put into chronological order, though the text would have to be altered after such an operation. What would the story itself lose? Probably the effect upon the reader of Jim's personality, and of Marlow's experience of that personality and its fortune. One important aspect of the particular effect achieved by Conrad's art is the contemporaneity, the coexistence, the simultaneity of the relevance of all the details in that subtle and tenuously interconnected history. The natural sequence of occurrences has been transmuted into the simultaneous existence of the human quandary in which chronological stages and links and continuities lose significance: time has turned into space.

One might perhaps challenge the validity of such a simplification, but it would be fair to admit its comparative justification if, for instance, we glance at Conrad's preceding Marlow story, *Heart of Darkness* (1899). The chronology of the inner narrative in that work is not distorted; it is, in fact, perfectly regular, though one or two narrative hints as to the future effect of certain experiences intensify the atmosphere of expectation. *Heart of Darkness* is an account of progression in space and its accompanying insight into the nature of things. In spite of the spatial organization of a network of linkages, the overall effect is one of movement, even of history, not of permanence and independence from transmission in time!

The texture of both works contains a number of recurrent, thematically significant images, the shorter fiction certainly not fewer than the longer one. It follows that the particular spatial effect of *Lord Jim* must depend on the way in which the story has been handled. It might be that the form of *Lord Jim* was dictated by the fact that a narrator is coping with the crisis in another person's life and is speculating about its meaning. In *Heart of Darkness* the narrator's experience itself is the object of attention, and in order to keep its outlines clear, the historical method may have been incumbent. But it is impossible to substantiate the connection between the narrative focus and chronology.

What is more, Conrad's last Marlow novel, *Chance* (1912), in spite of its even more intricate structure (which removes the core of the story from the reader by yet another intermediate narrator), does not strike us as a spatial construct. Compared to *Lord Jim*, the apparatus of the narrator in *Chance* is, in fact, multiplied, and the object under observation is not so much a single hero as a particular situation involving more than one character. Most of the characters have a double role: they play a part in the story, but in addition every one of them communicates, more or less directly, his own observation about some stage of the story. Envisaged from the angle of structure, the relationship between Marlow and Jim is, in comparison, much simpler. Marlow's discoveries and his meditations coincide with the revelation of Jim's character and his inner adventures. In *Chance* the relationship between the narrators themselves, that is, between characters only indirectly or partly connected with the central situation, is minutely observed and elaborated in detail, so that it practically becomes a subject for a separate novel. Therefore, the basic story, which unites all the characters, does not coincide with the history of its detection and comprehension. It takes a long time before it is realized that the former story has an autonomous course and that it is more than a pretext for an investigation of the character and behavior of the narrators and interpreters themselves. From this opposite angle, the narrators look as if they are parts of a superimposed machinery blurring the view and preventing access to the moral core of the story. Thus there appears to be a tension between content and form, substance and method.

Marlow's own procedure in *Chance* is not the same as that in *Lord Jim*. The story does not come to him in the course of his normal engagements; rather, it unfolds as evidence produced in a precisely established series of auditory sessions. What he does is rationally to reconstruct the case for Flora, to ascertain the facts from which her state of mind can be judiciously inferred; but in *Lord Jim* he participates in Jim's plight by feeling that he himself is personally involved, through the universal significance of what Jim does.

The irrelevance of the method in *Chance* in relation to the subject matter becomes obvious beyond any doubt in the second part of the book. Here Marlow is no longer a direct witness but merely retells, in an omniscient third-person manner, what he was told by Powell. In both parts, then, the method by which Marlow conducts his inquiry and by which he reproduces it must be intellectual and aloof. The whole book appears to be a misdirected effort to grasp and present a human situation which, being outside the scope of the author's most intimate moral preoccupations as well as his personal experiences, fascinated but did not temperamentally appeal to him. He uses it for a sentimental reassessment of some basic values in which he always wanted to believe: the moral superiority of the disciplined frankness of sea life against the suffocating complications on shore.

This lengthy analysis of the faults of a pretentious failed novel indicates that a necessary element for the achievement of the effect of spatiality—that is, the simultaneous significance of a novel in its total extension—may be the quality of realization, of illumination, of an intuitive awareness of its noumenal quality: the vision of significance that informs the whole story. This vision is present in *Heart of Darkness* too, yet it is experienced as being prepared in stages and then, at a moment of sudden insight, illuminates the path covered as well as the journey back and its consequences: "It was the farthest point of navigation and the culminating point of my experience. It seemed somehow to throw a kind of light on everything about me—and into my thoughts."[16]

My own reluctance to attribute spatiality as a dominating form to *Heart of Darkness* despite its texture and its admirably integrated set of symbols suggests that spatial form is a subjective category the application of which depends on individual appreciation. Does the work in question strike one more as an image of a complex *situation* or as that of an *enfolding* process?

If, according to the argument that has been put forward, *Heart of Darkness* basically does not belong to spatial fiction, this concept would apply even less to a novel like *Crime and Punishment*. Reflexive reference is not enough to create "spatial" fiction. What is needed is a way in which the temporal sequentiality of the story is neutralized by an appropriate abandonment of chronological presentation. *Lord Jim* appears to satisfy this requirement, though lack of space prevents me from demonstrating it at greater length.

In examining the function of time sequence in the creation of spatial form, the criteria established in studying *Lord Jim* may be

16. Conrad, *Heart of Darkness* (Harmondsworth: Penguin, 1975), p. 11.

applied to other novels to which this concept can be attributed. For heuristic purposes they may be divided into four groups:

(1) Novels with a continuous fable that develops in an ascertainable way, however intricate their story might be. The intricacies in the composition are due to the narrator's difficulties in achieving psychological insight and coordinating the various characters' judgments, and even more to inescapable ambiguities that arise continually in the act of understanding. *Lord Jim* may be considered as a prototype in this group, and as interesting variants Ford's *The Good Soldier* and Faulkner's *Absalom, Absalom!* deserve separate study. An important subdivision in this group consists of works with an apparently comparable but basically simpler time structure, of which several will be briefly considered.

(2) The novels of subjective exploration that share many facets of lyrical organization largely based on the stream-of-consciousness technique. The process of narration is not commented upon even in its omniscient portions. Instead, a large portion of the story coincides with the time-looping vagrancy of the characters' minds. The underlying story has no intrinsic significance, and the symbolic values that one feels in the text are due to the thematic interplay of connotations. This is true both of works based entirely on regular syntactic and lexical conjunctions, however personal and original, and of those relying largely on fragmentation, punning, and other types of verbal play. Proust and Joyce can be mentioned as extreme examples of the two possibilities, and theirs are the works usually cited as typical of spatial form in fiction.

(3) The multivolume (or multipart) novel in which the examination of spatial form involves the temporal parallelism betweeen the semiautonomous parts that go into the production of one novel (like Faulkner's *The Sound and the Fury)* or an integrated series (like Durrell's *Alexandria Quartet).* Each part in itself may belong to any of the other types or may not be spatial at all.

(4) The novel of indeterminate sequentiality. This group includes many works belonging to the French *nouveau roman* and a large variety of experimental fiction that can be related to this structurally fascinating avant-garde tendency.

Some interesting and important works will share features of more than one group, and two, as models of different types, will be described later: a French one, Claude Simon's *Flanders Road,* and

one from Latin America, *The Green House* by the Peruvian author
Mario Vargas Llosa.

To deal with the problems of time sequence in all the four groups
would far exceed the space at my disposal. It will be necessary to
restrict this study to the first group, the only one in which the actual
sequence of events as played against the layers of fictional time in
the organized narration, is in itself a key to the work's spatial organization.

How close Ford Madox Ford's *Good Soldier* (1915) is to *Lord Jim*
becomes apparent when one considers a book Ford wrote even later,
Joseph Conrad: A Personal Remembrance (1924). He maintains
that that book is "a novel exactly on the lines of the formula that
Conrad and the writer [i.e. Ford] evolved."[17] If you write of a character, "you must first get him in with a strong impression, and then
work backwards and forwards over his past." According to his and
Conrad's ideas, he maintains, a novel was to be "the rendering of an
Affair. . . . the whole novel was to be an exhaustion of aspects," the
end of the novel revealing "the psychological significance of the
whole" (p. 137). The novel, as he had written a few years earlier,
should render "one embroilment, one set of embarrassments, one
human coil, one psychological progression."[18]

These general principles have obviously been extracted from the
very techniques of *Lord Jim* and *The Good Soldier*. The cautious
narrator is only one item in the complex structure of relativity—the
gradual, subjectively directed revelation of fact. *The Good Soldier* is
a more homogeneously woven pattern, a less dramatically evolving
structure, than Conrad's, devoid as it is of Conradian bold strokes of
unfrustrated melodrama. The narration, however, elaborates a human embroilment just as difficult to explicate as that of *Lord Jim*.
Hesitatingly, groping for facts, it gradually establishes circumstan-
tial justification for the action and the narrator's experience of it.
The rhythm of events, the unity of occurrence, and the illumination
that arises cause the novel to be *one* total impression of the kind that
Conrad's work has been said to be.

The structure of relationships in *The Good Soldier* is perhaps not
subtler but is certainly even more complicated than that of Conrad's

17. Ford, *Joseph Conrad: A Personal Remembrance* (Boston: Little, Brown,
1924), p. 136.
18. Ford, *Thus to Revisit* (London: Chapman and Hall, 1921), p. 44.

novel. There is not just one axis of a give-and-take relationship between narrator and hero but a "little four-square coterie"[19] in which the narrator has an equal share. The relationship between any two of these characters is in constant flux, since with each of Ashburnham's new love affairs the relationships toward his wife, his mistress, and his mistress's husband are modified, and new tensions among the rest of the group are introduced. Imperceptive, naive, even somewhat obtuse, the narrator, Dowell, in his "moral flabbiness"[20] is not—like Marlow—the author's persona, who shares the author's values and contributes to the overall pattern and its very limitations. Seemingly erratic, the novel is beautifully composed: as in *Lord Jim*, the initial narrative situation is not chronologically the last one from which an ultimate retrospective can be given. Basically the story moves through "piecework chronology,"[21] but each stage is part of a rich arabesque of forward-pointing and back-ward-amplifying hints. Though the presentation is by no means static, it achieves at each moment some kind of omnitemporal quality: all its phases coexist simultaneously in the created novelistic space.

Absalom, Absalom! (1936) belongs to the same category of spatial fiction as *Lord Jim* and *The Good Soldier*, but it constitutes a different model, one in which the method of the earlier novels is even more radically exemplified; and the notion of spatiality is as justified as is possible in narrative works. For *Absalom, Absalom!* presents a process of interpretation and discovery conducted by several narrators and not simply by one. Shreve and Quentin receive information and opinions from Mr. Compson and from Rose Caulfield and integrate them with their own speculation, conjecture, and imaginative reconstruction, and fill in the gaps.

Like the other two novels, this one contains an important development toward its very end, a development that takes place after the main part of the narrators' compound discourse has already been performed. Thus the very end of the novel coincides with a thematic thrust that somehow illuminates all the preceding action and lends it

19. Ford, *The Good Soldier* (Harmondsworth: Penguin, 1946), p. 13.

20. H. Wayne Schow, "Ironic Structure in *The Good Soldier*," *English Literature in Transition*, 18 (1975), 210.

21. Ibid., p. 207.

meaning. The main hero, Sutpen, is removed from almost all of the narrators' direct experience, and we know him less intimately than Jim or even Ashburnham. The layers of narration are more numerous than in the preceding spatial novels (for example, the experience of Sutpen, Rosa's story, Mr. Compson's comment, Quentin's retelling, Shreve's interpretation). Despite the fact that each narrator has a distinct tone or style (some of which have been associated by critics with different cultural epochs), the collective result of this mutual complementary effect appears as a unique story with a radically fragmented time scheme and a great deal of repetition with variation. A situation will be suddenly revealed and on later occasions returned to several times. Gradually it will be accounted for within the context of other situations, earlier and later.

Thus the narration shuttles to and fro, joining together events from all stages of the story; its general movement with its accompanying piecemeal interpretation and detection has been called a "circling in." The feeling of concentration is heightened by the fact that all that occurs takes place in a few houses or a few estates, within one narrow geographic region and during a definite period of historical crisis. Since the historical facts and atmosphere are psychologically relevant and directly motivate the behavior of characters, the story is an examination not only of Sutpen's relationships but also of the nature and meaning of the South as a cultural and historical entity. The biblical title and classical references contribute to the timeless significance of this historically circumscribed set of events.

The spatial quality of *Absalom, Absalom!* is created even by the novel's theme: the rise and fall of a mighty house as a metaphor of the historical destiny of the South. The story is informed by a philosophical vision: the central event that gives meaning to the South is the Civil War, and its moral core is the ambivalent feeling about the racial relationships that necessarily involve the guilt of self-aware oppressors. The mechanism of cause and effect loses its sequential character and is seen as a dynamic copresence of both poles. Any moment in the story can be felt as pointing to the past and as being pregnant with its own consequences. The fate of Jim and the tenuous contacts of the couples in *The Good Soldier* make simple stories compared to the complex interlinked relationships among narrators and actants—each person assuming both functions as we review layer upon layer in each situation in the story.

It would be possible to tell the story in linear form, but then the meaning of this copresence of events would be lost. Faulkner's narrative method is functionally related to his imagination and his vision of man. The story as it exists covers up the minor contradictions (slips by the author?), conflicting assertions, and inconsistencies that it contains. Yet to say that "any attempted summary of the plot of *Absalom* is . . . necessarily impossible" is itself an unnecessary exaggeration, even though the motives for Henry's killing of Bon are unclear. "Always the novel returns to one basic question: did Thomas Sutpen's second son kill the first because he had a quadroon mistress, or because the marriage to his sister would be incestuous, or because of the miscegenation?"[22] The story as it is told allows for this mystery to remain unknown because its three motifs radiate throughout the mores and the manners of the Faulknerian South far beyond the confines of this novel: they are a central knot in the spatial organization of *Absalom, Absalom!*

The logic of its specific form—and of the Modernist view of the complex of history—can be illuminated by a highly interesting external parallel: the structure of *Wuthering Heights* (1847). The function of Heathcliff is analogous to that of Sutpen, and the interconnections of the two narrators' accounts (those of Nelly Dean—ancestress of Rosa Caulfield!—and Mr. Lockwood) point toward a source of Faulkner's inspiration. There is, however, an important difference between the two novels: the fortunes of the two main generations are, in Emily Brontë's novel, never as completely entangled as they are in Faulkner's; a mellowed wisdom and a coming to terms with life is finally brought about—some kind of human growth and progress is effected, and it can be followed through the stages of Mr. Lockwood's sensible report. Heathcliff's Gothic demonism—parallel to Sutpen's—does not prevent conjectures from getting answered and the puzzling situations from being accounted for. This is why *Wuthering Heights*—a most unusual nineteenth-century novel, though in style and sensibility definitely belonging to the Romantic wake—does not create the kind of spatial form that we

---

22. Floyd C. Watkins, "What Happens in *Absalom, Absalom!?*" *Modern Fiction Studies*, 13 (1967), 80.

see in the beginning with *Lord Jim*, in spite of its superficial similarities in chronological distortion and interlocked narrative strands.

Side by side with this line one encounters throughout twentieth-century fiction works in which the story has a broken-up chronology, though it is simpler to follow than that of *Wuthering Heights*. Essentially they allow us to study spatial form in narrative in a purer form than do the more difficult examples that we have discussed, where leitmotifs and subjective narrative perspectives somewhat obscure the problem of pure narrative sequence. A model example of research in that illuminating category of spatial fiction is Jeffrey R. Smitten's examination of Conrad's *Secret Agent* (1907).[23] It is a novel that deserves the same attention as *Nostromo* (1904), which Albert J. Guerard sees as "a more radical example of spatial form than *Lord Jim*." His reason is that *Nostromo* does not pretend to be "the oral narrative of a free wandering memory."[24]

This means that the difficulties, even the possible arbitrariness of the author's handling of chronology, should be a quality in itself, and yet Guerard complains of the technical clumsiness in this "great but radically defective novel" (p. 203). Most of its several beginnings take place in the harbor of Sulaco, and so the moment when their various incidents happen blend in the reader's mind. "The Custom House is the solid immovable object on which the novel nearly founders" (p. 207). Yet "it could be argued . . . that the chronological dislocations and distortions of emphasis may reflect a theory of history as repetitive yet inconsecutive, devoid of reason, refusing to make sense. The method would then reflect the material in an extreme example of organic or imitative form" (p. 215). The very concentration of the action through many historical changes in a precisely delineated, narrow geographical area gives the reader the impression that the book is spatially organized.

The example of *Nostromo* seems to corroborate the opinion implied earlier in this essay that in novels where spatiality depends on the handling of the story more than on recurring thematic imagery, the term "spatial form" will largely be used impressionistically. And

---

23. Smitten, "Flaubert and the Structure of *The Secret Agent*: A Study in Spatial Form," in *Joseph Conrad: Theory and World Fiction*, ed. Wolodymyr T. Zyla and Wendell M. Aycock (Lubbock: Texas Tech Press, 1974), pp. 151–166.

24. Guerard, *Conrad the Novelist* (New York: Athenaeum, 1967), p. 210.

yet, again, the effect of worthwhile spatial organization cannot depend merely on a shuffling of chronology. Fitzgerald used retrospect creatively in *The Great Gatsby* (1925), though modeling the novel loosely on *Lord Jim* and *Heart of Darkness*, thus bringing about a less extreme innovation. In the first and still reprinted version of *Tender Is the Night* (1934)—a work less concentrated and elliptic—the retrospective composition seemed to the author to spoil the story line of the process of Dick Diver's degeneration and of the hourglass symmetry in the development of the two main characters.

When the author presents a story without intermediate narrators, the reader is more aware of the actual story line than when the story is conveyed in what is presented as the natural order in a narrator's mind. This can be illustrated by a novel in which the involuted order of sequences is explicitly demonstrated by the dates in the chapter headings, as it is in Aldous Huxley's *Eyeless in Gaza* (1934). The number of points in time that are presented is limited: the situations beginning on certain dates in 1902, 1912, 1926, 1933, and 1934 develop over the ensuing days or even months. Huxley's narrative is not as fluid as Conrad's, Ford's, or Faulkner's in the novels considered before; it is clear at each point whether we are reading a third-person account, a diary, or a direct confession. The story is one of linear growth, but there are five lines starting at different moments in historical time, each gradually developing. Glancing at the chapter headings, the reader knows that there are several strands removed in time and intermixed chronologically, but running parallel to one another. It is soon realized that an awareness of Anthony Beavis's relative maturity and of his opinions at each stage is necessary if we are to perceive the theme and its meaning.

But why the simultaneous development from the five initial points? And do they make for a unified field of coexisting strands of action, for spatial form? Indeed they do, because Anthony's embracing of mysticism—his growing insight and its ensuing commitment—is seen as part of one unique human situation: instead of a *Bildungsroman* we have an account of a pacifistic revelation that begins from various focuses that eventually fall into one. The technique, carefully calculated by its rationalistic author, works well, but one has the feeling that a single linear story would not have been utterly dissimilar from what Huxley actually achieved. The significance of its spatial effect should not be underrated, but it cannot be put in the same category with that of *Nostromo*, let alone *Lord Jim*, *The Good Soldier*, and *Absalom Absalom!*.

When, however, in Malcolm Lowry's *Under the Volcano* (1947) the action is concentrated within twenty-four hours, in a narrow area topographically and culturally reminiscent of *Nostromo*, its frequent retrospectives pertinent to the mood and behavior of the characters in the present produce authentic spatial form: this is a tragedy—displaying the last stage in the fall of the hero—with a unity of time, place, and action; but it is also a symbolic narrative that has been very consciously structured. In Robert Penn Warren's *All the King's Men* (1946), we are back with the fictional technique of narrator-toward-protagonist, as in Conrad, Ford, and Faulkner, but the verbal patterns are less taut and an abundance of realistic circumstantiality allows easier reading. The presentation of private lives in terms of public and political issues, of individual destiny in terms of historical significance, with the additional dimension of a parable from the past added: the Faulknerian inspiration contributes to our seeing the narrative interconnections as much more than technical adroitness. The retrospective telling with its gaps and significant detours makes the consequences and ultimate insights completely absorb the initial causes. However, the more relaxed the technique is and the more it concedes to traditional telling, the less fully does it seem to impress us as a spatial construct, and this applies to the whole series discussed.

On the basis of the foregoing analysis, one can speak of three types of narrative organization which, through their handling of time sequence, create spatial fiction with a continuous, ascertainable fable:

(1) Works making up a complex unity of narrative strata, internally connected through thematic recurrence. The problem of interpreting what is recalled and narrated becomes itself one of the work's main themes (*Lord Jim*, *The Good Soldier*, *Absalom*, *Nostromo*).

(2) Works based on connections between narrative and memory, where what is revealed in the retrospective portions becomes part of current memory (*Under the Volcano*, *All the King's Men*). The novels by Conrad, Ford, and Faulkner that belong to the first type also possess the characteristic feature of this one, while Warren's work partly possesses theirs.

(3) Works depending for their effect on the way in which separate strands of the narrative are collocated. *Eyeless in Gaza* is a spatial fiction thanks to the author's handling of separate time sections on what is essentially one and the same level of narrative. This feature occurs in other types of work, too, but plays a minor role in producing the effect of spatiality.

Though the handling of time in all three types is based on some aberration from linear temporality, the actual quantity of chronological looping is not decisive for the production of spatial form. Nor does it matter whether the time shifts belong to the sequential rhythm of the authorial voice or to the way in which personalized narrators relate the story. What is decisive is whether the order and relationship of time sequences functionally contribute to the impact of the novel's totality. In addition, a novel of this group, if it is to be experienced as spatial, must result in some kind of vision, an insight of universal relevance, perhaps in what Conrad means when he says through his narrator in *Under Western Eyes*—a novel not far from the spatial quality of some of those that we have discussed—that some "moral discovery . . . should be the object of every tale."[25] But this discovery—its structural significance has already been pointed out, in connection with *Heart of Darkness*—is not merely moral; it is deeper and more compelling. Smitten, in the context of his discussion of *The Secret Agent,* speaks of "an artistic pattern which resolves itself in a final stasis of illumination embracing at once all portions of the narrative."[26] In the present analysis this quality has not been stressed, for it has been frequently pointed out in earlier critical assessments of the works under consideration. It is a quality that these spatial fictions share with those we have called the novel-as-poem (Woolf, Proust, etc.). Smitten refers us to Robert Scholes and Robert Kellogg, according to whom in the twentieth century "plots began to be developed which were based on rearranging time so that the resolution became not so much a stasis of concluded action as a stasis of illumination."[27] Yet if the traditional novel ends in a stasis of concluded action and the novel-as-poem in a stasis of illumination, the spatial novel based on a continuous fable and on

25. Conrad, *Under Western Eyes* (London: Dent, 1947), p. 67.
26. Smitten, "Flaubert and the Structure of *The Secret Agent,*" p. 164.
27. Scholes and Kellogg, *The Nature of Narrative* (New York: Oxford University Press, 1966), p. 235.

nonlinear narrative time achieves its resolution through both kinds of stasis.

The crucial importance of illumination in a work like *Lord Jim* or *Absalom, Absalom!* indicates that in a merely technical analysis, however exhaustive, no enumeration of recurrences and thematic collocation, of recognizable symmetries and contrasts, can ever reach the spatial effect of the whole.

There is spatial fiction to which a technical description will do almost full justice, but it does not belong to the model we have been discussing. It belongs to what we have classified as group four (the novel of indeterminate sequentiality). We will not go into the fascinating, entertaining patterns created by the surfaces of the French New Novel but discuss only one of its specimens, Claude Simon's *Flanders Road* (1960), which shares some important qualities with those I am studying: I wish to show what it has in common with our model and where it differs from it.

To show how Simon has radicalized some of Faulkner's indeterminacies in the structure of the novel, several of his works could be cited, but the most characteristic and perhaps most exciting example seems to be *Flanders Road*. In a style full of Faulknerian mannerisms and idiosyncracies, such as excessive use of the present participle and of phrases like "as if," "and this too,"[28] he elaborates upon a crucial situation in compound sentences that fixate aspects of one and the same situation. His novels are "a compendium of Faulknerian favorite devices"[29] with the purpose of presenting "the contiguity, the coexistence and the simultaneity of recollections of different moments in time in our mind."[30] His purpose is "to telescope time so that we *see everything at once* instead of in succession, to convert narration in time into a picture in space."[31] And perhaps, he really does achieve as complete a spatialization of time as has ever been carried out in a novel that describes historical action and successive human interrelationships.

---

28. John Fletcher, *New Directions in Literature* (London: Caldar and Boyars, 1968), p. 121.

29. W. M. Frohock, "Faulkner and the 'Roman nouveau': An Interim Report," *Bucknell Review*, 10, No. 3 (1962), 189.

30. Ibid., p. 124.

31. Vivian Mercier, *The New Novel from Queneau to Pinget* (New York: Farrar, Straus and Giroux, 1971), p. 277.

Like Faulkner starting his plan for the story of *The Sound and the Fury* with little Caddy's muddy drawers, Simon started with the image of a dead horse, and as Faulkner's novel is composed by telling the same story four times,[32] so Simon's "cavalrymen return three times in their wandering" toward the dead horse.[33] There are further repeated situations: the triangle scene between de Reixach, Corrine, and Iglesia in the stable is reproduced in the references to an analogous relationship connected with the antique family picture of an earlier de Reixach. These images recur through the narrative, which, developed with great intensity, is difficult to follow. The incidents from various periods melt into one another: juxtapositions are established, identities suggested, sequences broken, and thematic unities disrupted. The narrator, Georges, not only refers to his own experiences but at the same time thinks of previous conversations and imagines scenes that he has not witnessed but that have a compelling, haunting quality for him while thinking about de Reixach's death. In working one's way through the cellular composition based on the "intertextuality"[34] produced by the various voices at different time levels, frequently changed within a single interminable sentence, one notices that the narrator's tone "differs also with his changing attitudes towards his story: he observes, remembers and conjectures with one voice, visualizes with another, reconstructs with a third and questions with a fourth."[35]

It is difficult not only to distinguish levels of narrative but also to disentangle the chronological order of the past events to which Georges's story keeps returning, amplifying and rephrasing each time. The actual focus of the narration—Georges in bed with de Reixach's widow, Corrine, after the war—is thoroughly hidden and can be established only by indirect, subtle clues that the reader can hardly be patient enough to perceive by himself even in repeated attempts.

The question poses itself whether all this cumbersome organization is meaningful. Like Faulkner's novels, *Flanders Road* achieves

32. *Faulkner in the University,* ed. Frederick L. Gwynn and Joseph L. Blotner (Charlottesville: University of Virginia Press, 1959), pp. 1, 6.
33. Mercier, *The New Novel,* p. 268.
34. Dominique Lanceraux, "Modalités de la narration dans *La route des Flandres,*" *Poétique,* 14 (1973), 249.
35. Morton P. Levitt, "Disillusionment and Epiphany: The Novels of Claude Simon," *Critique* (Georgia), 12, No. 1 (1970), 58.

a conjunction of history and individual fate, and critics claim for
Simon's works a vision "of the disillusionment of man, of the be-
trayal of human ideals and values by a universe that is eternally
hostile, and especially so when man is most idealistic."[36] But the
technique seems to have a gratuituousness by far exceeding that of
Faulkner's idiosyncracies. In opposition to the works discussed
above, in Simon's the basic story ("fable") is not continuous but is
rather a series of flashes that sometimes can be put into an actual
time order only with great difficulty and little certainty.

Although the narration constitutes an almost uninterrupted flux, it
returns over and over to a series of discontinued insights, rather than
establishing a story *line*. The number of points in time that are
presented is so limited that they could almost be counted. These
features place it with works that can be grouped as novels of indeterminate sequentiality, works of Alain Robbe-Grillet, for instance,
rather than subsume it under the model inherent in our first group,
headed by *Lord Jim* as a prototype. One must admit that it is a
radical development, a transformation of the group's basic characteristics.

One of the basic models offers a wealth of possibilities for the
development of new, highly inventive, and imaginative forms. By
way of contrast with the work of Claude Simon, let us glance at
Mario Vargas Llosa's *The Green House* (1965). The novel deals
with life in the Peruvian jungle and the small towns by the river and
on the edge of the desert. It presents a fictional world based on a
genuinely historical, though probably slightly mythicized, culture—
partly inspired by Faulkner. It does not imitate the composition of
any of Faulkner's novels, but it does use his structural techniques,
even more systematically dividing strands of action into separate
sections, which through each of the book's five parts reappear in the
same order.

The story of Lalita (who in the narration never seems as if she has
a central position) from her provincial girlhood through her mar-
riages to the smuggler Fushìa and the river pilot Nievo joins the
history of the building, burning, and second lease of the Green
House brothel. In fact, one character only, Bonifacia—the Indian
girl, first servant in the Monastery, then servant friend to Lalita,

36. Ibid., p. 45.

later married to an army sergeant, finally whore in the Green House—brings the two strains of the action together. But they can hardly be called stories: the techniques of each of the recurring sets of sections is different, but the action never seems to progress except through infinitely small variations in the talk or the descriptions, or in slight modifications of occurrences—such as the soldiers' repeated struggle with Indians in the swampy reaches in the jungle. Any time we infer that events have actually moved forward, we are surprised! Yet in each of the four parts of the book, through the five sections of each, the time sequences recur in a regular rhythm. Each set of sections takes place at a different point in the overall action, and the characters in each are usually different ones—sometimes conversations of various groups of people are intermixed on the same page—and we have the feeling throughout much of the novel that we are reading our way through a mosaic of fictional vignettes, rather than through an integrated action. Thus an awareness of narrative trajectory is replaced by an overview of constantly copresent areas of fictional action in which the initial situations recur and only at the very end join into one circuitous thread, perceived intermittently but recognizably belonging to a whole.

A generalized description of compositional technique, like the present one, does not pay justice to the liveliness, humor, and vitality underlying this post-Faulknerian structure. Yet within each section there are repetitions or slight variants upon each dialogue or anecdotal incident—reminiscent of the deliberately mystifying devices of the French New Novelists. No narrative focus, no central occurrence or basic situation, no epiphanically radiating sense, no all-informing significance seem to dominate the novel, as they do in Faulkner, Conrad, and Ford. In a different way from Claude Simon's work, Vargas Llosa's novel is a hybrid belonging both to groups one and four within our division of spatial fiction.

Every year brings new experiments worth considering within the orbit of our theme. One wonders, however, whether under the heading of spatial form and narrative time sequence we are justified in expecting basic innovations. Time sequence, we have seen, presupposes some kind of continuous action, which in most spatial fiction is conveyed through some kind of systematic or patterned chronological distortion with a logic of its own. Radical experiment in fiction has lately been geared toward involving the reader in the actual production of the work that has a concomitant the abolishing of significant time-conditioned fictional action. To remain on Latin American soil, an exciting, entertaining, and intellectually exacting experiment like Julio Cortazar's widely acclaimed *Hopscotch* (1963) is basically a rumbustious neopicaresque sequence of adventures. The basic innovation is the choice left to the reader to insert or not between chapters, scrupulously though sometimes misleadingly, marked additional passages mainly dealing with intellectual argument without direct thematic purport to the place in the text to which they are assigned.

A different and even more extreme freedom is left to the reader in a work like Marc Saporta's *Composition No. 1* (1962), which consists of a package of loose leaves that can be put into any order the reader cares to invent. The theory behind this innovation is that of Umberto Eco's "open work," in which the interpreter—the reader of the score or the performer—of a work by Pousseur or Stockhausen does not interpret a completed score but intervenes in the work, determining the duration of the tones or their sequence in an "act of artistic improvisation."[37] It is clear, however, that a literary work of this sort cannot pretend to deal with any kind of narrative sequentiality unless one thinks of a string of anecdotes or, in Saporta's case, a long series of vignettes without references to any of the other fragments, though of course the same characters, in situations of the same type as on other leaves, appear and can be put into any arbitrary order. Since, given an infinite number of possible permutations, no single one can possess significance,[38] experiments or games of this sort go beyond the subject that we have been considering.

37. Eco, *L'oeuvre ouverte*, trans. Cahntal Roux de Bezieux (Paris: Seuil, 1965), p. 15.

38. The interconnections that necessarily exist between the 144 constituent parts of an infinite number of series, would give the work a spatial character. But the author's own note on the dust jacket, while claiming significance for his text, is witness to the triviality of what it says: "The reader is asked to cut these pages like a pack of cards. To lay them out, if he wants, with his left hand like a soothsayer. The order in which the leaves turn out in the game will direct X's destiny.

"For time and the order of events regulate life more than the nature of these events. Certainly, there is a frame imposed by History: a man's presence in the maquis, his participation in the occupying troups in Germany, these belong to a determined epoch. Equally, the facts which have marked his childhood cannot be presented like those that he lived through as an adult.

"Yet it is not insignificant to know whether he met his mistress, Dagmar, before

In conclusion, let us briefly sum up our main findings. Spatial form in fiction is achieved either through a network of recurring motifs (when there is no continuing developing social or physical action in the forefront—basically this includes the mental action of reminiscence and anticipation), or through a pattern of forward-and-backward moving in time that plays against the chronological order of events. The two types do not exclude each other, but whereas Joseph Frank and most critics of modern literature have closely studied the first, we have tried here to concentrate on a general overview of the other.

Lord Jim was taken as a provisional general model. It has been shown that a narrative focus is important for the establishment of the nonchronological account of events, and that a basic situation radiating some kind of noumenous significance can be said to embody the main themes of such works.

It might be possible to define this group as spatial novels with a continuous story. Other types of spatial fiction I have classified in three further categories. Their features might now be briefly outlined in the light of the preceding analysis of the first and, genetically, earliest group.

In the second category belong works usually associated with the stream-of-consciousness method, though these seem to present only a special case within a somewhat large basic category or group that also includes Proust. Since no meaningful continuous story line can be worked out even when the recurring motifs are examined for that purpose, the stream-of-consciousness technique or the roaming memory by itself lends such works the status of spatial fiction. Yet since their spatiality does not depend on the story level, one would not apply to them the statement by Scholes and Kellogg that within twentieth-century narrative the achievement of a stasis of illumination means that "the missing pieces of the temporal jigsaw puzzle" are "all finally in place and the picture therefore complete."[39]

---

or after his marriage; whether he abused little Helga as an adolescent or as a mature man; whether the theft of which he is guilty happened under the cover of the Resistance or in less troubled times; whether the accident which he suffered has any connection with the theft—or the rape—or whether it happened during the escape.

"It depends on the interlinking of circumstances whether the story ends happily or badly. A life is composed of multiple elements. But the number of possible ways of composition is infinite."

39. Scholes and Kellogg, *The Nature of Narrative*, p. 235.

A third category consists of works made up of seemingly auton-omous parts that roughly coincide in time but coexist in some kind of tension due to the different points of view and the ensuing differ-ent interpretations of facts. Chronology—and its distortions within such a cycle and its separate sections—is a significant aspect of the general perspective of these novels and the interrelationship of their parts.

The most radical experiments with time seem, however, to belong to the fourth category, which includes a wealth of new fictional structures thought out mainly in France or inspired by French tech-nical innovations. In such works it is impossible to put events into any kind of even incomplete chronological order. The events de-scribed repeat themselves with variations: the actual level of fiction-al reality cannot be distinguished from illusions, remembrances, imaginings—so events themselves become recurring motifs, dis-turbing and misleading. This fourth group, except for the more extreme ambiguity of the motifs in it, is spatial in the sense of the stream-of-consciousness group but without the kind of symbolic reverberation that would give metaphoric significance to the action. The indeterminacy and lack of significance of the actual order may be an indication that spatial narrative fiction is dying into some new category for which the traditional genre names, like "novel" or "story," are no longer adequate.

The larger part of this essay has dealt with fiction in which the sequence of events is played against the layers of fictional time in the organized narration. This in itself is a key to the spatial organi-zation of such works. These novels belong to a historical model that follows the traditional type of sequential fiction, usually realistic, occasionally with elements of fantasy. In literature in English we can identify its beginnings with the incipient Modernism of Conrad and see it achieve its culmination with Faulkner. Variations, in-spired especially by Faulkner, occur later; examples range from Claude Simon in France to Mario Vargas Llosa in Peru. The spatial organization of new fictional forms that develop between and after the two world wars depends on what seems to be a logical extension of the principle commanding the spatial functioning of earlier types. One difference between the two main types has, however, to be recognized. When the attribute of spatiality is applied to works of the *Lord Jim* type, it seems largely to depend on a subjective inter-

pretation of particular literary effects produced by the juxtaposition
of distinct time segments and the repeated resumption of particular
situations. More objectively evident signs of spatiality occur in the
Modernist and post-Modernist use of collocation and juxtaposition
of verbal motifs.

IV

The Theoretical Context of Spatial Form

7

Spatial Form in the Context of Modernist Aesthetics

James M. Curtis

"The twentieth century has addressed itself to arts of juxtaposition as opposed to earlier arts of *transition*."[1] This statement by Roger Shattuck in 1958 represents a late stage in a long process of development in Modernist criticism whose key document, Joseph Frank's "Spatial Form in Modern Literature," appeared in 1945. This mode of critical thought raises interconnected issues, such as the relationship between criticism and philosophy, the relationship between literature and the other arts, and the intriguing, dialectical relationship between national traditions and cosmopolitanism which characterizes much of twentieth-century thought in general. Yet to understand these issues themselves, one needs to interpret them in the context of the discussions of space and time in modern thought, especially in science and philosophy.

Science and philosophy have had a particularly important relationship in Western thought since the triumph of Newtonian physics, which posited a uniform space and time existing independently of any observer, and Kant's acceptance of uniform space and time as inherent modes of thought. In terms of the philosophy of science, Newton and Kant defined what Thomas S. Kuhn calls a "para-

1. Roger Shattuck, *The Banquet Years: The Origins of the Avant Garde in France, 1885 to World War I*, rev. ed. (New York: Vintage, 1968), p. 332.

digm," a set of rules that make rational investigation possible; Kuhn
states that the work of people who define paradigms meets two
criteria: "Their achievement was sufficiently unprecedented to
attract an enduring group of adherents away from competing modes
of scientific activity. Simultaneously, it was sufficiently open-ended
to leave all sorts of problems for the redefined group of practitioners
to resolve."[2] To understand Kuhn's concept of a paradigm, one
needs to keep in mind his assumption that the mind does more than
evaluate "raw facts"; since facts and theory interact, Newton and
Kant to some extent *created* the principles they embodied in their
work; contrary to popular belief, they did not *discover* previously
existing but unknown principles. Thus a paradigm shift, and a re-
definition of physical reality, occurred when Einstein's relativity
theory denied the existence of uniform space and time.

"Paradigm," a grammatical term, has great relevance for critics
who produce verbal responses to verbal works of art. In this essay, I
argue that Frank's "Spatial Form in Modern Literature" represents a
paradigm shift in the theory of prose and that it appeared as a
response to a particular situation in critical theory, a situation re-
sembling certain situations in science.

The validity of scientific theories depends in large measure on
their ability to predict phenomena: thus when anomalies (phenomena the theory cannot explain) occur, a crisis results. If the crisis
proves sufficiently severe, only the emergence of a new paradigm
will resolve it. Like the sciences, the arts experienced crisis after
crisis in the first quarter or so of the twentieth century as innovative masterpieces appeared at a bewildering rate. As a result, criticism rapidly became what Kuhn calls "a crisis-ridden field," as it
attempted to explain and interpret the hermetic, enigmatic works
that have now become the classics of Modernism.

For various reasons, working out a theory of modern prose became more difficult than working out a theory of modern poetry.
With the exceptions of Viktor Shklovsky and Mikhail Bakhtin in
Russia, virtually none of the great Modernist critics were doing
innovative work with prose. Whereas many influential poets had
written, and were writing, about poetry, few novelists wrote about
their work. Indeed, Gide constitutes a striking exception as the only

2. Kuhn, *The Structure of Scientific Revolutions,* 2d ed. (Chicago: University of
Chicago Press, 1970), p. 10.

major theoretician-practitioner of the novel in Europe during the twenties. Yet the works of four authors posed seemingly unsolvable problems: Tolstoy and Dostoevsky on the one hand, and Proust and Joyce on the other. Critics who had grown up on nineteenth-century realism unconsciously generalized their assumptions about, say, Dickens and Balzac to apply to all literature. Crisis resulted when the facts—novels by these four artists—failed to fit the theory, and in the twenties we find critics again and again confessing their failure to assimilate these artists to any existing theory. Such statements characterize a group that has not achieved what Kuhn calls "normal science," for meaningful investigation requires a generally accepted paradigm. Because purely literary categories offered little help, critics turned to space and time; and a treatment of space and time, directly or indirectly, involved Kant.

As Einstein attacked Newton's physics, many of the important philosophers of the last century or so have attacked Kant's philosophy. Although Nietzsche's work offers the best-known example of explicitly anti-Kantian thought, those who wished to deal with time and space found themselves drawn into a confrontation with Kant. Of all those who participated in the anti-Kantian movement, William James and Henri Bergson have the greatest immediate relevance.

James interests us here because of a remarkable article, "The Perception of Space," which he published in *Mind* in 1887. After a lengthy analysis of our sensations of space, he concludes with a historical survey of treatments of the subject in philosophy. He has this to say about Kant:

> The essence of the Kantian contention is that there are not *spaces,* but *Space*—one infinite continuous *Unit*—and that our knowledge of *this* cannot be a piecemeal affair, provided by summation and abstraction. To which the obvious reply is that, if any known thing bears on its front the *appearance* of piecemeal construction and abstraction, it is this very notion of the infinite unitary space of the world. It is a *notion,* if there ever was one; and no intuition.[3]

James does not use that very important word for him, "pluralism," but the implicit pluralism in his treatment of sensation clearly makes an acceptance of Kantian uniform space impossible. Early in the

3. James, "The Perception of Space," *Mind,* 12 (1887), 542. Here and below, I follow James's capitalization and emphasis.

article, for example, he asserts, *"If spatial feelings are to be perceived alongside of each other and in definite order they must appear as parts in a vaster spatial feeling which can enter the mind simply and all at once."*[4] The very idea of "spatial feeling" clearly implies a more complex organization than that which uniform space would create. Strikingly enough, James even used the term "spatial form," although in a very different way from that in which Frank was to use it over half a century later: "We have shown that, within the range of every sense, experience takes *ab initio* the spatial form" (p. 30). He means that one can understand the perception of space in terms of each individual sense; for James, this fact alone refutes Kant. James's own attitudes led him to concentrate on more pragmatic studies than the meaning of space, but the philosopher with whom people generally associate him, Henri Bergson, did essential work with this problem.

Bergson shared some important assumptions with James: both took human consciousness, not abstractions, as the essential concern of philosophy. Bergson proceeds in a different way, however—by insisting on the *distinction* between time and space. These two, he announces in the conclusion to his first book, *Essay on the Immediate Data of Consciousness* (1887), "are no more in us than outside, but the very distinction between inside and outside is the result of time and space."[5] Bergson's strenuous criticism of Kant stems from his belief that "Kant's error was to have taken time for a homogeneous milieu" (p. 119). When one thinks of time and space as identical, what Bergson calls "the deeply rooted habit of developing time in space" (p. 81) appears. Spatialized time, as in the phrase "historical perspective," allows only discrete succession of unrelated events and thus destroys the possibility of the continuity of life itself.

Hence, "The whole difficulty of the problem which concerns us comes from the fact that perception is represented as a photographic view of things" (p. 188). Twenty years later, in *Creative Evolution* (1907), this comparison becomes an analogy between perception in the modern age and a movie projector, which shows a discrete series

4. Ibid., p. 11.
5. Bergson, *Oeuvres* (Paris: Presses Universitaires de France, 1959), p. 153; my translation.

of pictures and thereby creates the impression of motion and continuity—but only the impression: "Let us imagine that the rapidity of
the flux (of individual pictures in the projector) becomes infinite.
Let us imagine . . . that the trajectory of the mobile T (time) is given
all at once, and that all past, present, and future history of the
material universe is spread out instantaneously in space" (p. 781).
Bergson's point is that a movie projector whose speed became infinite would spread out all time in space. We can recognize this as
an extreme statement of the spatialization of time, of course; if
past, present, and future can somehow, if only theoretically, be
spread out instantaneously in space, this necessarily implies a rigid
determinism, since the future already exists. And it was the deterministic, mechanical concept of spatialized time that Bergson
wished to refute.

History has its own logic, however, and this passage from *Creative Evolution* gave rise to one of the most fruitful misunderstandings in intellectual history; time meant discrete sequence to Modernists, no matter how much they read and admired Bergson, and
time implied determinism, evolution, social progress, and the like—
in short, all things against which they were rebelling. If time represented the old world, space represented the new; they proclaimed
themselves proponents of space and structure, not time and sequence. And they seized upon Bergson to justify their abolition of
time; in the process, they completely reversed his original meaning.
But no one seems to have noticed or minded, and the question of
right or wrong obviously has no relevance to anyone who wants to
understand the development of critical thought.

By associating space with structure, Modernists could associate
structure with meaning, and meaning with eternal, mythical existence; as they witnessed the disintegration of the world into which
they had been born, they sought permanent meaning all the more
vigorously. For many Modernists, art had ceased to express moral
absolutes and began to express ontological absolutes. (To be sure,
some—like Eliot—wished to equate the two.) Moreover, this
change has an analogy in the development of science, for Einstein's
physics did not eliminate absolutes in physical theory either; rather,
it redefined these absolutes. Einstein denied absolute status to time
and space, and attributed it instead to the speed of light. Nowhere

did Modernists carry through the analogous development, the attribution of absolute meaning to literature, more vigorously than in England.

T. E. Hulme first became well known as England's most enthusiastic champion of Bergson, and (to risk a pun) he spread the gospel of space among his numerous gifted friends. He characterized Bergson's work (often paraphrasing or simply translating long passages) as "The Philosophy of Extensive Manifolds." Given Hulme's seminal role in the formation of Imagism, the denial of historical time soon became a common concept among the British avant-garde. Ezra Pound anticipated a general attitude only by a little when he wrote in *The Spirit of Romance* (1910): "It is dawn at Jersualem while midnight hovers above the Pillars of Hercules. All ages are contemporaneous. It is B.C., let us say, in Morocco. The Middle Ages are in Russia."[6] However, this essay concerns the use of space and time as critical concepts, and thus it concentrates on the decade when Bergsonians of various kinds matured—the twenties.

The decade begins with T. S. Eliot's *The Sacred Wood* (1920), and ends with G. Wilson Knight's *The Wheel of Fire* (1930), for which Eliot wrote an introduction. Both works had immense influence, both dealt with poetry, and both proclaimed their allegiance to space, and their rejection of time. In his introduction to *The Sacred Wood,* Eliot describes the critic's concern with tradition in the following way:

> It is part of the business of the critic to preserve tradition—where a good tradition exists. It is part of his business to see literature steadily and to see it whole; and this is eminently to see it *not* as consecrated by time, but to see it beyond time; to see the best work of our time and the best work of twenty-five hundred years ago with the same eyes.[7]

As for Knight, in the first chapter of *The Wheel of Fire,* he states that he does not wish to find fault with this or that aspect of Shakespeare but to understand his work, and each play, as a totality; he proposes to do this in terms that both recall Bergson and anticipate Frank:

6. Pound, *The Spirit of Romance* (New York: New Directions, 1968), p. 5.
7. Eliot, "Introduction," in *The Sacred Wood* (London: Methuen, 1950), pp. xv–xvi.

But to receive the whole Shakespearian vision into the intellectual consciousness demands a certain and very definite act of mind. One must be prepared to see the whole play in space as well as in time. . . . A Shakespearian tragedy is set spatially as well as temporally in the mind. By this I mean that there are throughout the play a set of correspondences which relate to each other independently of the time-sequence which is the story. . . . This I have sometimes called the play's "atmosphere."[8]

Knight seems to have synthesized philosophy and poetry here; he has applied Baudelaire's correspondences to the relationships among the various parts of the work, and he has clearly understood the implications for criticism of spreading time in space. Like a good Modernist, Knight strongly rejects the nineteenth century's emphasis on the story, on character, and on morality. Moreover, he generalizes the attitudes of his own age, as we expect an ahistorical critic to do:

What I have called the "spatial" approach is implicit in our imaginative pleasure to a greater or a less degree always. And it is, probably, the ability to see larger and still larger areas of a great work spatially with a continual widening of vision that causes us to appreciate it more deeply, to own it with our minds surely, on every reading . . . [p. 4]

Although the details of Knight's analysis do not concern us here, we should notice that Knight consistently refers to Shakespeare's "poetry," not to his "plays," and, indeed, suggests that the performances of the actors and actresses, the sets, and so forth, do not deserve the critic's attention.

Thus we find that Hulme, Pound, Eliot, and Knight all equate poetry with creativity in general; the twenties, a wonderfully productive period in the history of the modern novel, lacked an aesthetics of the novel. Three books that appeared almost simultaneously in the late twenties responded to this crisis in the critical paradigm: Edwin Muir's *The Structure of the Novel* (1928); E. M. Forster's *Aspects of the Novel* (1927); and Wyndham Lewis's *Time and Western Man* (1927). All three men were artists themselves, of course, and all three used the time-space opposition to interpret and classify prose works. But here the resemblances end and the differences begin.

8. Knight, *The Wheel of Fire* (London: Oxford University Press, 1930), p. 3.

Muir states on the first page that "the object of this book is to study the principles of structure in the novel."[9] Acutely aware of the shortcomings of current criticism of the novel, he characterizes its vocabulary as "ridiculously inadequate." Like Frank later, he mentions the affinities among the arts and associates them with time and space: "The annihilation of time in the statue and of space in music has in reality the effect of making both absolute" (p. 90). Time and space give Muir an ahistorical typology that distinguishes between the "dramatic novel" and the "character novel": "the imaginative world of the dramatic novel is in Time, the imaginative world of the character novel in Space" (pp. 62–63). While Muir places no value judgment on time as opposed to space, he reverses the usual meaning of the words: "In the one [the dramatic novel in time] we shall find a loosely woven pattern, in the other [the character novel in space] the logic of causality" (p. 64). In fact, Muir's criticism anticipates such later books as Gaston Bachelard's *The Poetics of Space,* for he analyzes the articulation of time and space in the works themselves and has some worthwhile things to say:

> In the dramatic novel in general the articulation can be evoked by calling to mind the different feeling of the time and space in various novels. In the dramatic novel in general the articulation of space is vague and arbitrary. London might be a thousand miles away from Wuthering Heights or Casterbridge. But from the London of *Vanity Fair* and *Tom Jones,* on the other hand, every place has its just geographical distance, and no part of England, no small town, no country estate or remote parsonage is inaccessible. [pp. 64–65]

This is a valuable kind of criticism, and we still do not have enough of it.

But once Muir has had his say on the eighteenth- and nineteenth-century British classics and takes up other works, he becomes less certain. He introduces a third classification to account for a striking anomaly: "Scattering all our generalizations, *War and Peace* seems to give a comprehensive picture of life both in time and space, and in spite of that to achieve universality" (p. 94). Muir therefore introduces a third classification, "the chronicle," to come to terms with *War and Peace.* In his rather disorganized discussion of Tolstoy, he also introduces a typical misinterpretation of Bergson when he says,

9. Muir, *The Structure of the Novel* (London: Hogarth Press, 1963), p. 7.

"The moment of aesthetic vision lifts us out of the flux" (p. 22). He seems to be referring to Bergson's belief in the holistic perception of the artist; but whereas for Bergson holistic perception creates the wholeness of time, for Muir it transcends time. Muir has no difficulty in identifying the major contemporary anomalies of the period:

> The two outstanding works of prose fiction of the present age are almost certainly *A la recherche du temps perdu* and *Ulysses*. Neither is in the reigning tradition of the chronicle; and both have been claimed as new forms. For contemporary reasons they demand attention. [p. 124]

Whatever they demand, they receive grudging praise at best from Muir. Of Proust, he says, "The form was legitimate, for it suited Proust's genius; but it is questionable whether it could ever be used by anyone else" (p. 126). Joyce fares less well: "*Ulysses* is a work of extraordinary literary virtuosity, and some of its technical innovations are striking; but in structure it is not revolutionary. Its faults are obvious: its design is arbitrary, its development feeble, its unity questionable" (pp. 126–127). Muir cannot perceive a structure in the work: "Mr. Joyce's insistence on the symbolical framework of the book is . . . a confession that it is formless in itself" (p. 128). Muir does not even apply his own ideas about the organization of time and space to a work for which they would have proven fruitful; in his terms, *Ulysses* is obviously a character novel.

Although Muir uses the time-space opposition, he does not choose between its poles; Forster, in *Aspects of the Novel*, does choose and says so flatly:

> Time, all the way through, is to be our enemy. We are to visualize the English novelist not as floating down that stream which bears all its sons away unless they are careful, but as seated together in a room, a circular room, a sort of British Museum reading room—all writing their novels simultaneously.[10]

Forster has the distinction of attempting to see literature whole—to see it spread in space—more consistently than anyone else at the time; yet unlike Eliot, he allows no development, change, or interaction in tradition:

10. Forster, *Aspects of the Novel* (New York: Harcourt, Brace, 1950), p. 21.

All through history writers while writing have felt more or less the same. They have entered a common state which it is convenient to call inspiration, and having regard to that state, we may say that History develops, Art stands still. [p. 38]

Like Muir, Forster knows his English classics, of course; with his warmth and wit, with the fullness of his humanity, he can apply a Modernist insistence on the difference between art and reality in an analysis of *Moll Flanders* and create a memorable passage of criticism.

But as the critic who lives in the age of post-Modernism rereads *Aspects of the Novel* (if only to savor its stylistic delights), he realizes that Forster abolishes history primarily in order to characterize more distinctly just those features of the novel—plot and character, for example—that historical critics had discussed. We miss such leitmotifs of New Criticism as "structure" and "ambiguity" in Forster; and when he comes to the anomalous works, he too has his difficulties.

Like Muir, Forster thinks that no one can classify Tolstoy and Dostoevsky. He claims, in fact, that no one can even analyze them. Thus he writes that "after one has read *War and Peace* for a bit, great chords begin to sound, and we cannot say exactly what struck them" (p. 63). As for Dostoevsky, he "is a great novelist in the ordinary sense . . . [and] he has also the greatness of a prophet, to which our ordinary standards are inapplicable" (p. 192). But if Tolstoy and Dostoevsky transcend ordinary standards, Joyce does not.

Agreeing with Muir that *Ulysses* is "perhaps the most interesting literary experiment of our day" (p. 177), Forster senses the Homeric parallels and their meaning. Yet he does not discuss *Ulysses* as an experiment; he has nothing to say about its style and offers comments like this:

The Night Town scene does not come off except as a superfetation of fantasies, a monstrous coupling of reminiscences. Such satisfaction as can be attained in this direction is attained, and all through the book we have similar experiments—the aim of which is to degrade all things and more particularly civilization and art, by turning them inside out and upside down. [p. 180]

This opinion of Joyce is surely the only thing that Forster shares with our final critic of the twenties, Wyndham Lewis.

No one would care to argue, I think, that Lewis made any discernible attempt to avoid prolixity and self-indulgence in *Time and Western Man,* or that he did not feel a strong, compulsive need to oppose any popular movement of the time. But to explain the attacks on the Ballet Russe *and* Joyce *and* Bergson and all the rest of it by Lewis's personality alone will not suffice. Cantankerous and wrongheaded though he was, Lewis was most emphatically not obtuse. The famous (or infamous) denunciation of Modernism by a prominent Modernist in *Time and Western Man* makes sense only if we remember that those who liked Bergson and those who dislike him misunderstood him in equal measure.

Needing somebody to denounce, Lewis denounced Bergson without reading him, as the following comments show.

> Time for the bergsonian or relativist is fundamentally sensation; that is what Bergson's *durée* always conceals beneath its pretentious metaphysic. It is the glorification of the life-of-the-moment, with no reference beyond itself and no absolute or universal value; only so much value as is conveyed in the famous proverb *Time is money.* It is the *argent comptant* of literal life, in an inflexibly fluid Time.[11]

Anyone who knows his Bergson can point out obvious errors here; contrary to what Lewis says, Bergson emphasizes that we *cannot* perceive the present "with no reference beyond itself"—we can perceive only the interaction of the past and present—and he explicitly denies that *durée* can have any relationship to number. But it forms no part of the present undertaking to judge Lewis as a philosopher; like Knight and the other Modernists, Lewis could think of time only as the discrete succession of homogeneous units. Logically, then, he believed that anyone who asserted the importance of time was asserting the importance of the Newtonian universe and everything it represented:

> The material had already collected into a considerable patrimony by the time Bergson was ready to give it a philosophic form. The darwinian Theory and the background of nineteenth-century materialistic thought was already behind it. Under the characteristic headings Duration and Relativity the nineteenth-century mechanistic belief had now assumed a final form. [p. 87]

---

11. Lewis, *Time and Western Man* (Boston: Beacon Press, 1957), pp. 11–12. Here and below, I follow Lewis's emphasis and capitalization.

Since, to put it mildly, Bergson's prose is far easier to read than Joyce's, we expect that a writer who can make Bergson out to be a representative of the very philosophy that he wished most of all to refute can misread Joyce just as egregiously. And, as we know, Lewis did just this.

Lewis took the affirmation of *durée* in *Ulysses* as an affirmation of Newtonian mechanistic time and dismissed the "homeric framework" as "only an entertaining structural device or conceit" (p. 84). A careful rereading of "An Analysis of the Mind of James Joyce" makes us realize that Lewis writes more on the occasion of Joyce (of Joyce as an Irishman, of Joyce as a representative of Dublin's "shabby-genteel" intellectuals, of Joyce as similar to Proust), than about him. When Lewis does write about Joyce, it is to criticize his style—he grudgingly admires it but prefers Flaubert's. Fortunately, however, he states clearly why he cannot come to terms with Joyce: "I regard *Ulysses* as a *time-book*; and by that I mean that it lays its emphasis upon, for choice manipulates, and in a doctrinaire manner, the self-conscious time-sense, that has now been erected into a universal philosophy" (p. 84). This "universal philosophy" of time as discrete sequence denied any possibility of ontological status to the meaning that Lewis and his generation believed themselves to be creating in their work. Lewis was a typical Modernist not only in his rejection of time but also in his preference for space.

> But the Time conception of Bergson seems to us entirely to misrepresent the rôle of Space, and, as it were, shuffle and transpose their respective "realities." So what we seek to stimulate, and what we give the critical outline of, is a philosophy that will be as much a *spatial-philosophy* as Bergson's is a *time-philosophy*.
>
> Regarding mind as Timeless, it is more at home, we find, with Space. . . . For the objective world most useful to us, and what may be the same thing, most "beautiful," and therefore with most *meaning*, and that is further to say in a word with most *reality*, we require a space distinct from Time. [pp. 427–428]

All that Lewis knew, or needed to know, was that he believed in space; anyone who had the audacity to proclaim or imply an allegiance to time became a clear and present danger.

But the twenties turned into the thirties, and even where Modernism did not become a crime against the state, as it did in Russia and Germany, the thirties produced relatively little critical theory about prose in Europe; since it was published at the very end of the war, Frank's "Spatial Form in Modern Literature" summed up, and solved, many problems of the earlier period—and in doing so he made possible much of the best critical work of the last three decades.

New paradigms often come into being when someone resolves anomalies by applying previously existing concepts in a new and startling way, as in Einstein's application of non-Euclidean geometry to physical problems. Frank's essay does just this, because he applies Modernist theory to Modernist prose; although he does discuss Eliot's *The Waste Land,* he devotes most of his attention to prose, and precisely to Proust and Joyce, whose works had previously proven intractable. Moreover, he gives an example of how his paradigm works in his detailed analysis of Djuna Barnes's controversial minor classic *Nightwood.* After the publication of "Spatial Form in Modern Literature," criticism of modern prose achieved what Kuhn calls "normal science," because it now had a paradigm.

Early in the essay, Frank quotes Pound's famous definition of an image, "that which presents an intellectual or emotional complex in an instant of time." The definition seems most appropriate for short forms like the Japanese haiku, which Pound admired so much, but he applies it to the long novel. Pound's definition lacks the specificity that would make it a viable critical concept. Frank, however, thinking of the emphasis on the synthesis of the arts beginning with Wagner and the French Symbolists, creates a very productive definition by reinterpreting Lessing's distinction, in *Laokoön,* between the spatial arts of painting and sculture and the temporal arts of music and literature. The terms of Pound's definition of an image—and critical practice for several decades—implied that literature, too, could become a spatial art. Frank asserts that it in fact has done so, when he defines spatial form as "the exact complement in literature . . . to the developments that have taken place in plastic arts. . . . Both . . . have . . . attempted to overcome the time elements involved in their structure."[12] In Frank's reading of Lessing, the old space-time

12. Frank, "Spatial Form in Modern Literature," in his *The Widening Gyre: Crisis and Mastery in Modern Literature* (New Brunswick: Rutgers University Press, 1963), p. 57.

opposition takes on a new meaning, which gives it two functions.

First, Frank's use of the space-time opposition introduces an essential element in paradigmatic thought: historicism. Thus Kuhn calls his first chapter "A Role for History," because distinguishing the past from the present—as Forster, for example, refused to do—means accepting the validity of each as a coherent paradigm. An acceptance of historicism means that Frank can interpret the literature of the past, as Lessing did, as temporal and sequential, and reserve space and structure for modern literature. Second, "spatial" here expresses the relations between the arts in a very practical way; it makes possible interpretation that proceeds by juxtaposing what Frank calls "word groups," as one visually juxtaposes the compositional elements of a painting or a piece of sculpture. In *The Waste Land*

> syntactical sequence is given up for a structure depending on the perception of relationships between disconnected word-groups. To be properly understood, these word-groups must be juxtaposed with one another and perceived simultaneously. Only when this is done can they be adequately grasped . . . [p. 12]

For the first time in modern critical theory we have here not merely a description of the problem but a procedure for dealing with it. Frank insists that each of the great works of Modernist literature forms a whole, and he gives a method for arriving at a perception of this whole. Whereas the stylistic virtuosity of Proust and Joyce confounded earlier commentators, Frank can tell us that "Joyce's most obvious intention in *Ulysses* is to give the reader a picture of Dublin seen as a whole" (p. 17) and explicate Proust's search for *temps perdu* as a means of going beyond time.

Frank's essay does not remain purely speculative, as Continental criticism often does; his detailed analysis of *Nightwood* connects the generalizations of his introduction with specific aspects of a specific work, and thus greatly increases the productivity of the paradigm in the future. I emphasize the point because this ability to deal with specific problems places Frank in the pragmatic American tradition that caused James to rebel against the immense authority of Kant in the first place.

I certainly do not wish to suggest that no one had done any important work on the Modernist novel before Frank's essay appeared, or that all work on the Modernist novel after it appeared derives from it. Yet a number of critics have successfully applied Frank's method to modern literature and to works from the nineteenth century and even earlier periods, and this phenomenon of transference strikes me as noteworthy. Although we are beginning to understand the psychology of reading, we have hardly begun to analyze the psychology of literary scholarship as a special case of this problem. Both Frank and Kuhn can give some hints about this.

Frank tells us that spatial form "asks its readers to suspend the process of individual reference temporarily until the entire pattern of internal references can be apprehended as a unity" (p. 13), and, more specifically, "Joyce cannot be read—he can only be reread" (p. 19). To explicate this seeming paradox, we must follow in the tradition of James and Bergson (as well as that of most phenomenologists) and analyze the critic's thought processes as he or she interprets. And here Kuhn's work on scientific revolutions becomes most helpful, because Kuhn makes a vital issue of perception. He suggests that "we may want to say that after a revolution scientists are responding to a different world."[13] Scientists, or thinkers of any discipline, "respond to a different world," because they have internalized a different paradigm.

I myself experienced this phenomenon several years ago. Although I did not know it at the time, I was becoming familiar with some of the same feelings that Muir and Forster knew so well, for I had been puzzling over the seemingly random recurrence of certain words and images in Tolstoy and Dostoevsky. The great novels produced an undeniable effect but did so in a way that defied analysis. Then, upon reading "Spatial Form in Modern Literature," I felt a sense of elation because I perceived the possibility of fitting these words and images into a pattern; I had found a way—only one of many, naturally—to account for those "great chords" that Forster considered so mysterious. I could, in short, find meaning where I had found only anomaly before, because I had, more or less by accident, found a paradigm.[14]

This matter of the critic's perception has another implication as

13. Kuhn, *The Structure of Scientific Revolutions,* p. 111.
14. See my "Spatial Form as the Intrinsic Genre of Dostoevsky's Novels," *Modern Fiction Studies,* 18 (1972), 135–154; and "The Function of Imagery in *War and Peace,*" *Slavic Review,* 29 (1970), 460–480.

well. It seems to me that to take seriously Frank's concept of perceiving simultaneously the word groups constituting a work written in spatial form means to construct a nondiscursive Gestalt as an operator for analyzing previously puzzling passages. I believe that Frank had some such possibility in mind when he said that one can only reread Joyce. One must read the text once in order to acquire its Gestalt and only then begin to interpret it. (Actually, in constructing a Gestalt for Chekhov's *The Seagull*, I found that the process took more than one rereading.)[15]

Certain analogies exist between this procedure and some of Saussure's key concepts in his *Course in General Linguistics*. A Gestalt such as this relates to the text very much as Saussure's *langue*— "the group of linguistic habits which permit a person to understand and to make himself understood"[16]—relates to *parole*, actual discourse in the language. Someone who hears an utterance in a language whose *langue* he has not internalized cannot understand it; likewise, someone who reads a work written in spatial form without knowing the Gestalt for that work, finds it puzzling and frustrating. Thus we have the relationship— text : Gestalt :: *parole* : *langue*.

Once we understand this analogy, we realize that other analogies exist between Saussure and Frank—or, more generally, between Saussure and Modernist criticism in general. Saussure's distinction between synchronic linguistics, the study of the changes in language, and diachronic linguistics, the study of relationships within a language at a given time, corresponds to the now familiar distinction in criticism between time and space. Saussure sounds very much like a Modernist critic when he complains that "ever since modern linguistics has existed, one can say that it has been completely given over to diachronics" (p. 118; my translation). His book, however, changed that by creating a very powerful paradigm for synchronic, or structural, linguistics.

These analogies between Saussure and Frank explain the striking similarities between "Spatial Form in Modern Literature" and another remarkably influential essay, "The Structural Study of Myth," in which Claude Lévi-Strauss applied Saussure's principles

15. See my "Spatial Form in Drama: *The Seagull*," *Canadian-American Slavic Studies*, 6 (1972), 13–37.

16. Ferdinand de Saussure, *Cours de linguistique générale* (Paris: Payot, 1960), p. 112; my translation.

to the Oedipus myth. Both Frank and Lévi-Strauss begin by stating that the material to be studied makes no sense if one looks for continuity from one part to another, and both go on to describe a similar method for dealing with the material. Whereas Frank works from the analogy between painting and literature, Lévi-Strauss works from Saussure's distinction between *langue* and *parole*. He takes the text as *parole* whose *langue* he wishes to elicit. Nevertheless, the essential similarity of what they do becomes clear in what Lévi-Strauss calls "the very core" of his argument:

> The true constituent units of a myth are not the isolated relations but *bundles of such relations,* and it is only as bundles that these relations can be put to use and combined so as to produce a meaning. Relations pertaining to the same bundle may appear diachronically at remote intervals, but when we have suceeded in grouping them together we have re-organized our myth according to a time referent of a new nature.[17]

Lévi-Strauss's "bundles of relations" correspond exactly to Frank's "word-groups," and Lévi-Strauss's "time referent of a new nature" denies sequence as a determining structure and uses juxtaposition instead.

In the United States from 1930 to about 1955, Saussure's linguistic theories met with hostile criticism from Leonard Bloomfield and his followers, who emphasized the external, taxonomic description of linguistic units. The Bloomfieldians disliked Saussure's emphasis on language as a system of internal relationships, and thus anticipated the terms in which Philip Rahv was to attack Frank.

Unlike most twentieth-century critics, Rahv prefers time to space. After describing spatial form as the result of a "fear of history," he asserts: "The fear of history is at bottom the fear of the hazards of freedom. In so far as man can be said to be capable of self-determination, history is the sole sphere in which he can conceivably attain it."[18] As his use of the words "freedom" and "self-determination" indicate, Rahv represents here the American tradition of Romantic individualism, which prizes discreteness above all. This tradition contains an essential paradox in that it defines human-

17. Lévi-Strauss, "The Structural Study of Myth," in *Structural Anthropology* (New York: Basic Books, 1967), p. 207; Lévi-Strauss's emphasis.

18. Rahv, *The Myth and the Powerhouse* (New York: Farrar, Straus and Giroux, 1965), p. 20.

ity in terms of its sociopolitical organizations, yet demands that those organizations not impinge on humanity. This ambiguity toward systemic relationships appears clearly in Rahv's preference for time over space and gives his work an old-fashioned quality in the present context. Rahv may well never have heard of Bloomfield, but a belief in meaning as consisting of externally defined discrete units certainly unites the two men. Ultimately, the differences between Bloomfield and Saussure, and Rahv and Frank, pit a particular version of American pragmatism (one that does not necessarily coincide with James's pragmatism) against a particular outgrowth of European idealism.

The developmental history of any significant concept in twentieth-century thought probably resembles that of other concepts in other, sometimes unrelated, disciplines. Generally speaking, the more fruitful a given concept has proven in the past, the more analogies one can find between it and other concepts. The concept of spatial form illustrates the point very well; the numerous analogies between it and other concepts give a historical justification for the intuitive feeling many of us had when we read Frank's essay for the first time, a feeling that it created new possibilities for understanding great works of art. No critical concept can do more.

8

The Aporia of Recent
Criticism and the Contemporary
Significance of Spatial Form

Ronald Foust

Paul de Man has recently written of a growing "crisis" in contemporary criticism. He attributes it to "the incredible swiftness with which often conflicting tendencies succeed each other. . . . What seems crisis-like is, among outer signs, the impatient competitiveness with which various disciplines vie for leadership."[1] This intellectual malaise can be seen as the result of an ancient aporia that divides students of literature into warring camps, each armed with a sense of the *either/or* nature of literature's "ontological form." The existential or "subjective" position commits the critic to an impossible attempt to interpret the text from the *inside,* while the formalist or "objective" position condemns exegesis to the monotony latent in the demand that texts be viewed always from the *outside.* The result is intellectual instability, confusion, and "crisis."

This essay assumes that the essential task of contemporary critical theory lies in the effort to resolve this crisis by developing a synthetic theory. It further assumes that spatialization is an essential feature of the critical act and that it will play a significant role in the development of any crisis-mediating synthetic criticism of the future. Therefore, while spatial form is of great value to practical

1. De Man, *Blindness and Insight: Essays in the Rhetoric of Contemporary Criticism* (New York: Oxford University Press, 1971), pp. 3–5.

criticism in the form in which Frank formulated it in 1945, its longer-term value as an essential component in a "newer" criticism demands that we expand certain latent implications in the theory of which Frank was not, perhaps, aware. But in order for it to be taken seriously enough to function in this role, it must have a theoretical base from which to withstand the accusations hurled at it by a host of often violent antispatialists who proclaim it a "life-denying" theory that would "reduce the history of literature to sameness and static juxtaposition."[2] Its relevance to contemporary criticism can be established only by clearing it of the charge that it is simply an outdated formalism and thus too easily reducible "to the status of a period aesthetic."[3]

My concern is not to develop a yet more fashionable avant-garde theory but merely to try to encompass the dichotomous poles of recent critical thought. Therefore, while no attempt is made to deny the real differences between the theories to be compared here, I want to interface them as much as is realistically possible. This essay emphasizes their shared characteristics as the first step in overcoming the crisis about which de Man writes. My purpose is to demonstrate the extent to which Frank's view "that the best criticism as well as the best literature is dialectical—the working out of a total form (or synthesis) from the interactions of chaotic opposites"[4] resembles the basic assumptions of myth criticism, Structuralism, and the view of Existential phenomenology that "the final product of the creative act is, then, a fusion in which both elements, the subjective and the objective, merge."[5] I shall emphasize spatial form's role as an embryonic precursor of these other critical formulas, all of which are linked by their participation in the modern holistic vision of the literary work as a system of interrelated systems, even when the result is variously called an "object," an "archetype," a "consciousness," or a "structure."

2. Philip Rahv, *Literature and the Sixth Sense* (Boston: Houghton Mifflin, 1969), p. 212. He was the first to formulate the typical attack that spatial form represents "a fear of history [which] is at bottom the fear of the hazards of freedom" (p. 214).

3. Frank Kermode in a letter to this writer dated August 17, 1974; quoted by permission of the author.

4. Joseph N. Riddel, review of *The Widening Gyre: Crisis and Mastery in Modern Literature*, in *Comparative Literature Studies*, 3 (1966), 74.

5. David Halliburton, *Edgar Allan Poe: A Phenomenological View* (Princeton: Princeton University Press, 1973), p. 22.

In his original essay Frank provided a *raison d'être* for spatial form by concluding that the characteristic quality of modern literature is its "transformation of the historical imagination into myth— an imagination . . . which sees the actions and events of a particular time only as the bodying forth of eternal prototypes." Since "modern literature has been engaged in transmuting the time world of history into the timeless world of myth," it is myth that forms "the common content of modern literature [and] that finds its appropriate aesthetic expression in spatial form."[6] Some years after Frank's essay, Mircea Eliade compared the modern "historical" to the primitive "mythic" imagination and reached a similar conclusion. He noted among modern intellectuals an interest in "the myth of cyclical periodicity," and concluded that one saw in them "a revolt against historical *time,* an attempt to restore this historical time . . . to a place in the time that is cosmic, cyclical, and infinite." He concluded by noting that the work of both T. S. Eliot and James Joyce "is saturated with nostalgia for the myth of eternal repetition and, in the last analysis, for the abolition of time."[7] The type of literature that this "nostalgia" produced was the main concern of Frank's original essay. Frank's essay, however, is not myth criticism *per se.* Since Northrop Frye is so closely associated with the theory of literature as myth, I shall take his position as the basis for a comparison between myth criticism and spatial form.

I begin by noting two differences between spatial form and Frye's theory of genres and archetypes. The most obvious is that Frank limits his discussion to modern literature, while Frye develops a theory the limits of which are the limits of literature itself. And though Frye has been criticized for overdetermining his archetype, Frank, with one exception, provides no specific determinations for his "prototypes." This means that Frye is interested in the classification of the mythic content of literature, whereas Frank is primarily concerned with myth as the *necessary* content for the achievement of spatialization. Despite these minor differences, however, Frye brilliantly elaborates the same basic structural insights that Frank had earlier developed.

6. Frank, "Spatial Form in Modern Literature," in *The Widening Gyre: Crisis and Mastery in Modern Literature* (New Brunswick: Rutgers University Press, 1963), p. 60.

7. Eliade, *The Myth of the Eternal Return, or Cosmos and History* (Princeton: Princeton University Press, 1971), p. 153.

As long ago as 1934 Maude Bodkin had written that fiction

> reaches us as a passage of experience never present in its complete-
> ness. The task of the reader, before he can criticize, is to refashion
> the novel out of the march of experience as it passed . . . [while in
> drama] the procession of experience is marshalled and concentrated
> at certain peaks; so that, recalling the images of these, we can look
> back upon the whole play as a living unity.[8]

Frye echoes this attitude thirty years later when he writes that the
critic must "see literature, not only as complicating itself in time, but
as spread out in conceptual space from some unseen center."[9] This
"reflexive" reading is essential to myth criticism and, in the concept
of reflexive reference, to the theory of spatial form.

Both Frank and Frye follow Lessing in distinguishing between
arts that move in time and those that are articulated in space. Frye
notes: "In both cases the organizing principle is recurrence, which is
called rhythm when it is temporal and pattern when it is spatial" (p.
14). He then distinguishes between rhythm and pattern as a difference between temporal form and spatial meaning. Thus, "We may
call the rhythm of literature the narrative, and the pattern, the simultaneous mental grasp of the verbal structure, the meaning or significance. We hear or listen to a narrative, but when we grasp a writer's
total pattern we 'see' what he means" (p. 14). He calls this narrative
motion "displacement," which signifies for him what is usually
meant by verisimilitude. It is "indirect mythologizing" which,
although it is a necessary component of the communication of significance, is not the center of interest for the *critic*. Thus both Frye
and Frank admit the necessity of the temporal element in literature,
but Frye removes critical interest to the spatial act of weaving from
the various rhythms one pattern of sound, one essential or significant
form. This means that although

> we may tentatively accept the principle that, in the direct experience
> of fiction, continuity is the center of our attention; our later memory,
> or what I call the possession of it, tends to become discontinuous.
> Our attention shifts from the sequence of incidents to another focus: a
> sense of what the work of fiction was all *about*. . . . [T]he incidents

8. Bodkin, *Archetypal Patterns in Poetry: Psychological Studies of Imagination*
(London: Oxford University Press, 1934), p. 9.

9. Frye, *Fables of Identity: Studies in Poetic Mythology* (New York: Harcourt,
Brace and World, 1963), p. 13.

themselves tend to remain . . . discontinuous, detached from one another and regrouped in a new way. [p. 23]

This spatial reading derives from a conviction that the *critical* significance of literature is to be found not in narrative dynamics, but in "patterns of imagery" that "derive from the epiphanic moment, *the flash of instantaneous comprehension with no direct reference to time*" (p. 15; emphasis added). Therefore, when the critic encounters a text, "the most natural thing for him to do is to freeze it, to ignore its movement in time and look at it as a completed pattern of words, with all its parts existing simultaneously" (p. 21).

This sketch does obvious violence to the diversity of Frye's insights and especially to his specific task of demonstrating that it is "part of the critic's business to show how all literary genres are derived from the quest-myth" (p. 17).[10] But this reduction is justified by my purpose, which is to suggest that while myth criticism does more consciously what is usually only implicit in Frank, they are both tending toward what we may call a Structuralist hermeneutic.

Significant parallels between spatial form and myth criticism abound: both analyses are nonjudgmental descriptions of verbal phenomena conceived of in a "double relation"—that is, as both autonomous and yet participatory in a historical process. Both conceive the function of literary structures to be projecting archetypes or prototypes that are nonetheless individual creations, a part of the poet's private symbol system. Literature performs a double function, since the private prototypes take on social significance by being mediations between the individual and his collective human environment.[11] But by far the most important similarity between the

10. Frye's commitment to the radical vision of a literary "urmythos" separates him from Frank, who makes no such assertion. There is a freedom of authorial choice in Frank's generalized "prototypes" that is missing in Frye's elaborate schemata. Frank closer to S. E. Hyman's position that "for literary purposes, all myths are not one . . . The writer can use traditional myths with varying degrees of consciousness (with Joyce and Mann perhaps most conscious in our time)." "The Ritual View of Myth and the Mythic," in *Myth and Literature: Contemporary Theory and Practice,* ed. John B. Vickery (Lincoln: University of Nebraska Press, 1966), p. 57.

11. Maude Bodkin was one of the first to point out this "double-relation": "When a great poet uses the stories that have taken shape in his fantasy of the community, it is not his individual sensibility alone that he objectifies," but also the collective yearnings and values of the group, and he "communicates that experience, at once individual and collective, to others" (p. 8). This appears to be the significance of T. S. Eliot's remark that Joyce's "myth method" had made "the modern world possible for art."

two is the insistence that meaning, which is latent, is drawn from the work only by an act of freezing structures whose manifest form is temporal.[12]

In a recent essay that relates Frye to G. Wilson Knight's concept of spatial form but that curiously ignores Frank's contribution, Geoffrey Hartman writes that Knight's

> concept of spatial form is thus related to what Frye will call "total form." . . . But Frye carries Knight's position a step further. He argues that whatever literary structure is in itself, it must be spatial to the critic. Interpretation, to grasp the work as a complete and simultaneous pattern, must ignore its movement in time. The spatial is now a form that enables the understanding of art and makes criticism possible as a progressive science.[13]

But this is also the sense of Frank's remark that modern literature cannot be read but only reread. It is also the sense of his description of the act of reading modern literature as one of suspending judgment and one's willful desire to be carried along a "stream" of narrative created upon, and reciprocally creating, the illusion of

12. This metaphorical act of "freezing" is the point at which the antispatialists attack both myth and spatial form as "life denying." The attack, however, is based on a misunderstanding, since spatial form is not a prescription for correct fictional form, but only a heuristic device for critical discourse. Neither it nor myth criticism need be taken as dogmas. For myth and spatialization are unlike dogmas in that "they are plastic and dynamic. They look to the present and the future. As Malinowski says, they are made *ad hoc* and are 'constantly regenerated.'" Richard Chase, "Notes on the Study of Myth," in *Myth and Literature*, ed. Vickery, p. 71. More recently John J. White has expanded this viewpoint: "Mythological works develop their motifs. . . . Development means change of attitude, shift of emphasis and a focus on a different part of the [mythic] prefiguration. Hence, prefiguration becomes a kind of unraveling commentary." White, *Mythology in the Modern Novel: A Study of Prefigurative Techniques* (Princeton: Princeton University Press, 1971), p. 112.

13. Hartman, "Structuralism: The Anglo-American Adventure," in *Structuralism*, ed. Jacques Ehrmann (Garden City: Doubleday, 1966), pp. 147–148. Frank is relegated to a footnote, p. 150, as one who has explored the significance of spatial form. Hartman discusses some relations between spatial form and myth criticism but disapproves of both techniques. On the other hand, Jackson I. Cope's excellent book on *Paradise Lost* utilizes spatial form as a tool of mythic analysis, while Murray Krieger has combined spatial form with a "phenomenological" concept of the archetype in an attempt to develop an "ekphrastic" poetics. See respectively *The Metaphoric Structure of "Paradise Lost"* (Baltimore: The Johns Hopkins University Press, 1962), and "The Ekphrastic Principle and the Still Movement of Poetry: Or *Laokoön* Revisited," in Krieger's *The Play and Place of Criticism* (Baltimore: The Johns Hopkins University Press, 1967).

logic and the fiction of temporal form. To this end Frank, before Frye, created a methodology and a rudimentary vocabulary for future criticism. He suggests an empathetic or interpretive reading based on a nonjudgmental acceptance of the vision embodied in the text. This requires a process not unlike phenomenology's bracketing. Next, by a process of cross- (reflexive) reference of juxtaposed word groups, the critic begins to establish a mental picture of the structural interrelations of metaphors, actions, and characterizations (Frye's "patterns of imagery," the phenomenologists' "themes"). When such a reading is successful, the critic should arrive at both a logical and a phenomenological significance. He should also arrive at an understanding of the unique double relation between the work and its social environment. Since artists "are always the most sensitive barometers of cultural change" (Frank, p. 55), they are the first to record for the society that consumes their work certain tendencies latent in it as a collective process. Thus the work stands in a double relation to the artist: in its contextual aspect it is subjective and centripetal, mediating between the artist and an ideal of order; in its referential aspect it is objective and centrifugal, mediating between the artist and contingent reality. That is, via its various prototypes the work mediates the distance between the artist and his society. Recovery of the writer's vision is attained by first considering the work an autonomous structure and then by metaphorically freezing it while simultaneously absorbing the aggregate of recurrent images and actions that give form to the presence in the text. This done, however, one should see the simultaneous interpenetration of *that* mind and *that* time and place. The real meaning of spatial form is this dialectical process that perpetually produces mediating double relations. It allows Frank to move easily from individual writers like Proust, Eliot, Joyce, Pound, and Djuna Barnes to their historical milieux and back again.

But spatial form is not, finally, simply myth criticism in a different guise, and it would be a mistake to view it as a rudimentary concept perfected by Northrop Frye. The fruition of spatial form can occur only in a hermeneutic Structuralism or, what is the same thing, in a renovated phenomenology.

Phenomenology's recent influence has been due to its opposition to the spatializing tendency in modern critical thought and its support of the temporal dynamics of literature in its character of subjectivity. Since it is the only major theory that presupposes the total subjectivity of both literature and criticism, its attraction resides in the claim to reconstruct, rather than to analyze, the original existential experience latent in a literary text. Since Gaston Bachelard's "phenomenology of the image" has influenced all the existential critics considerably, we can use him as a link between them and Frank.

Like the other existentialists, Bachelard posits meaning in language, but, unlike them, he disregards the work as a totality and posits value entirely in the "reverberative" power of isolated images that, having no past, create themselves spontaneously. For Bachelard the poetic image "does not duplicate present reality, and is not the echo of the past. . . . [It] has no true causes"; instead, the power of images is that they "*reverberate* in the reader's consciousness and lead him to create anew while communicating with the poet."[14] "Reverberation" is the special function of poetry; it is described as a dialectical potency that overcomes the sense of contradiction informing Bachelard's vision. Thus for Bachelard "poetic language expresses the continuous tension within a substance. It is by virtue of the dialectic of opposite qualities that poetic matter fascinates" (Gaudin, p. xxxii). The synthesizing image renews itself through its immediate and perpetual contact with the material archetypes (earth, air, fire, and water). The synthesis of contradictions is achieved dialectically by the creation of "poetic relationships which enrich the world" and which "must be studied simultaneously as isomorphic and unique" (Gaudin, p. xxxiii).

Bachelard's theory of literary perception disregards any other facet of the text, and that distinguishes his poetics from Frank's. But he resembles Frank and Frye—despite his temporal vocabulary—in that he stresses the epiphanic or timeless quality of individual images or, at most, of groups of related images apprehended simul-

14. Colette Gaudin, *On Poetic Imagination and Reverie: Selections from the Works of Gaston Bachelard,* trans. Gaudin (Indianapolis and New York: Bobbs-Merrill, 1971), p. xix. In "Suffused-Encircling Shapes of Mind: Inhabited Space in Williams," *Journal of Modern Literature,* 1 (1971), 549–564, Cary Nelson produces a Bachelardian reading of Williams that combines spatialization with phenomenology.

taneously as an archetype. He seems to have been trying to do for
the image what Frank attempted to do for entire texts—that is, found
a theory of literary perception on the basis of the epiphanic power,
the reverberative or reflexive suggestiveness, of images conceived
of as dynamic but coordinated entities. And his belief that we do not
really "know ourselves in time" is almost identical with the motive
Frank assigns for the modern preoccupation with mythic prototypes.
Rather than taking man's temporal identity for granted, Bachelard
intuits that "all we know is a sequence of fixations in the spaces of
the being's stability, a being who does not want to melt away, and
who, even in the past, when he sets out in search of things past,
wants time to 'suspend' its flight. In its countless alveoli *space
contains compressed time*. That is what space is for."[15] It is the
literary technique for objectifying this impulse that Frank charts and
calls spatial form.

The Geneva School of existential critics are all indebted in one
way or another to Bachelard's poetics. The basic assumption uniting
critics as various as Marcel Raymond, Albert Beguin, Georges
Poulet, Jean Rousset, Jean-Pierre Richard, Jean Starobinski, and
J. Hillis Miller has nothing to do with specific critical practices.
Instead, it has to do with their agreement about "the nature of criticism itself. For the Geneva critics literature is a form of consciousness . . . [They] are relatively without interest in the external form
of individual works of literature."[16] Therefore,

> The criticism of consciousness is a criticism of the author's experi-
> ence conveyed in a text, and of his active consciousness at the mo-
> ment of creation. . . . It is the consciousness of individual subjective
> perceptions, or of an all-encompassing general existence, and exists
> in a special mental region of "interior distance."[17]

The critic's attempt to reproduce with exact fidelity the emotional
"traces" embodied in the text or "mental universe" requires the
suspension of all a priori presuppositions. It also requires that an
author's consciousness be viewed as a temporal flow or energy

15. Bachelard, *The Poetics of Space*, trans. Maria Jolas (Boston: Beacon Press,
1969), p. 8; emphasis added.
16. J. Hillis Miller, "The Geneva School," *Critical Quarterly*, 8 (1966), 306–
307.
17. Sarah N. Lawall, *Critics of Consciousness: The Existential Perspectives of
Literature* (Cambridge: Harvard University Press, 1968), pp. 5–6.

rather than as an objective form. Yet consciousness, which is an essence capable of being reconstructed by empathetic participation, exists only in the formal structures of words that comprise the text and is not to be confused with an actual historical figure. In order for the critic to participate in this consciousness, he must develop

> a systematically empathetic approach in which he tries to re-create the experience embodied in the text. He must subordinate his own subjective personality to a new subjective identity which is gradually created and revealed in the course of the book. . . . Because they define a work as the expression of an individual personality, their reading is openly personal. [Lawall, pp. 6–7]

Whatever their individual differences of practice, all the "critics of consciousness" uphold "the main existential premise of an empathetic reading as opposed to an exterior judgment based on form" (Lawall, p. 8).

Theoretically none of this is either objectionable or novel; Frank, as well as Poulet or Miller, calls for a participatory reading of the work. At worst it is a quaintly displaced Romanticism dominated by a desire for an empathetic experience whereby one shares in a superior creative personality. And at its best it has reawakened a generation of critics trained in the complacencies of the New Criticism to literature's vitality and essential mystery. This is an experience that criticism was, perhaps, near to forgetting, and Existentialism has been useful to literature to that extent. Since the Existentialists' dogmatic insistence on the exclusive temporality of literature is a part of our aporia, however, we must insist that they violate two of their own basic tenets. I do this neither to discredit an interesting critical mode nor to establish an unreal isomorphism between it and spatial form, but only in order to move in the direction of a compromise solution to the problem.

The Existentialists' origins are in Husserl's phenomenology and Heidegger's temporal metaphysics. The first calls for an "objective" (i.e., scientific) description of the object of analysis, one that can only be achieved by putting it momentarily in parenthesis. This procedure is called "bracketing," and it amounts to an attempt to suspend value judgments. Ideally this act of willful empathy will result in a "self-dispossession," leading to a subjective identity of near coextensiveness of the critic's personality with that of the "author" hypothesized in the text. Its ideal objective is the reconstruction of the creative act at its source. But as Robert Scholes has pointed out,

> the "subjectivity" of hermeneutic criticism can never be entirely subjective. The critic who "recovers" the meaning of any given work always does so by establishing a relationship between the work and some system of ideas outside it. This may be a theory of man, or as with Poulet a theory of "human time," but the theory must be there in order to justify the critic's presence . . . Interpretation, however subjective, must justify itself by bringing something external to the work, if only the subjectivity of the critic, which is different from that of the artist.[18]

This necessary presupposition means that implicit value judgments—prior to the text and antithetical to a truly presuppositionless empathetic approach—creep back into their practical criticisms. For example, when Poulet encounters Lamartine, a writer who depicts "unsuccessful resolutions of metaphysical conflicts," we note that a "certain standard, and with it a sense of judgment, re-enters this empathetic approach" (Lawall, p. 99). With the exception of Maurice Blanchot's blankly pessimistic fatalism, these critics demand an affirmation of existence as the price of appreciation, and the "loss of a sense of being is, of course, a failure according to these existential tenets" (Lawall, p. 100). Thus the very object of Existential analysis—the recreation of the immediacy of a vital, comprehensive unconsciousness latent in the text—is defeated by the creation of

> a second work which is abstract, general, and far too removed from the impact of the original text. . . . [T]he original consciousness is narrowed down from a rounded, universal, comprehensive structure (the work) and funneled into the single voice hypothesized behind it . . . This experience is assumed to be the same as the author's . . . and the whole procedure is justified by such a quasi-biographical method. [Lawall, pp. 131–132]

The attempt at complete identity between critic and text, besides being impossible, severely limits their range of subjects. But recently David Halliburton has produced a phenomenological reading of Poe in which he writes that "*inter*subjectivity is a relation between, not a condition of, complete identity. 'I' am never completely

18. Scholes, *Structuralism in Literature: An Introduction* (New Haven: Yale University Press, 1974), p. 9.

'thou,' whether 'thou' be another person or a literary work. The process of identification might better be termed an alignment or a coming-near-to" (Halliburton, pp. 27–28). This is a less romantic approach, but it is the right one for phenomenology to take, since it admits the finally impenetrable mystery at the heart of the literary experience. It also loosens the dogmatic rigidity that so severely limits most existential interpretation.

Martin Heidegger, the other major influence on phenomenology, commits the "critics of consciousness" to an interpretation of literary consciousness as solely temporal, as a "flow" or an "energy." Although there is nothing intellectually objectionable in this position, we must take the position of both Northrop Frye and, more recently, Murray Krieger and insist upon the necessity of spatial assumptions and language *for the literary critic*. And, of course, the "critics of consciousness" also spatialize, as all critics must, although they deny the importance of it. J. Hillis Miller's analyses of Eliot and of Hardy and Poulet's analysis of Proust are clear examples not only of the necessity of spatialization for the critic, but also of the influence of the spatial form hypothesis on their work. Miller has this to say of Eliot's early poetry:

> Human time in Eliot's early poetry has the same qualities as subjective space. There is often a spontaneous spatialization of time, so that a poem exists in a perpetual present. The simultaneity of parts is guaranteed by the fact that past, present, and future exist at once for the imprisoned ego. The reader must hold all the images of a poem in his mind at once, and set each against the others in order to apprehend the full meaning.[19]

In a recent work on Hardy, Miller uses language that almost seems to have been written by Frank:

> To say "pattern" is to use a spatial term. . . . The change from infatuated movement forward to a detached seeing of the past is also a change from time to space. Detachment spatializes time, freezes it into a fixed shape . . . [The narrator sees] all moments in time as simultaneously present, juxtaposed side by side in a spatial design. The movement in orientation from future to past is a transformation of time as it is lived from moment to moment into the spatialized time

19. Miller, *Poets of Reality: Six Twentieth-Century Writers* (New York: Athenaeum, 1969), p. 145.

of a permanent destiny . . . [This is a] change in relation to life from existential temporality to spatialized time.[20]

The importance of spatial form to Miller's interpretation is undeniable.

Turning to Georges Poulet's reading of Proust, we find that it, too, is in perfect accord with Frank's: "Proustian time is time spatialized, juxtaposed."[21] This interpretation defines Proust's vision as being that of a "static, panoramic (spatial) time. Time and space blend into a total experience, a *cogito*" (Lawall, p. 77). Poulet

conceives of Proust's time as a static, panoramic, *spatial* vision . . . [since to Proust] places and moments are fragmentary indications of a still unseen unity. They are so many pieces of a spatial existence to be fitted together, so that Proust's real task is . . . to establish a comprehensive pattern.

   The end of this task is not temporal, but spatial. [Lawall, pp. 106–107]

Thus Poulet's metaphoric "cogito" is spatial and functions as a formal device, a strategy for organizing his interpretation. By interpreting the existential category of temporality literally rather than heuristically, few critics have seen that "time for Poulet is not a chronological sequence but, instead, a process of connecting and differentiating among different 'points,' that is, the process of making lines and shapes, of giving form to *space*."[22] This is a spatial or cognitive activity, and Poulet's technique of "connecting and differentiating" among disparate verbal elements is a process similar to Frank's reflexive reference of juxtaposed word groups.

   Poulet is justly famous as a seeker after literary beginnings; the thrust of his criticism is always a dialectically conducted search for the literary "cogito" responsible for the originating impulse that finds its adequate expression in the creation of a literary text. It has never been explicitly pointed out that Frank also utilizes a dialectical

20. Miller, *Thomas Hardy: Distance and Desire* (Cambridge: Harvard University Press, 1970), pp. 197–198.
21. Poulet, *Proustian Space,* trans. Elliott Coleman (Baltimore: The Johns Hopkins University Press, 1977), p. 106.
22. Leo Bersani, "From Bachelard to Barthes," in *Issues in Contemporary Criticism,* ed. Gregory T. Polletta (Boston: Little, Brown, 1973), p. 97.

method to seek out in the works of Proust, Joyce, Eliot, and Djuna
Barnes the originative impulse that, given adequate expression only
in language, defines the peculiar quality of twentieth-century literature. And, finally, the reason is the same in both criticisms: it is
the quest for the transcendence of time. The Existentialists' claim to
originate a critical program that deals completely and adequately
with the dynamic human time to be found in literature is typically
presumed to oppose the spatialists' search for moments of literary
transcendence. Uncritical acceptance of this claim simply avoids the
felt contradictions in this admittedly attractive criticism by ignoring
one of its latent dimensions. Again using Poulet as our representative, we should note J. Hillis Miller's startling remark that the image
of an "internal milieu" is so habitual with Poulet that

> his thought may be defined as fundamentally spatial. . . . In his most
> recent work he has yielded overtly to the spatializing tendency of his
> criticism. . . . Throughout the whole history of Western thought
> Poulet explores the varieties of spatial relation . . . With each of his
> authors Poulet goes as far as he can toward the attainment of this
> *totum simul,* human equivalent of divine simultaneity and ubiquity.[23]

To draw from this the conclusion that spatial form and phenomenology are more closely related than has been admitted is not
to deny that spatialization in both Miller and Poulet is used to arrive
at conclusions usually different from Frank's, nor is it to deny that
their intentions are different from his. But since what is needed in
criticism is a third way of talking about literature that denies neither
its existential "dynamism" nor its spatiocognitive "significance," the
point bears emphasizing. It is not a question of totally embracing or
repudiating either of the two positions, since it is such unskeptical
enthusiasm that has led to our current crisis. A more fruitful
approach would be a third way of viewing the two whereby they are
both assimilated to a broader ideological movement on the basis of
their similarities. This cannot be done, however, until what is simply arbitrary in them has been established, defined, and excluded.
     We can apply to spatial form Sarah Lawall's remarks about the
relationship between Structuralism and phenomenology by saying
that both existential and spatial-form critics "are like the structural-

23. Miller, "The Literary Criticism of Georges Poulet," *Modern Language Notes,*
78 (1963), 483–485.

ists in that they do form patterns of experience, do relate the work to a history of ideas, and do speak of a pre-verbal experience at the base of literature" (Lawall, pp. 118–119). We can also say that spatial form, like Structuralism and phenomenology, "focusses on the meaning-giving process and emphasizes the active constituting role of the human participant in that process." The essential difference is that while "existential phenomenology takes the high road on which the fully conscious subject exercising his freedom brings meaning into existence, structuralism takes the low road, on which a universal but latent and unconscious human mind inscribes its deterministic architecture everywhere."[24] And spatial form treads a middle ground between these two extreme positions.

Seen from a fresh perspective, spatial form may be able to mediate, if not annihilate, the distance separating phenomenology from Structuralism. As we shall see, Frank's theory has much in common with the Structuralist idea of system, while sharing the existential passion for the empathetic and nonjudgmental dialectical method. Spatial form is a metaphor for the art work as a combined space-time event. This is also the way the "critics of consciousness" interpret the literary experience; and it is certainly the specific real meaning of Poulet's "cogito." Therefore, although Frank's historical assumption (of alternating period art styles responding to cultural stability and hysteria) and his conclusion (that the common content and the function of modern literature is the projection of universal "prototypes") are capable of being viewed as deterministic and reductive, this is a mistaken interpretation of the theory. As we have seen, there is nothing generically deterministic in the use of either spatialization or mythic materials. Like all else, they are simply some of the writer's materials; everything depends upon his treatment of them.

Throughout the midsection of his essay, in which he applies his theory to selected modern authors, Frank uses the notion of myth in the modern sense to mean a sophisticated device allowing writers to find an adequate structuring technique for their visions in an otherwise formless epoch not conducive to the production of integrated works of art. He interprets this use of myth as a *conscious* manipulation by the artist that reflects modern man's existential freedom

24. Vernon W. Gras, *European Literary Theory and Practice: From Existential Phenomenology to Structuralism,* ed. Gras (New York: Dell, 1973), p. 15.

(why the choice of one prototype rather than another? why is it introduced at one point rather than at another? etc.). Spatial form's perpetual oscillation between freedom and determinism and between artist and society should not be viewed as a failure of critical imagination. Rather, it is this very dialectical quality that lends the theory its particular strength and accounts for its longevity. It is also the quality guaranteeing that spatial form cannot be either totally excluded from more fashionable critical modes, such as phenomenology, or ever completely reduced to another mode, such as myth criticism.

Myth criticism has run its theoretical course, while phenomenology is at the height of its influence. Despite phenomenology's current importance, however, "the literary imagination has moved through existentialism and into structuralism in our time" (Scholes, p. 99). But if Structuralism is easy to name as the chief contemporary critical mode, it is considerably more difficult to define, for it "is at present only a methodology with ideological implications. But it is a methodology which is seeking nothing less than the unification of all the sciences into a new system of belief. This is why its ideological implications, incomplete as they are at present, strike us forcibly" (Scholes, p. 2). Scholes operates from the now common "crisis" assumption according to which recent history has been characterized by "the fragmentation of knowledge into isolated disciplines so formidable in their specialization as to seem beyond all synthesis" (p. 1). He sees Structuralism as "a response to the need . . . for a 'coherent system' that would unite the modern sciences and make the world habitable for man again" (p. 2). Spatial form is not an outmoded "period aesthetic" chiefly because it participates in the progressive development of Structuralist thought in our time.

Although there is no simple definition of Structuralism, one nonetheless can construct a rudimentary description of its latent ideological tendencies, and the model so described should correspond at important points to the theory of spatial form. In its simplest and most general sense, "structuralism is a way of looking for reality not in individual things but in the relationships among them" (Scholes, p. 4). That is, the Structuralists "stress a functional interrelationship of elements . . . [They] are concerned with reaching behind the appearances of man's behavior (or better, analyzing what these appearances have in common) to get at the *manner* in which they work" (Lawall, p. 16). Structuralism has inherited the banner of the major intellectual movement of our time: the shift from absolutist or substantialist thinking to that of descriptive, functional, and relational thinking. Thus Structuralism is a relativistic hypothesis. In contradistinction to Existentialism's absolute moral a prioris of choice, freedom, authenticity, and the sense of history, Structuralism is led to

> an attack on the liberal notion of historical truth . . . Put simply, Sartre feels that men live in history and seek refuge from it in myth; while Lévi-Strauss feels that men live in myth and seek refuge from it in history. For Lévi-Strauss, history is a myth that men make up for their own satisfaction. But what looks like progress to the historian is only transformation or displacement to the structuralist. [Scholes, pp. 194–195]

History, then, like any man-made object, is a fiction; but it is a pragmatic and collective fiction, not a solipsistic one. Therefore, rather than passing judgment on the supposed value of any system, the Structuralist is concerned to uncover its rules of functioning. In this it functions as a kind of cultural psychoanalysis concerned with uncovering latent constitutive tendencies in aggregates rather than in individual personalities. Its only a priori is the assumption that all things made by man are, at bottom, logical—that is, governed by some constituting code that can be deciphered. The Structuralist starts from "a relational perspective, according to which it is neither the elements nor a whole that comes about in a manner one knows not how, but the relations among elements that count. In other words, the logical procedures or natural processes by which the whole is formed are primary, not the whole, which is consequent on the system's laws of composition, or the elements."[25] As Fredric Jameson has recently pointed out, the Structuralist is not interested in "things" but only in

> differential perceptions, that is to say, a sense of the *identity* of a given element which derives solely from our awareness of its *differences* from other elements, and ultimately from an implicit compari-

25. Jean Piaget, *Structuralism*, trans. Chaninah Maschler (New York: Harper and Row, 1970), pp. 8–9.

son of it with its own opposite . . . Thus the dominant category of
structuralism as a method is the concept of the binary opposition.[26]

The binary opposition is a measure of the differential relationships
(similarity, difference) between things compared, rather than an
analysis of the things themselves. This is familiar to students of
spatial form as a version of Frank's reflexive reference, whereby
meaning is derived by a meticulous cross-referencing of word
groups juxtaposed with one another for the purpose of allowing the
mind to make partial, immediate identifications of images,
metaphors, puns, and the like. It also allows the reader to distinguish
a perpetually shifting variety of levels of contrast, thereby placing
the contrasted elements at momentary rest in the reader's mind at
various levels of an imagined hierarchy of metaphors. While at rest
they continue to resonate ("reverberate"), awaiting augmentation
and, finally, completion as the total pattern(s) of the work becomes
clear in the simultaneous (spatial) grasp of the work's *significant*
form.

Structuralism is based on three key ideas: "the idea of wholeness,
the idea of transformation, and the idea of self-regulation" (Piaget,
p. 5). All three elements must be found together in any single
phenomenon before it can be called a "structure." Together they
constitute a "system," which can be described as "a self-regulating
system of transformations," where transformation means "an intel-
ligible change, which does not transform things beyond recognition
at one stroke, and which always preserves invariance in certain
respects" (Piaget, pp. 36, 20). Such a description does not ignore the
subjectivity of experience, since "transformation" and "self-
regulation" are simply Structuralism's equivalents of phenomenology's "intention" and "significance" (Piaget, p. 52). For our purpose,
then, the most significant element of Structuralist thought is its definition of a system as "a complete, self-regulating entity that adapts
to new conditions by transforming its features while retaining its
systematic structure" (Scholes, p. 10).

26. Jameson, "Metacommentary," *PMLA*, 86 (1971), 14. Edmund Leech has
recently criticized the idea of "binary oppositions and mediating middle terms" as an
obscurantism that actually signifies "little more than the Hegelian triad of thesis,
antithesis, synthesis." He sees it as being merely a semantic substitution masking a
traditional concept in a misleadingly "revolutionary" language. Leech, *Claude Lévi-
Strauss* (New York: Viking, 1970), p. 127.

By interpreting Frank's theory structurally, we can see reflexive reference as a process of self-regulation whereby one system (the reader) interpenetrates the significance formed by the consciousness latent in another system (the text) through the transformational device of the juxtaposition of word groups. Viewed solely as elements or "things," these word groups are, of course, static; but they are not just elements, they are elements of a synergic whole. The reader's active response to the latent life of the text, or system, initiates a process from which existential as well as logical significance is derived by participation in the re-creation of the text. What is resurrected is a heterocosm consisting of the subjectivity of the reader, the "subjectivity" of the "author," and the objectivity of the spatial "thing," the book itself. Nothing could be less "life denying" than such a process.

Allied to the Structuralists' preoccupation with the idea of system is their concern with the autonomy of its language. The point that most interests the literary critic is the Structuralists' insistence that "language is an autonomous system whose signs derive their meaning from inner relationships and not by designating things. Intelligibility is a function of the relationships and oppositions of terms in a system" (Gras, p. 13). Like the literary critic, the Structuralist is first of all interested in "the system within the work (the words, syntax, ideas, plot, etc.) which together help produce a given esthetic effect and make an integral whole" and which leads him to the position that the "work itself is to be studied as a totality or system before it is to be related to other systems—historical, social, biographical, or other."[27] But once such relationships and their various significances have been established and the entity has been defined as a system, the step that completes the Structuralist process is that whereby the text and its latent consciousness is related to its extraliterary context. The establishment of a system is only preparatory to the basic Structuralist goal, which is "to explore the relationship between the system of literature and culture of which it is a part" (Scholes, p. 10). Thus the Structuralists' dialectical method first establishes an individual system's autonomy and then places it into a context of aggregate autonomous systems, all of which have meaning solely by virtue of being in relation with one another. Rather than killing the

27. Richard and Fernande DeGeorge, "Introduction," in *The Structuralists from Marx to Lévi-Strauss*, ed. the DeGeorges (Garden City: Doubleday, 1972), p. xxi.

subject through an overobjectification, as has often been claimed, this attitude frees the critic to see the interpenetrative vitality—the social as well as the psychological value—of the "system of literature."

At this point we should confront more directly the charge that Structuralism kills the subject of its inquiry, since this is also the basic criticism of spatial form. Vernon W. Gras has written that in Structuralism "the subject, no longer constituting but constituted, merely participates as one of the terms in a set of functions" (Gras, p. 16). We can refute this oversimplification by analyzing the critical position of Roland Barthes.

Barthes has defined "the goal of all structuralist activity" as an attempt "to reconstruct an 'object' in such a way as to manifest thereby the rules of functioning (the 'functions') of this object. Structure is therefore actually a *simulacrum* of the object, but a directed, *interested* simulacrum. . . . The simulacrum is intellect added to object. . . . It is man himself, his history, his situation, his freedom." Therefore, "it is not the nature of the copied object which defines an art. . . . It is the fact that man adds to it in reconstructing it."[28] Once the system to be studied has been identified, one must "find in it certain mobile fragments whose differential situation engenders a certain meaning" (Barthes, p. 160). He calls this process "dissection." The next step, "articulation," requires that one then discover in these fragments "certain rules of association," or "recurring units," since "it is by the regular return of the units and of the associations of units that a work appears constructed, i.e., endowed with meaning" (Barthes, p. 161). The purpose of this process is neither to "kill" the subject, nor to neglect it by pretending that its individuality is totally absorbed in that of a collective mind. Rather, it serves to highlight "the strictly human process by which men give meaning to things" (Barthes, p. 161). Therefore, "the object of structuralism is not man endowed with meanings, but man fabricating meanings . . . *Homo significans*: such would be the new man of structural inquiry" (Barthes, p. 162).

Barthes's "fragments" are conceived of as mobile, not static, and the thrust of the technique he describes is dialectical: like both spatial form and phenomenology, it attempts to unite subject and

28. Barthes, "The Structuralist Activity," in *European Literary Theory and Practice*, ed. Gras, pp. 158–159.

object in a form of coherence that is an expression of the creating subject's freedom simply because it *is* coherent—that is, siphoned out and cleared of the blockages of contingency. Both Frank's "word groups" and Barthes's "dissection" allow for a "disintegration" of the system into images, while "reflexive reference," or the rapid and continual juxtaposition of these images, corresponds to the constitutive activity that Barthes calls "articulation." Both are attempts to manifest "the rules of functioning" of a subject by bringing to light the essential rhythmic impulse, the "recurring units," at its source. In both cases this is done by the rapid and shifting process of establishing differential relationships between fragments meaningless only *as* fragments.

What criticism has not stressed is that spatial form is primarily a theory of perception that focuses on the reading process. Its prime rule—similar to both phenomenology's "empathy" and Structuralism's "dissection/articulation"—is that the reader must engage the text on its own terms in a strenuously participatory reading that attempts to re-create the experience embodied in it. Meaning, as Frank implies, resides somewhere between the past activity of the author and the present activity of the engaged reader. This point of view is in keeping with recent phenomenological reading theories calling for empathetic participation while admitting the impossibility of actual coextensiveness between reader and text.[29]

Spatial form is, then, clearly related to both Structuralism and phenomenology in several ways: all three search for the latent, preverbal origin of literary expression, with spatial form doing this in order to make coherent the metaphysical impulse behind experimental literature's notorious "obscurity"; each utilizes a basically dialectical approach, with each masking its findings in a suitable vocabulary; and they all emphasize the meaning-giving process in a particular "order of words" as originating from bundles of relations within the work, rather than from direct reference between word (in the text or system) and thing (in the extraliterary historical process). This is the mental comparison and contrast of differentials implicit in Frank's reflexive reference, in the Structuralists' binary oppositions, and in the Existentialists' "back and forth" technique of search-

29. See the first chapter of Halliburton, and Wolfgang Iser's *The Act of Reading: A Theory of Aesthetic Response* (Baltimore: The Johns Hopkins University Press, 1978).

ing for a hypothesized authorial cogito in the text. And, finally, they all require, at least theoretically, a strenuously empathetic or presuppositionless reading whereby the reader re-creates the text's significance by an act of participation in its essential constituting rhythms and properties.

There are also two significant points of distinction between the positions of the Existentialists, on the one hand, and of Frank and the Structuralists on the other. One is their disagreement about the temporal element in literature: for the Existentialists it is diachronic and historical, for Frank and the Structuralists it is synchronic and "mythic." And while the Existentialists assign supreme importance to a consciousness that literally *is* the text, both Frank and the Structuralists emphasize the partially unconscious function of the creative ego and its subordination to a collective mind—that is, its function as a mediation between an individual personality and a broader psychosocial category. This explains why the Structuralist can see literature as both autonomous and yet as a method "to explore . . . the culture of which it is a part." The parallel with spatial form lies in Frank's conscious intention to analyze the psychic malaise embodied in the works of certain individual writers for the sake of declaring that they were, after all, not only individual writers but also mediations, instruments through which flow "eternal prototypes" giving form to their time. This is perfectly in keeping with Structuralist thought, which declares that any system—literary, economic, political, religious—is a metonymy for the aggregate of other communication systems inside a historical and cultural context. Since they see "the work of art as a cosmic symbol or metaphor, containing within itself and in terms proper to itself a global account of the human world which engendered it,"[30] the art work can legitimately be used as Frank uses it—to explore, analyze, and define the prominent structural features of its epoch.

A third way of talking about literature must be developed if criticism is to overcome the naive antinomies between "subject" and "object," "form" and "content," "history" and "myth," and "time" and "space" that now dominate it and contribute to its crisis atmosphere. For literary form is neither solely one nor the other: it is neither completely temporal nor spatial. Instead, we should begin to

30. Sheldon Nodelman, "Structural Analysis in Art and Anthropology," in *Structuralism*, ed. Ehrmann, p. 91.

interpret literary works as homeostatic organisms. Such a view would see a text as an articulation of *printed* sounds interrelated by the artist with varying degrees of conscious intention and success for the purpose of regulating its own internal conditions in such a way as to produce and permanently maintain a state of equilibrium within itself and its various extraliterary environments. Equilibrium requires change, "flux"; but this must be *ordered* change, change that is transformational rather than revolutionary, that has a future only because a present is still related to, while falling out of, its own past. To achieve this equilibrium, criticism needs a theory of assimilation. A biological concept, assimilation "is the process whereby the organism [text] in each of its interactions with the bodies or energies of its environment fits these in some manner to the requirements of its own physico-chemical structures while at the same time accommodating itself to them" (Piaget, p. 71). An assimilative critical hypothesis would be ecological in the broadest and truest sense, since it would be a form of complementarity engendering equilibrium and perpetuation rather than competition and novelty. Its purpose would be to allow us to "conceive of a literary history that would not truncate literature by putting us misleadingly *into* or *outside* it" (de Man, p. 164). This approach would be, in the truest sense, an *empathetic* approach. Some such "equilibrium" or "assimilative" critical approach seems the only way to overcome our present critical aporia and the crisis it has engendered.

Whatever direction the course of critical theory may take in the future, the inevitability of spatial language by the critic allied with the undeniably elliptical and discontinuous quality of "obscure" twentieth-century literature assures the student of spatial form that it will occupy a major place in future literary studies and in the writing of any systematic history of criticism dealing with the ferment that is the art of criticism in our time.

9

Spatial Form:
Thirty Years After

Joseph Frank

I

Ever since 1945, when my article "Spatial Form in Modern Literature" first appeared, it has continued to exercise influence and arouse discussion, even if, to put it mildly, it has not always met with agreement.[1] Very recently, however, I have become aware that such discussion has become more widespread than in the immediate past and that my ideas seem to have taken on an increased actuality as a result of new developments in criticism. The existence of the present volume is the best proof of such an assertion; and when I was approached for a possible contribution, it seemed to me that the time was ripe to do something I had long thought about vaguely—without, up to the present, finding the proper occasion to stir me to action. What I had long wished to do was, in the first place, to answer the numerous criticisms of my ideas which had accumulated over the years, and to which—partly because I had become preoccupied with other problems—I had never bothered to reply. Further, in

1. Frank, "Spatial Form in Modern Literature," in *The Widening Gyre: Crisis and Mastery in Modern Literature* (New Brunswick: Rutgers University Press, 1963), pp. 3–62. All subsequent citations are to this version.

the course of my readings I had gradually become aware of many
points of contact between the notion of spatial form and some of
the views now being advanced under the aegis of French Structuralism; and I had nourished the hope of someday being able to comment on the intriguing concordances I could make out.

The invitation to contribute to the present collection provided a
welcome incentive to accomplish both these objectives; and the
following pages will be devoted to doing so as best I can. Most of
the essay will be taken up with a reply to critics, in the hope of
clearing away misunderstandings that may have arisen because of
my prolonged silence in the face of attack. This has left a number of
unanswered questions in the minds of many readers, and I shall
endeavor to clarify them as I go along. Since my most important
critics retain the original perspective of my essay, which viewed
spatial form exclusively as a particular phenomenon of avant-
garde writing, I shall continue to do so myself in these sections even
though this no longer represents my own point of view. In the last
four sections, however, I shall discuss the relation of my own ideas
to the more general theory of a literary text now beginning to
emerge, and which, as I shall try to show, includes spatial form
(regardless of whether the term is used or not) as one of its essential
categories.

Before going on to answer critics of spatial form in detail, it
seems essential to establish a point that has generally been misunderstood. Far too many readers have assumed that I was a fanatical
partisan of experimentalism in all its varieties simply because my
attitude toward it was analytical rather than condemnatory and because I tried to understand the moderns in their own terms. Certainly
I admired the work of all the writers that I discussed; but, without
feeling it necessary to be too self-assertive, I thought it clear that my
own attitude was not that of an advocate or defender. At the very
beginning of the essay, in talking about Lessing, I remarked that I
wished to use his ideas solely as descriptive, and not at all as norma-
tive, categories. "Lessing's insights may be used solely as instruments of analysis, *without proceeding to judge the value of individual works by how closely they adhere to the norms he laid down* . . .
For what Lessing offered was not a new set of opinions but a new
conception of aesthetic form" (italics added). These sentences were
perhaps not as clear as they might be, and have probably been read

to apply only to Lessing's own evaluations; but they were meant to indicate my own position as well. They were emphatically *not* intended to imply a positive valuation of Modernist works simply because the latter *violate* Lessing's norms. My aim, like that of Ortega y Gasset in his *Dehumanization of Art,* was to work out descriptive categories for a new literary phenomenon, not to establish the rules of a Modernist critical canon.

All through the essay, as a matter of fact, I kept indicating that I was setting up what Max Weber called an "ideal type"—now called a "model"—rather than describing what was empirically and literally true in any particular case. In speaking, for example, of the "space-logic" of reflexive reference that governed modern poetry and of the necessity "to suspend the process of individual reference temporarily until the entire pattern of internal reference can be apprehended as a unity," I specifically labeled this the definition of a model. "This explanation, of course," I added in the next sentence, "is the extreme statement of an ideal condition rather than of an actually existing state of affairs." Years later, when I revised the essay for inclusion in *The Widening Gyre,* I omitted this sentence and replaced it by what I thought would be an unmistakable indication of my continuing skepticism about spatial form *à outrance.* Noting the formal resemblance between Mallarmé's *Un coup de dés, The Waste Land,* and the *Cantos,* I remarked that the ambition of modern poetry to dislocate "the temporality of language . . . has a necessary limit. If pursued with Mallarmé's relentlessness, it culminates in the self-negation of language and the creation of a hybrid pictographic 'poem' that can only be considered a fascinating historical curiosity." Concrete poetry has never seemed to me to have much interest or much future—though I have a sneaking sympathy for its practitioners because I have spent so much time thinking about what they are trying to do.

Similarly, my remarks about various novels (with the exception of *Nightwood*) were by no means intended as "readings" of these works in any definitive sense, and I assumed my reader would understand that I was focusing only on those formal elements necessary to make clear the spatiality of their structure. This did not mean that I thought other aspects of these books inferior, insignificant, or unworthy of notice. Roger Shattuck, whose own writings I greatly admire, has carried on an amicable polemic with me over the years concerning my comments about *Remembrance of Things Past*. He believes that my exclusive focus on the final "stereoscopic vision" of Proust, the attainment of an extratemporal spatial perspective in which the narrator can view his life as a whole, somehow is intended to downgrade all the other multifarious experiences of his life. "But we are dealing with a linear story which Proust carefully and properly called *a search*," Shattuck reminds me. "Far more aptly it could be represented as a climb to the top of the mountain . . . that allows one's gaze to move at will from feature to feature and to take it in all at once. That view is essentially *spatial* [italics added]. But it does not and cannot abolish the climb that took one to the summit, and the temporal order of events in that climb."[2]

There is really no quarrel here between Shattuck and myself; we have merely undertaken to do different things, and my narrower point of view was necessitated by my purpose. I can only add that, at the time I wrote, the linear aspects of Proust's search—the social and psychological dimensions of his work—had already been amply discussed in the critical literature (after all, I had cut my teeth on *Axel's Castle*); but nobody had quite seen, with as much clarity as I thought necessary, the point I was trying to make. Indeed, almost twenty years later, it was still being hailed as a valuable new insight in France when Georges Poulet published his book *L'espace proustien*. And in a penetrating discussion by Gérard Genette entitled "Proust palimpseste," several years later, a footnote informs the reader that "lost time is not, for Proust, as a widely spread misunderstanding would have it, the 'past,' but *time in a pure state,* that is, in fact, by the fusion of an instant of the present with an instant of the past, the contrary of time that flows: *the extra-temporal, eternity.*"[3] My limited focus in giving Proust's novel what Genette calls "une lecture structurante" would thus still seem to be an emphasis that has not lost its usefulness.

II

What has struck me in general, while reading through the reactions to my article that have accumulated over the years, is how little

2. Shattuck, *Marcel Proust* (New York: Viking, 1974), p. 116; see also my review of Shattuck's *Proust's Binoculars* in *Partisan Review*, 31 (1964), 135–143.
3. Genette, *Figures I* (Paris: Seuil, 1966), p. 40; my translation.

specific objection has been taken to my actual arguments or analyses. Most of the discussion has turned on the larger cultural implications of the artistic tendency represented by my examples, not with what I had to say about them. Only two of my critics, so far as I am aware, dealt with my ideas as such and tried to refute them within the terms I had established.

One of the earliest is G. Giovannini, who is interested in the methodological problem of a comparative study of differing art forms and who approaches the issue of spatial form from this point of view.[4] Unfortunately, it is a point of view that leads to a total misunderstanding of what I was talking about. Giovannini assumes, for example, that I was influenced by John Peale Bishop, who claimed "that since space (as well as time) is a deeply rooted concept of the mind, it inevitably informs poetic structure." Bishop's article, in the first place, came out simultaneously with my own and could thus hardly have influenced it; secondly, I was not interested in arguing any such general thesis or applying "a method based on the notion of time and space as comparable or quasi-identical," as Giovannini claims. Following Lessing, I very carefully distinguished between the two as *not* comparable, but showed that, *within* literature, the structure of modern works took on aspects that required them to be apprehended spatially instead of according to the natural temporal order of language.

Giovannini's fundamental error is to assume, simply because I began with Lessing, that I was interested in the old *ut pictura poesis* problem and was maintaining that literature could attain the spatial effects of painting. Thus he remonstrates that the "instantaneous fusion of fragments in *The Waste Land*" is not "an imitation of spatial art" (as if I had claimed that it was!), but rather "a technique of concentration and rapid shift without transitions, a technique that is probably a development of elements within a literary tradition." These words are meant as a criticism because I am supposed to be arguing that Eliot's effects were those of painting; but of course I was doing no such thing. Giovannini pays no attention whatever to my specific disclaimer on this point, contained in the remark that Pound defines the image "*not as a pictorial reproduction* but as a unification of disparate ideas and emotions into a complex presented

4. Giovannini, "Method in the Study of Literature in Its Relation to the Other Arts," *Journal of Aesthetics and Art Criticism*, 8 (1950), 185–195.

spatially in a moment of time" (italics added). As should be clear by now, Giovannini's failure to grasp my ideas is so complete, and his criticisms accordingly so wide of the mark, that there is little point in continuing to discuss them any further.

A much more perceptive critic is Walter Sutton, whose article, "The Literary Image and the Reader," stresses that, since reading is a time-act, the spatialization of literature can never be entirely achieved.[5] Sutton evidently overlooked the qualifications I had made on this point myself; but in any case, as I responded briefly to him in *The Widening Gyre*, "this has not stopped modern writers from working out techniques to achieve the impossible—as much as possible." I think it will be instructive, though, to consider his arguments a little more at length on this occasion.

One of his major criticisms is directed against my remarks on the space-logic of modern poetry and my contention that readers are required to suspend the process of reference temporarily until the entire pattern of *internal* references can be apprehended as a unity. But what, he asks, "is going on in the mind of the reader during the process of reading? . . . Presumably nothing, since consciousness in time has somehow been suspended." On the basis of this last (but totally unwarranted) inference from my text, Sutton triumphantly concludes that such a *"nothing* is inconceivable. We are in a realm beyond criticism, beyond theory." Certainly we should be if I had really said that *nothing* was going on in the mind of the reader of modern poetry; but of course I had made no such nonsensical assertion. I merely stated what has become a platitude—and what I can now put in more precise linguistic terminology—that the synchronic relations *within* the text took precedence over diachronic referentiality and that it was only after the pattern of synchronic relations had been grasped as a unity that the "meaning" of the poem could be understood. Naturally, to work out such synchronic relations involves the time-act of reading; but the temporality of this act is no longer coordinated with the dominant structural elements of the text. Temporality becomes, as it were, a purely physical limit of apprehension, which conditions but does not determine the work and whose expectations are thwarted and superseded by the space-logic of synchronicity.

5. Sutton, "The Literary Image and the Reader: A Consideration of the Theory of Spatial Form," *Journal of Aesthetics and Art Criticism*, 16 (1957), 112–123.

Another of Sutton's objections is leveled against my assertion that in the poetry of Eliot and Pound, "syntactical sequence is given up for a structure depending upon the perception of relationships between disconnected word-groups" (i.e., a structure of juxtaposition rather than of sequence). "In all cases," he retorts, "one could hardly say that there is no relationship in time of the *apparently*-dissociated images of these poems. Their relationship in time is in fact the concern of the poet"; and Sutton points to the ironic contrast between Prufrock and Hamlet, as well as the "contrast between the classic past and the vulgarized present in Pound's 'Mauberley,'" to prove his point. It is clear here that Sutton and I are simply talking about different things: he is referring to the *thematic* meaning conveyed by the time contrasts in the poetry, while I am talking about the temporality of *language*. The time contrasts he refers to emerge, all the same, from the juxtaposition of word groups syntactically unrelated to each other, which means that significance is no longer determined by linguistic sequence.

Such thematic use of time contrasts returns at the end of Sutton's article, in a more relevant context, when he takes issue with my contention that spatial form can be correlated with the substitution of the mythical for the historical imagination. "I must particularly disagree with Mr. Frank's statement," he says, "because works like *The Waste Land* and the *Cantos* and *Nightwood* are so obviously works of the historical imagination—of a skeptical, self-conscious awareness of the predicament of modern man as a victim of cultural decay." Sutton here neglects to inform the reader that I made this very point myself and spoke of "the source of meaning" in the *Cantos, The Waste Land,* and *Ulysses* as being "*the sense of ironic dissimilarity* and yet of profound human continuity between the modern protagonists and their long-dead (or only imaginary) exemplars" (italics added). But I argued that, by yoking past and present together in this way, these contrasts were felt as "locked in a timeless unity [which], *while it may accentuate surface differences,* eliminates any feeling of sequence by the very act of juxtaposition" (italics added).

There is thus no argument here about the immediate impact of these works in creating an ironic sense of contrast between past and present; but Sutton denies the deeper meaning that seemed to me implicit in their formal novelty—the "profound human continuity" that they took for granted. To buttress my position I can cite some words of Eliot himself, who, in the same year he wrote *The Waste Land*, saw a performance of *Le sacre du printemps* given by the Ballets Russes in 1921. This work, he observed, "brought home . . . *the continuity of the human predicament*: primitive man on the dolorous steppes, modern man in the city with its despairing noises, *the essential problem unchanging*"[6] (italics added). Such is the feeling underlying the shock effects of the contrast in all the texts I spoke about; and I was concerned to disengage this latent ahistoricity contained in what seemed a skeptical and self-conscious historical imagination. Certainly the latter was there; but it was striving to transform itself into myth.

The great works of Modernism are thus analogous, it seems to me, to those examples of medieval sculpture or book illustration in which figures from the Old and New Testaments, classical antiquity, and sometimes local history are all grouped together as part of one timeless complex of significance. Erich Auerbach has explained the assumptions underlying such significance in his famous article on "Figura";[7] but while no such unified system of meanings and values of course exists for the moderns, the latter attain a similar effect in purely formal terms.

6. Monroe K. Spears, *Dionysus and the City* (New York: Oxford University Press, 1970), p. 80.

7. Auerbach, "Figura," in his *Scenes from the Drama of European Literature* (New York: Meridian Books, 1959), pp. 11–76. Shortly after making the above comparison between the techniques of Modernism and Auerbach's conception of "figura," I came across the following passage in Julio Cortazar's remarkable experimental novel, *Hopscotch*. It is contained in the reflections of a novelist, Morelli, who is obviously Cortazar's artistic *alter ego* and serves as commentator. "To accustom one's self to use the expression *figure* instead of *image*, to avoid confusions. Yes, everything coincides. But it is not a question of a return to the Middle Ages or anything like it. The mistake of postulating an absolute historical time: There are different times *even though* they may be parallel. In this sense, one of the times of the so-called Middle Ages can coincide with one of the times of the Modern Ages. And that time is what has been perceived and inhabited by painters and writers who refuse to seek support in what surrounds them, to be 'modern' in the sense that their contemporaries understand them, which does not mean that they choose to be anachronistic; they are simply on the margin of the superficial time of their period, and from that other time where everything conforms to the condition of *figure*, where everything has value as a sign and not as a theme of description, they attempt a work which may seem alien or antagonistic to the time and history surrounding them, and which nonetheless includes it, explains it, and in the last analysis orients it towards a transcendence within whose limits man is waiting" [italics in text]. *Hopscotch*, trans. Gregory Rabassa (New York: New American Library, 1975), pp. 488–489.

Eisenstein has pointed out that the juxtaposition of disparate images in a cinematic montage automatically creates a synthesis of
meaning between them; and this supersedes any sense of temporal
discontinuity.[8] More recently, Robbe-Grillet has made the same
point in speaking of the lack of time depth in his novels: "The
cinema knows only a single grammatical modality: the present of the
indicative."[9] The juxtapositions of disparate historical images in
Joyce, Pound, and Eliot also bring the past into the present of the
indicative; and in doing so they turn history into myth. (Cassirer
defines the mythical imagination precisely in terms of the lack of
such a "dimension of depth," a lack of differentiation between foreground and background in its picture of reality.)[10] One has only to
compare this with, for example, the classical historical novel to feel
the difference immediately; what is stressed in this characteristic
nineteenth-century genre is the *pastness* of the past, the gulf created
by historical time that separates the world of the novel irrevocably
from the present of the reader or that clarifies the process of transition from one to the other. It is amusing to see Sutton illustrating my
point, while thinking to refute it, by his remark that Eliot's image of
Mr. Eugenides, the commercial traveler from Smyrna, is "the de-
based modern counterpart of the ancient trader who brought the
mysteries of the fertility cults to the West." Exactly: he is part of the
same timeless pattern in a different guise.

III

For the most part, as I have said, the criticisms directed against
spatial form have been aimed not so much against the concept
itself as rather against the kind of literature that it helps to explain
and, presumably, to justify. This is certainly the case with Philip
Rahv's influential essay "The Myth and the Powerhouse," invari-
ably cited among the most powerful criticisms of spatial form.[11]

8. Sergei Eisenstein, *Film Form and Film Sense*, ed. and trans. Jay Leyda (New
York: Meridian Books, 1957), p. 307. This edition consists of two books paginated
separately; the reference refers to the second volume, *Film Sense*.
    9. Alain Robbe-Grillet, *Pour un nouveau roman* (Paris: Minuit, 1963), p. 164;
my translation.
    10. Ernst Cassirer, *The Philosophy of Symbolic Forms*, 3 vols. (New Haven: Yale
University Press, 1955), II, 96.
    11. Rahv, "The Myth and the Powerhouse," in his *Literature and the Sixth Sense*
(Boston: Houghton Mifflin, 1969), pp. 202–215.

Rahv was greatly incensed by the rise in prestige of myth as a focus of cultural attention, and he set out to deflate it as a valid response to the acute sense of cultural crisis that he freely acknowledged to exist. He cites the evidence given in my essay as proof of "the turn from history toward myth" that he deplores; he remarks that *Finnegans Wake*, which I had not mentioned at all, "is the most complete example of 'spatial form' in modern literature"; and he concedes that "Joseph Frank's definition of the form is extremely plausible." No argument is made that my analysis does not accurately grasp the modern situation; but Rahv nonetheless opposes it on other grounds.

One is that "he [Frank] too readily assumes that the mythic imagination is actually operative in the writers he examines. But the supplanting of the sense of history by the sense of mythic time is scarcely accomplished with so much ease; the mere absence of the one does not necessarily confirm the presence of the other. For my part, what I perceive in Pound and Eliot are not the workings of the mythic imagination but an aesthetic simulacrum of it, a learned illusion of timelessness." I must confess that these sentences baffled me for some time because I could not quite grasp of what I was being accused. But they seem to mean that I believed Pound and Eliot to have *literally* reverted to the condition of primitives, to have forgotten all about time and history, and to be truly living in—and writing out of—a mythical imagination untouched by their situation as moderns. Of course no such absurd idea had ever entered my head, nor could I see how it might have been suggested by anything I said; what I was talking about was precisely "the aesthetic simulacrum" I was supposed to have overlooked. Rahv, it seems to me, was just creating a straw man in order to pretend to disagree, while actually accepting all my conclusions. There is no difference between what I say and his own presumably opposing assertion that "they [Pound and Eliot] are as involved in historicism as most contemporary writers sensitive to 'the modern situation,' but in their case the form it takes is negative."

In the remainder of his essay, Rahv does not so much attack spatial form as articulate his dislike of the negative response to history that it expresses. "The fear of history is at bottom the fear of the hazards of freedom. In so far as man can be said to be capable of self-determination, history is the sole sphere in which he can conceivably attain it." What these words really mean, on close scrutiny, is very difficult to decide; if they simply assert that man as a species lives in an empirical world and can act only within its limits, then one can hardly object to such a resounding platitude. Otherwise, they may be taken as the expression of a personal position about which there is very little to say—except that the greatest modern writers have felt quite the opposite, and that Rahv's animadversions hardly help us to understand why. One would have to be either a fool (which Rahv emphatically was not) or a fanatic to claim that after the experiences of the first three quarters of the twentieth century, there are no good grounds for refusing to worship before the Moloch of "history" in the old starry-eyed nineteenth-century fashion, with its built-in theological postulates. Lévi-Strauss has neatly exposed the intellectual naiveté of such a blind faith in history in his polemic with Sartre (*La pensée sauvage*); and we now see such faith as part of the same Western ethnocentrism that Worringer discarded long ago as a criterion for the plastic arts. It is time to stop allowing the same position to influence our discussion of literature as well.

To return to literature, however, the implication of Rahv's words, very simply, is that modern writers should not employ forms that negate history and time. But he is too sophisticated a critic and polemicist, and perhaps too much a genuine admirer of modern literature, to express such a position overtly. Instead, he skirmishes with spatial form so as to avoid the considerable embarrassment of having to attack Pound, Joyce, Eliot, et al., and thus end up sounding like the veriest Philistine (or, perish the thought, Irving Babbitt or Paul Elmer More). Rahv's problem is that he was unable to reconcile his literary taste with his ideological convictions; and while this inconsistency does him honor (it was the source of his great services to American literature as editor of *Partisan Review*), it does not make his polemic with spatial form either cogent or convincing. What it expresses is really a concealed opposition to Modernism as a whole, which his own critical judgment refused to allow to gain the upper hand; and in attacking critics rather than writers he found some relief from the pressure of his internal contradiction.

Rahv's commitment to history clearly derives from his residual Marxism; and a much more detailed attack on spatial form, using almost the same terms, can accordingly be found in a book that seems to have escaped general notice. It is, as a matter of fact, a quite valuable book, written by the East German Anglicist Robert

Weimann and called *"New Criticism" und die Entwicklung Burger-licher Literaturwissenschaft* (1962). Weimann's work is very well informed and contains one of the best historical accounts I am famil-iar with of the background, origins, and theories of the Anglo-American New Criticism; but since he writes as an orthodox Marx-ist, his attitude is inevitably hostile. Nonetheless, the tradition of German *Gründlichkeit* rescues the book from being simply a parti-san polemic and gives it independent value. A special section is devoted to the analysis of the New Critical theory of the novel, and in a separate chapter spatial form is discussed under the title: "The Negation of the Art of Narrative."

Weimann expounds the main lines of the essay quite faithfully, and even, at times, with accents of appreciation. After quoting my description of spatial form in *Ulysses,* for example, he says: "As a contribution to the interpretation of the so-called avant-garde novel, this may not be without justification. Frank, who relies primarily on examples of this kind, is able in this way to analyze Joyce's work and his 'unbelievably laborious fragmentation of narrative struc-ture.'" What Weimann objects to is not the insight offered by such analysis, but rather what he calls "the apologetic tendency" that he detects in the essay. "Like other interpreters of modern bourgeois prose," he writes, "Frank also sees 'not only a history of dissolution and destruction, but one of creative discovery and achievement'" (the phrase in single quotes is from the German critic Fritz Martini). So far as I do not regard modern experiments in the novel as ipso facto a sign of creative decadence, this is unquestionably true. But I should wish to add that there are as many mediocre experimentalists as banal naturalists, and I do not think literary quality simply a matter of adopting this or that technique. Weimann wishes to prove, however, that I set up fragmentization of narrative and atemporality as a positive aesthetic and critical norm; and this gives him a bit of trouble.

He manages, nevertheless—by taking a passage completely out of context and interpreting it in a way that is misleading. Early in the essay, expounding the implicit assumptions of the poetics of the image, I remarked that "if the chief value of an image was its capacity to present an intellectual and emotional complex simul-taneously, linking up images would clearly destroy most of their efficacy." To an impartial reader, it should be perfectly clear that I was simply developing the logic of the aesthetics of the image; but Weimann finds it polemically useful to turn my remark into a value judgment. "Because the New Critic affirms *only* the atemporal and fragmentized, that is, autonomous *image,* temporality and sequence in the novel are labelled as a lack of 'efficacy.'" From here it is easy for Weimann to accuse the New Critics—impersonated by myself— of having constructed an aesthetics of the novel "conceived as an apologetic for imperialistic artistic decadence"(!).

Weimann, all the same, has a clear and honest position, which allows him to state the issues without equivocation and, unlike Rahv, to take a consistent stand. Despite his obvious moral distaste for *Nightwood* ("homosexuality and sodomy are merely two links in a long chain of human aberrations"), he is capable of agreeing that my spatial conception "finds in Djuna Barnes's experimental novel . . . a not uninteresting self-confirmation." But of course Weimann staunchly refuses to acknowledge the *legitimacy* of any such experimentation, and he objects to the Modernist *mélange des genres,* which, as he rightly sees, has substituted lyric for narrative principles of organization in the novel. Like so many other partisans of "history," who believe that their devotion to time and change entitles them to strike poses of moral superiority, Weimann also paradoxically hangs on for dear life to the immutability and virginal inviolability of the literary genres. Everything else in human life is supposed to be transformed from top to bottom in the name of "progress," and humankind is invited (ordered?) to participate in the fray with whoops of joy, but hands off the sacrosanct rules of narrative art! "The loss of the temporal dimension," he writes warningly, "means the destruction of the specific narrative effect, namely, the representation of temporal processes, developments, mutations, changes, etc." And this is reprehensible because, "in back of the aesthetic negation of narrative stands the ideological negation of *self-transforming reality,* the negation of the historicity of our world." Like Rahv, Weimann also thinks it is morally inadmissible for mankind, even if it prefers to do so, to take refuge in art from "historicity." And the Russians, who at least have the courage of their convictions, bring out bulldozers to break up outdoor exhibitions of abstract art by their younger painters, curiously indifferent to the glories and achievements of the historical process.[12]

12. An extremely sophisticated Marxist treatment of the problems of Modernism in the plastic arts, which touches on the same theoretical questions as in literature,

IV

Of all the attacks on spatial form over the years, by far the most interesting, subtle, and critically productive has been that of Frank Kermode. Unquestionably one of the best critics now writing in English, Kermode exhibits a responsiveness and sensitivity to the passing scene, a wide-ranging intellectual curiosity, and an unerring instinct for the major problems that few contemporaries can match. And from the very first moment that he embarked on his career as a critic—from the moment that he ceased being a Renaissance scholar and emerged as the most interesting and provocative analyst of Modernism in English—he has been concerned with issues that culminate in his rejection of spatial form. Indeed, after reading most of his relevant work, it seems to me that even if the theory itself were proven worthless, it would still have been of value in providing some of the stimulus for Kermode to have written *The Sense of an Ending*. But of course I do not think the theory worthless. I think, rather, that in opposing it as strenuously as he does, Kermode is operating under something of a delusion: in reality, by the time he finished his book he had accepted everything about spatial form except the terminology. Let me see if I can document this conviction and also offer some reason for the puzzling "space-shyness" (to adapt a term of Worringer's) that he continues to exhibit.

Kermode's first important work, *The Romantic Image*,[13] is a delightful and original exploration—full of piquant detail about French music-hall dancers—devoted to the historical background of what he calls the Romantic-Symbolist tradition in English literature—that is, the tradition of Modernism, whose roots go back to Blake and Cole-

---

may be found in R. Bianchi Bandinelli, *Organicità e astrazione* (Milan: Feltrinelli, 1956). The author, recently deceased, was Professor of Archeology and Greek and Roman Art at the University of Florence, an eminent scholar and an important member of the Italian Communist Party.

Bianchi Bandinelli's brochure, which contains some extremely interesting pages on regression in art, refers to Worringer only in passing and does not mention *Abstraction and Empathy*; but he sees abstraction in modern art in exactly the terms that Worringer defined. Refusing to condemn it outright ("non si tratta, dunque, di pronunziare una condanna"), he considers it as the inevitable product of the sickness of capitalist culture, doomed to disappear in any case and be replaced by humanism once the contradictions of that culture have been resolved in the new Communist society.

13. Kermode, *The Romantic Image* (London: Routledge and Kegan Paul, 1957).

ridge and whose career he traces up through Pater, Yeats (the key figure), and the twentieth-century Modernists Eliot and Pound. This tradition, as Kermode ably defines it, turned the artist into the purveyor of some sort of irrational wisdom supposedly superior to commonsense knowledge and reason; it isolated him from the world and the ordinary concerns of men; and its ideal was to overcome the dissociation of thought and feeling which, in modern culture, had resulted from the rise of science and rationalism and the triumph of the latter over religion and tradition. The Dancer became so important a symbol in this aesthetic because, in the expressive human body, this dissociation is healed; some sort of revelation, some sort of gleam of what Mallarmé called "l'incorporation universelle de l'idée," is accomplished through the spectacle of dance. The same is true of music, whose purity, according to Pater and (earlier) of Schopenhauer, all the arts aspire to emulate and attain. The ideal of this aesthetic was a nondiscursive art, breaking with ordinary life and its trivial concerns, aristocratic and elitist in relation to plebeian mortals, seeking to rise above what Kermode calls, in a typical phrase, "the ordinary syntax of the daily life of action." Implicit in Modernism is the desire "to recover those images of truth which have nothing to do with the intellect of scientists, *nothing to do with time*" (italics added).

Kermode's attitude to this movement, which he depicts so well, was fluctuating and ambiguous, composed of that mixture of attachment and withdrawal that he holds up as one of the chief virtues of Edmund Wilson, a critic he greatly admires. It would have been impossible for Kermode to have written so well of Yeats without the attachment; but the withdrawal is equally evident when he attacks Eliot's theory of a "dissociation of sensibility" as lacking any historical grounding, and indicates his distaste for the divorce of art from life and of poetic meaning from ordinary discourse. He speaks admiringly of Yvor Winters's assault on the Romantic-Symbolist tradition and considers one of "the main issues of modern poetic" to be "the unformulated quarrel between the orthodoxy of Symbolism and the surviving elements of the empirical-utilitarian tradition," which, we are assured, "is characteristically English." It is a pity, he says, that "the movement of the 'thirties away from aesthetic monism, the new insistence on the right to discourse, even to say such things as 'We must love one another or die' (as Auden does in an exquisite poem) has ceased." Well aware that the Romantic-Symbolist tradition was still dominant, he nonetheless looks forward, in conclusion, to the end of its reign and the restoration of Milton and Spenser to the central position from which they had been dethroned; for once that has been accomplished, "the dissociation of sensibility, the great and in some ways noxious historical myth of Symbolism (though the attempt to see history in terms of the Image was noble) will be forgotten."

Kermode's attitude to the Romantic-Symbolist tradition, as we see, is both reverential and dismissive; it performed a noble function in its time, but its time has passed, and it should now be interred with full military honors. The reason is not so much literary—not that he prefers long poems to short ones or wishes poetry again to appeal to the common reader—but rather, it seems to me, practical and "empirical-utilitarian." The new poetic that he looks forward to, he explains, "would be remote from the radicalism of Blake, have little to do with the forlorn hopes of Mallarmé, and less with the disastrous *dérèglement* of Rimbaud. *We have perhaps learnt to respect order, and felt on our bodies the effect of irrationalism, at any rate when the sphere of action is invaded by certain elements of the Romantic rêve"* (italics added). It is this translation of the Romantic-Symbolist tradition into the realm of action, the acceptance of its irrationalism in the sphere of life and politics, that finally accounts for Kermode's hostility. The term "spatial" is used once in the book, and then only in a glancing reference to the "holistic" criticism of G. Wilson Knight; but opposition to what the word designates lurks in the background nonetheless. For we should remember that Kermode has identified the Romantic-Symbolist hostility to the intellect of the scientists (the *source* of its irrationalism) with the effort to escape from time.

V

As we come to *The Sense of an Ending* from *The Romantic Image,* we hear, as the French say, an entirely different *son de cloche.*[14] A great change has occurred, and it may confidently be attributed to Kermode's fascination with that quintessential Roman-

14. Kermode, *The Sense of an Ending* (New York: Oxford University Press, 1967).

tic-Symbolist poet Wallace Stevens, to whom, in the interim, he had devoted an excellent little book.[15] In any case, there is no longer any talk, in *The Sense of an Ending,* about the ordinary reader, poetry as discourse, or the empirical-utilitarian tradition. Man now lives in a world whose contours are provided, not by the intellect of the scientists, but by the myths of Crisis, Apocalypse, Decadence, and the End, and by the existential need to give shape and pattern to the unendurable meaninglessness of pure temporal duration. Just as, according to Wallace Stevens, the poetic imagination projects its metaphors on bare materiality to endow nature with metaphysical significance, so the imagination of Western man, living in the rectilinear time of a crumbling Judeo-Christian civilization, projects the myths of his religion onto the course of events and locates within such structures the meaning of his own life.

What is striking about all this, from my point of view, is not so much Kermode's change of intellectual front (probably less radical than I make it out to be), but rather the shift in attitude toward time that it illustrates. Time, for the earlier Kermode, had been something unproblematic and taken for granted; it was the world defined by the intellect of the scientists and known to the ordinary man (though the two are scarcely the same). To live uncomplicatedly in time, all the same, was to escape the temptations of the Romantic *rêve* and also, presumably, to resist the danger of translating its irrationalism into action. But Kermode has since learned that man's relation to time is much more complex; experimental psychology has persuaded him that we say "tick-tock" because to repeat "tick-tick" endlessly is a burden that humans cannot bear; where there is a beginning we want an end, a human pattern, the music of the spheres, not simply the hum and buzz of repetition ad infinitum. The intolerable time of sheer chronicity creates a problem that humanity has had to cope with since the beginning of *its* time; and humanity has done so either in the myths of its religions, or, when such "supreme fictions" no longer inspire faith, in the secular fictions of art and literature. Myths are thus fictions that one believes to be true and that inspire actual behavior; fictions are what we know as works of art, whose definition has always been that we are aware of their status as being fictive, a seeming, an illusion, *Schein*—or, if we are positivists, downright lies.

---

15. Kermode, *Wallace Stevens* (Edinburgh: Oliver and Boyd, 1960).

This distinction is very important for Kermode because it helps him out of an extremely ticklish dilemma. No longer able to rely on the intellect of the scientists as a criterion of truth, and, as he had once done, using it as a weapon to demolish the dangerous fantasies of the Romantic *rêve,* he feels exposed to the charge of now accepting all the irrationalisms he had once castigated so vehemently and so justifiably. And indeed, if what gives meaning to human life is simply one or another myth, how is one to choose between those competing for the allegiance of the modern mind? "If *King Lear* is an image of the promised end," Kermode writes with commendable candor, "so is Buchenwald"; "both stand under the accusation of being horrible, rootless fantasies, the one no more true than the other." Kermode rather evades this issue of the relativity of values instead of meeting it head-on, though I should be the last to criticize him for having adopted a flanking strategy—the greatest modern minds all leave us equally in the lurch at this point. But he copes with it, in his own way, by the distinction between myth and fiction. Fictions can "degenerate into myths whenever they are not consciously held to be fictive. In this sense anti-Semitism is a degenerate fiction, a myth; and *Lear* is a fiction." There would seem to be no ambiguity about these terms and what Kermode means by them: so long as we remain within the realm of art, so long as fictions remain *conscious* fictions, we do not have to worry about myth and its dangers.

I shall return to this important point and examine how Kermode uses (or abuses) it in a moment; but first I should like to focus on what seems to me the most fruitful insight in his book. This insight is that the plots of our literature are, to a great extent, dependent on the pattern of expectations established by the apocalyptic and eschatological imagination of our culture, and that the former can be seen to have developed out of the latter. Using the language of theology, Kermode points out that plots presuppose "that an end will bestow upon [a] whole duration and meaning . . . Within this organization that which was conceived of as simply successive becomes charged with past and future: what was *chronos* becomes *kairos*" (meaning, by this latter term, the meeting of past and future in a present that Kermode calls "historical moments of intemporal significance"). Elsewhere, he speaks of plots as being the "purging" of "mere successiveness . . . by the establishment of a significant relation between the moment and a remote origin and end, by a concord of past, present and future." Plots therefore seem to work *against* the flow of time and to keep alive, or to create, an indigenous kind of unity overarching and reshaping the constraints of pure temporal linearity.

One can imagine an innocent reader, ignorant both of Kermode's intellectual history and of the terminological warfare of contemporary criticism, thinking it perfectly appropriate to conclude that plots thus exhibit a tendency to counteract time by spatializing its flow—that is, to create relations of meaning detached from pure succession. To be sure, in most literary works before the mid-twentieth century (the great exception, of course, being *Tristram Shandy*), such plot relationships remain in the background and are firmly subordinate to temporal continuity; but Kermode has performed a valuable service in pointing out their nature as embryonic nonlinear structures. He rejects with great decisiveness, however, any idea of using such a term as "spatial" to characterize these forms. "Such concords," he says, "can easily be called 'time-defeating,' but the objection to that word is that it leads directly to the questionable critical practice of calling literary structures *spatial*. This is a *critical fiction* that has regressed into a *myth* because it was not discarded at the right moment in the argument [italics added in last sentence]. 'Time-redeeming' is a better word, perhaps." Nor is this the only passage in which Kermode breaks a lance against "spatial" and "spatial form"; he carries on a continual polemic against the use of these terms all through his book.

Somewhat later, for example, he speaks of St. Augustine reciting his psalm, in which "he found . . . a figure for the integration of past, present and future which defies successive time. He discovered what is now erroneously referred to as 'spatial form.'" Rather than use this latter term, Kermode prefers to reach back to Thomas Aquinas and resurrect his concept of *aevum*. This is a word for the time of the angels, neither the eternity of God nor the transience of mere mortals; a duration out of time but, as it were, coexisting with it. "It [the *aevum*]," Kermode assures us, "does not abolish time or spatialize it"—as if the latter term meant the abolition of time entirely, though it is employed only to refer to the same sort of intemporal *organization* of temporality that Kermode analyzes. Despite his efforts, however, Kermode does not succeed entirely in freeing his own ideas from "spatial" contamination, for later he does speak of

Spenser's poetic use of the "time-defeating *aevum*"; and in distinguishing between the older moderns and the newer generation, who revive the lineage of Dada and Surrealism, he remarks: "But they [the men of 1914] were intellectuals and space-men, not time-men with a special interest in the chaotic present." If so, then why protest so strenuously against using "spatial" terms in reference to their work?

Questions of terminology are of course insignificant, and I am much more interested in the obvious analogies between Kermode's ideas and my own than in arguing on behalf of my particular set of labels. All the same, Kermode's stubborn opposition to my terms is rather an odd phenomenon. Why such hostility to a critical vocabulary? And why, in particular, does such hostility cause Kermode to lose control of his own categories and to misuse them so lamentably?

For how, it may be asked, is it possible for a "critical fiction" to regress into a myth? Critical fictions, after all, are literary criticism and refer to literature; nothing at all is said by Kermode or has been said by those who call some literary structures "spatial" (myself among others) which transfers the argument from the realm of fiction to that of myth as Kermode has defined it (Buchenwald, the Gulag Archipelago, the Second Coming, etc.). Clearly, Kermode's animus against the word "spatial" has loaded it with such an affective charge that he is unable to cope with it properly even inside his own framework of ideas. Or rather, what he does, in classic psychoanalytic style, is to project his own animosity onto others and to turn them into a scapegoat. For it is he himself who makes "spatial form" into a "myth," not those he accuses of failing to drop the term at the right stage of the argument. It is he who refuses to treat it as a neutral critical fiction, perhaps useful or perhaps not; it is he who fills it with a "mythical" content that finally allows him, in a phrase quite unworthy of his usual fairness and good sense, to speak of "the spatial order of the modern critic or the closed authoritarian society"—as if the two really had anything in common, and as if to refer to the one necessarily meant to approve of the other.[16]

16. For the sake of the record, and in view of the unpleasant insinuation contained in the quoted phrase, I should like to cite a passage from my article "Reaction as Progress: Thomas Mann's *Dr. Faustus*," which originally appeared in a review of the book published in 1949: "It is hardly possible any longer to overlook the union in modern art of the most daring intellectual and aesthetic modernity with a rejection of

How is one to account for this intense hostility to the spatial that
Kermode exhibits to such an alarming degree, which he never justifies or explains and which causes so lucid a mind to land in such
confusion? Why should the critical fiction of spatial form invari-
ably be equated in his book with the myth of Fascist totalitarianism?
Part of the answer can no doubt be found in the long-established
association in his mind between the "abolition of time" and the
practical effects of "irrationalism," which, as we have seen, goes
back to *The Romantic Image.* Another link becomes clear in the
remainder of the passage from which the above quotation was taken.
Here Kermode is talking about the reactionary politics of the Anglo-
American moderns (Yeats, Eliot, Pound, Wyndham Lewis); and
Lewis, who at one point openly supported Hitler, quite clearly is
Kermode's *bête noire,* whom he cannot refer to except in accents of
loathing. "He [Lewis] painted on a theory that the closed society of
'abstraction'—an anti-kinematic[?], anti-humanist society, ruled by
fear—much like the fiction of Worringer, was the best for art." And,
a bit later, he says that Lewis wanted to get rid of "democracy and
all the 'Bergsonian' attitudes to time and human psychology, all the
mess which makes up a commonplace modern view of human real-

---

humanism and liberalism, and a preference—both formally and ideologically—for
the primitive, the mythical, and the irrational. To be sure, this has not necessarily
resulted in an alliance with the forces of political retrogression; nor did it do so, we
should remember, in the case of Leverkuhn himself, whose music was considered
Kulturbolschewismus by the masters of the Third Reich. Still, the careers of Knut
Hamsun, Ezra Pound, and Drieu la Rochelle; the political pronouncements of Yeats,
Eliot (in the mid-thirties), Wyndham Lewis, and Gottfried Benn; the proto-Fascist
tendencies in the work of D. H. Lawrence and Stefan George—all this reveals to
what extent Thomas Mann has managed to raise to the level of sovereign art the
problematic nature of modern culture itself. As modern life has become more and
more rationalized, mechanized, and industrialized, art has been driven into a more
and more frenzied and violent assault on a world in which the total dimension of the
spirit has been reduced to a stiflingly materialistic utilitarianism. The legitimacy and
necessity of such a revolt is beyond question; yet its danger is no less evident. For it
is an uncomfortable but inescapable truth that, if some of our noblest artistic expres-
sions were to be translated to-morrow into practical, political terms, the result would
only be to play into the hands of some form of tyranny and oppression." *The
Widening Gyre,* pp. 158–159. So far as I can judge, Kermode has never read
Dr. Faustus—which, if true, is a great pity. No modern novel comes closer to the
heart of his own preoccupations; and Mann would have perhaps taught him not to
make facile identifications between Fascism and avant-garde art while at the same
time remaining fully aware of their disturbing relations. No totalitarian regime has
tolerated the avant-garde, whatever the latter's overt politics may be, or whether the
regime uses the slogans of the right or the left.

ity." Lewis, it will be recalled, was the most vigorous and loquacious English champion of space and spatiality against the time flux of Bergsonism. It is evidently of Lewis that Kermode thinks whenever these words cross his horizon (lumping poor, innocent Worringer into the hateful complex for good measure); and the words thus release the deep-rooted antagonism to Lewis that goes back again to those unforgettable years when Fascist "irrationalism" was wreaking its havoc on the modern world.

VI

It is difficult for me to quarrel with someone for whose feelings I have so much sympathy, and whose social-political antipathies I fully share. But just as noble sentiments do not necessarily make good poetry, so admirable moral convictions do not always guarantee against muddled thinking. I should, therefore, merely like to say two more things about Kermode's reaction. One is that my own use of spatial categories was inspired not by Wyndham Lewis (I had not even read *Time and Western Man* when I wrote my article), but by Lessing, a good Enlightenment liberal, the foe of anti-Semitism, the friend of Moses Mendelssohn, the author of *Nathan der Weise*, etc.; in other words, Kermode's associations are not my own, and there is no reason why his should be accepted as obligatory. More seriously, it is time that English critics overcame their provincialism, took a closer look at the literature of some other countries, and realized that the experimental Modernism linked in England with right-wing political sympathies had quite other affiliations elsewhere.

A much more balanced view of this matter has been given by the Mexican poet and critic Octavio Paz, whose *Children of the Mire* is, in my opinion, the most profound recent interpretation of the modern literary situation. He writes:

Modern literature is an impassioned rejection of the modern age. This rejection is no less violent among the poets of Anglo-American modernism than among the members of the European and Latin-American avant-gardes. Although the former are reactionaries and the latter revolutionaries, both were anti-capitalist. Their different attitudes originated in a common aversion to the world of the bourgeoisie. . . . Like their Romantic and Symbolist predecessors, twentieth-century poets have set against the linear time of progress and history the instantaneous time of eroticism or the cyclical time of analogy or the hollow time of the ironic consciousness. Image and humor: rejections of the chronological time of critical reason and its deification of the future.[17]

It is no longer permissible, it seems to me, for English critics never to take account of other "modernisms" in elaborating their views. It is really no longer permissible to identify the revolt against chronological time in modern literature as a whole—a revolt that has led to the experimental techniques analyzable in spatial terms—with the repulsive social-political ideas of a few (or one) of the Anglo-American writers of the post–World War I generation. Kermode has remarked, in a letter released for publication, that he believes the theory of spatial form to be merely a relic of the past, an outmoded "period aesthetic."[18] This may very well be true; critical theories date

17. Paz, *Children of the Mire*, trans. Rachel Phillips (Cambridge: Harvard University Press, 1974), pp. 109–110.

18. The letter is cited by R. E. Foust, p. 180 above.

In his reply to the initial publication of this portion of my essay in *Critical Inquiry*, Kermode continued to insist that Modernism as an international phenomenon "was powerfully associated with the extreme Right" and that there is "overwhelming evidence" to prove this true. See "A Reply to Joseph Frank," *Critical Inquiry*, 4 (1978), 579–588. If it is not true, he candidly admits, "my whole position would be much weakened." So far as this implies that Modernism tends to be associated more with the Right than the Left in the broad sense (of course not with official Communism), then I equally insist that it is not true, and to that extent Kermode's case is quite weak. The quotation he offers from Renato Poggioli (certainly international enough for anybody) does not prove anything because it is a reply to the assumption that "aesthetic radicalism and social radicalism, revolutionaries in art and revolutionaries in politics" (*The Theory of the Avant-Garde*, trans. Gerald Fitzgerald, New York: Harper and Row, 1971, p. 95), automatically or even predominantly go together. This is, of course, not the case; but neither is the opposite true—namely, Kermode's position that Modernism and Fascism are tied together in some fundamental way. Since Kermode accepts Poggioli as competent to speak on the issue, let me offer another quotation: "We must deny the hypothesis," Poggioli writes, "that the relation between avant-garde art (or art generally) and politics can be established a priori. Such a connection can only be determined a posteriori, from the viewpoint of the avant-garde's own political opinions and convictions" (p. 95). The question at issue, then, as Kermode rightly states, is "whether it was proper for [him] to assert a relationship between modernist spatialising and political and cultural fascism." What does Poggioli say on this point? "Actually . . . the only omnipresent or recurring political ideology within the avant-garde is the least political or the most antipolitical of all: libertarianism and anarchism" (p. 97). So that while it was perfectly proper for Kermode to assert his relationship for the English situation, this national connection does not, as he always tends to assume, have any general applicability or validity.

very rapidly, especially in our time of a frantic quest for novelty in the arts. More relevant, however, is that Frank Kermode himself cannot view this idea *except* in such period terms, exclusively in relation to his own experiences and those of his generation in the Second World War. All this is perfectly human and perfectly comprehensible; but it does indicate an unwillingness to move beyond a fixed point, to evolve, and to develop a less traumatized perspective. In any case, it scarcely justifies a condemnation of spatial form as a theory that no longer has any connection with the literature of the present. On the contrary, the very forcefulness of Kermode's attack would seem to indicate that the theory is far from moribund; and when he quotes Robbe-Grillet to the effect that, in the *nouveau roman*, "le temps se trouve coupé de sa temporalité," he may well have suspected that spatial form is alive and well and very much at home in Paris.[19]

Such considerations should help to explain why Kermode reacts so vehemently and so illogically to any possibility that his own ideas might be thought to resemble a theory of spatial form. They also help to clarify why, though he is so close and careful a reader of Spenser, Shakespeare, Sartre, Yeats, Wallace Stevens, and others, he seems incapable of referring to my article without falling into some egregious error or misapprehension. Joseph Frank, he writes, "implied that although books are inescapably of the element of time, their formal organization is to be apprehended as spatial; one would read them twice, as it were, once for time and once for space." But, so far as I am aware, I implied no such thing: what I said was that *certain* works of twentieth-century literature, because of their experiments with language and narrative structure, forced a reader to approach them as a spatial configuration rather than as a temporal continuum.

Again, speaking of *Ulysses*, Kermode says rightly that it is full of contingency; hence he thinks it unlikely that, as I said, Joyce believed "a unified spatial apprehension of his work would ultimately be possible." Presumably to refute my point of view, he cites Arnold Goldman, who remarked that since *Ulysses* is full of nonsignificant coincidences, "we are forced to carry ultimate explanations to the

19. It is not without significance that in 1972 the article was still considered interesting enough to be translated into French: "La forme spatiale dans la littérature moderne," *Poétique*, 10 (1972), 244–266.

novel's end." This is precisely what I say myself, more elliptically, in the oft-quoted assertion that *Ulysses* cannot be read but only re-read; the unified spatial apprehension *cannot* occur on a first reading, though Joyce postulated it as the basis of his formal structure. So far as Proust is concerned, Kermode remarks that Marcel, in the recognition scene, "is not talking about spatial form" (who said he was?) and that "the experiences reserved for permanent meaning, carried out of the flux of time, surely do not make a pattern in space." Perfectly true! My point was that "by the discontinuous presentation of character Proust forces the reader to juxtapose disparate images [of his characters] spatially, *in a moment of time*, so that the experience of time's passage is communicated directly to his [the reader's] sensibility" (italics added). What I meant was not that the characters made "a pattern in space" (I used no such phrase) but that the reader must perceive the identity of past and present images of the same characters "in a moment of time, that is to say, space."

Whether Frank Kermode has read me rightly or wrongly is hardly a matter of earthshaking consequence; and I should not have wearied the reader with the above demonstration if I were not persuaded that a more important issue was involved. I wish to show that there are no *substantive* gounds for the quarrel that Kermode has chosen to pick with my ideas. I am motivated not primarily by the puerile desire for self-vindication, but because I think it crucial to sweep away the obfuscation that this supposed disagreement tends to create. Actually, as I stated at the beginning of this discussion, it seems to me that Kermode has *accepted* the substance of my ideas (call them by whatever name you please), while pretending to be their most determined antagonist. And in fact, as I have suggested, we have both developed different parts of the same theory.

My own contribution relates to twentieth-century literature, where spatialization enters so fundamentally into the very structure of language and the organization of narrative units that, as Kermode is forced to concede, "Frank says quite rightly that a good deal of modern literature is designed to be apprehended thus." His insights deal with the literature of the past, where spatialization (or, as he calls it, plot concordance) was still a tendency that had by no means yet emerged in as radical a manner as in modernity. Both may be seen and should be seen as part of a unified theory linking experimental Modernism with the past in an unbroken continuity, and which view the present, not as a break, but rather as a limit-case, an intensification and accentuation of potentialities present in literature almost from the start. One of Kermode's essential aims in *The Sense of an Ending* was precisely to argue in favor of continuity, and to reject the schismatic notion that a clean break with the past was either desirable or possible. It seems to me that he succeeded better than he knew, and that in polemicizing with spatial form he merely perpetuates a schism that the deeper thrust of his own ideas has done much to reveal as nugatory and obsolete.

What is necessary for the future, in my view, is to recognize that we now have the basis for a unified theory of literary structures and to work to fill in the outlines already sketched. Indeed, Kermode's extremely suggestive ideas about the relation of such structures to the religious and apocalyptic imagination pave the way for fruitful historical correlations between certain types of structure and certain kinds of collective imaginative experiences. Can we work out any sort of relations between the two in more detail? Why should the picaresque plot have dominated the novel for so long? Why should the much tighter Gothic structure have taken over in the late eighteenth century? These are some of the questions that immediately suggest themselves and that Kermode has opened up for further exploration. It is because his ideas on this score seem to me so promising that I have taken this much trouble to try to exorcise the needless argument between us, and to clear the way for the possibility of genuine progress toward a theory of literature grounded both in psychology and in history.

VII

Even though, in the preceding pages, I have defended myself vigorously—and, I hope, effectively—against what seems to me incomprehension and unjustified cultural-political antagonism, it should not be imagined that I think my article immune to criticism. Far from it; and if I were writing today, I should make one important change. The necessity for such a revision was brought home to me by a just comment contained in the excellent book of Hans Meyerhoff, *Time in Literature*. Meyerhoff picks up my term "symbolic reference" and also cites my remark that Joyce attempted to create in *Ulysses* "the impression of simultaneity for the life of a whole teeming city"; but he criticizes me for "failing to recognize the importance of the distinction between physical and psychological time" and also for not discussing "the correlation between the structure of psychological time and the structure of the self."[20] Both these criticisms are very relevant; and they point to a weakness in the essay that may be traced back to a single source.

This source, as I now realize, is the accidental circumstance that my work took its origin in a preoccupation with *Nightwood*. While unquestionably a work of remarkable literary quality, *Nightwood* was not destined, as the passage of time has shown, to exercise a major influence on the course of the novel;[21] quite the contrary, its poetic texture, which transforms the world into "soliloquists' images,"[22] has remained something of a sport technically speaking. Much more influential have been the efforts of stream-of-consciousness writers like Joyce, Faulkner, and Virginia Woolf to break up language itself so that it reproduces the movements of consciousness on either the reflexive or prereflexive level. Only this latter effort highlights the difference between physical and psychological time and calls into question the unity of the self. Despite my remarks on Joyce and Proust, I did not pay sufficient attention to these issues, because neither arose in relation to *Nightwood*. Hence what I now consider a rather unbalanced perspective in my essay— not so much because of the amount of space devoted to *Nightwood*, but rather because of the neglect of the main line of novelistic development in which spatial form appears in its sharpest contours and with the richest philosophical-cultural implications.

Wylie Sypher has noted "the loss of the self" as one of the dominant tendencies of both Modernism and post-Modernism;[23] and such loss is, of course, another symptom of what I called "the transmutation of the time-world of history into the timeless world of myth." The self no longer feels itself to be an active, individual force operating in the real world of history and time; it exists, if at all,

20. Meyerhoff, *Time in Literature* (Berkeley and Los Angeles: University of California Press, 1955), p. 152.

21. Melvin J. Friedman, *Stream of Consciousness: A Study in Literary Method* (New Haven: Yale University Press, 1955), pp. 261–262.

22. Ralph Freedman, *The Lyrical Novel* (Princeton: Princeton University Press, 1963), p. 278.

23. Sypher, *Loss of the Self in Modern Literature and Art* (New York: Vintage, 1964).

only through its assimilation into a mythical world of eternal prototypes. I remarked on this tendency in the concluding pages of my
essay but could have discussed it more effectively in the context of
the dissolution of the self in stream-of-consciousness fiction.

Even though this modification is the only major change that, with
the benefit of hindsight, I should wish to make in my original text,
this does not mean that I think my essay exhausts the discussion of
the problem. Quite the contrary, it merely initiates a continuing
exploration of a question whose larger implications have only recently begun to become clear. The developments in literary criticism
in recent years have created a new context within which the idea of
spatial form can now be situated and whose effect has been greatly
to extend the range and applicability of the concept as I first pro-
pounded it. This context has arisen from the fusion of anthropology,
information theory, structural linguistics, and literary criticism
which began with the Russian Formalists, was carried on in the
Prague Linguistic Circle, and now goes by the name of French
Structuralism. The theories of this critical movement have shown
not only that spatial form is a concept relevant to a particular phenomenon of avant-garde writing but also that it plays a role, even if
only a subordinate one, throughout the entire history of literature.
The radical nature of the experiments of literary Modernism succeeded in bringing spatial form to the general attention of critical
consciousness; but now that the novelty has worn off, it has become
possible to locate it in relation to a much wider literary horizon.
Spatial form, so far as I can judge, is at present in the process of
being assimilated into a much more general theory of the literary
text; and I should like to conclude these reconsiderations with some
remarks on the ways this is being done.

VIII

Such a development is obviously occurring (or has already occurred, to a large extent) with regard to poetry, largely as a result of
the growing influence of the theories of Roman Jakobson. My own
views were worked out without a knowledge of Jakobson's articles;
but Lessing and modern literature had led me to similar conclusions,
even though I was not able to express them with the exact terminology that Jakobson could command as a professional linguist. It may

seem surprising, at first sight, that such a similarity of views should have emerged by chance; a little reflection, however, shows that Jakobson's ideas and my own had numerous points of contact (even if not personal ones). Jakobson after all, was formed in the atmosphere of Russian Futurism, and as a young man was a personal friend both of Khlebnikov and Mayakovsky. The ideas about poetry circulating in the prerevolutionary Russia of his youth had many similarities with those which influenced Eliot, Pound, and the Anglo-Americans: both drew from the common source of French Symbolist aesthetics.[24] Hence, even though I had available only Anglo-American criticism and French literary criticism of the 1930s (now much, and very unjustly, underestimated in its own country), both Jakobson and I were working in the same cultural climate. And one should remember, in any case, that experimental Modernism is a world-wide movement whose formal features as a whole remain quite similar across national boundaries.[25]

Jakobson's views are thus rooted in his own experience of poetic Modernism; but they take their systematic point of departure from Saussure's theory of poetic language. Saussure had no connection, so far as I am aware, with the avant-garde (Symbolist) literature of his own day; yet if someone had wished to design a theory of language adapted to rationalize Modernist poetry, he could not have done better than this retiring and socially conservative scion of the Genevan aristocracy. For Saussure defines the sign not as the union of a name with a thing, but rather of a sound image with a concept; in other words, language is now seen as a self-enclosed system of sound images and concepts. "Meaning" is defined in terms of the differential relations within the system, not in terms of the relation of the sign to a reality external to language itself. Such a view of language harmonizes with that of modern poetry, where referentiality is relegated to a secondary position or disregarded entirely and the internal relations of words to each other play a predominant role. Jakobson saw this relationship and used it as the basis of his theory of poetic language; and though I did not have Saussure at my dispos-

---

24. See the excellent discussion of Jakobson's relation to modern poetry in Tzvetan Todorov, *Théories du symbole* (Paris: Seuil, 1977), pp. 339–352.

25. In Russia, Khlebnikov, Mayakovsky, Pasternak, Biely; in England, Pound, Eliot, Joyce, Virginia Woolf; in France, Rimbaud, Mallarmé, Apollinaire, Proust, now the *nouveau roman*.

al, what I said about the "space-logic" of modern poetry is quite similar. "The primary reference of any word-group [in a Modernist poem]," I wrote, "is to something inside the poem itself," i.e., the system of self-reflexive signs that constitute the text. And I added that the "space-logic" of such self-reflexiveness "demands a complete reorientation in the reader's attitude toward language." Actually, such a reorientation had already taken place in linguistics under Saussure's influence; and the impact of Jakobson's work, both as linguist and literary critic, has led to its general acceptance as part of modern literary awareness.

Jakobson's now classic definition of poetic language in terms of information theory, contained in his article "Linguistics and Poetics,"[26] incorporates this space logic of modern poetry into a much wider framework; but such space logic, all the same, receives the place of honor by being assigned the function of a universal poetic signifier. There are, Jakobson says, six factors involved in the sending and receiving of any message: sender, message, receiver, context, contact (the physical or psychological medium), code. Each of these factors gives rise to a different linguistic function; and though all are contained in any message, one or another, in any particular case, may have greater dominance in the hierarchy of functions. A poetic message is distinguished by the dominance of the *message itself*, in preference, for example, to the dominance of the (extralinguistic) context. I had called the same phenomenon "the principle of reflexive reference" in modern poetry. In a poetic message, Jakobson explains further, "*the poetic function projects the priniple of equivalence from the axis of selection into the axis of combination*" (italics in text). What this means is that the organization of words in the poem ("the axis of combination") is no longer controlled, as in ordinary language, exclusively by the syntactical order of whatever language is being used; the latter is counterbalanced by the "principle of equivalence" between words, based on their inner relations of similarity or dissimilarity, synonymy or antonymy, which governs the axis of selection. Such a principle of equivalence usually determines the *choice* of words in any ordinary message, but not their combination in a sequence. In a

26. Jakobson, *Essais de linguistique générale* (Paris: Minuit, 1963), pp. 209–248. I refer to Jakobson's English essay in French translation because the latter is more easily accessible. A similar selection of Jakobson's work in English is badly needed.

poetic message, then, the customary order of combination is over-laid by an order based on equivalence—that is, by a space-logic running counter to the linear temporality of syntactical structure.

Jakobson's analysis of Baudelaire's "Les chats," written in col-laboration with Lévi-Strauss, is an attempt to demonstrate the dense network of linguistic equivalences that underlie the poem and are integrated with its syntactical construction. Such application of Jakobson's views to particular poems has excited a great deal of controversy, and details of his readings, it has now become clear, are quite vulnerable. The trouble seems to be that in interpreting the poetry of the past, Jakobson tends to approach it *as if* it were already modern—as if the purely grammatical and linguistic structures of equivalence totally dominate the semantic level.[27] This is, of course, far from being the case; but he has nonetheless succeeded in demon-strating the existence of a supporting and complex structure of such equivalences in poems far from difficult in the modern sense. Jakob-son has thus made a fundamental contribution to the study of poetic language; and in so doing he has proven that there is a space-logic of greater or lesser degree in all poetry. The point at which such space logic becomes completely dominant—the point at which it breaks loose and entirely disregards the sequential order of syntax—is the point at which Modernism begins.

IX

As the essays in the present volume make clear, it was not so much in relation to poetry as to the novel that the notion of spatial form made its greatest impact. It focused attention on the opposition between the temporal nature of the narrative medium (language) and the experiments of such novelists as Joyce, Proust, and Djuna Barnes, who broke up narrative continuity in order to portray either the prereflexive stream of consciousness or the interweaving time shifts of memory, or who composed in terms of symbolic imagery. Systematic experiments with point of view and time shift had begun much earlier with James, Conrad, and Ford, not to mention the occasional sporadic anticipations of Sterne and Diderot. But only in

27. As Gérard Genette has recently shown, Jakobson has constantly wavered in his attitude toward the relation of sound and significance in poetry. See "Formalisme et langage poétique," *Comparative Literature*, 28 (1976), 233–243.

the works of the great Modernists, soon followed by Faulkner, Dos Passos, and a host of others (recent examples are the French *nouveau roman* and the Latin-American *nueva novela*) did the break with narrative sequence first become a significant aesthetic phenomenon.

Lessing proved immensely helpful and suggestive in providing me with a way of discovering how to grasp this evolution of form in narrative; for while I was not at all concerned with his particular problem—the rivalry between poetry and painting as imitative media—his emphasis on language as a linear-temporal structure gave me an insight into the dominant formal peculiarity of the avant-garde novel. Not that novelists were trying to portray space in any literal sense, but their experiments led them in a direction counter to the physical-perceptual nature of their medium. Lessing had advised poets to prefer action to description and not to dwell on picturesque details, because action harmonized better with the linear-temporal character of language. Of course, he said nothing about the novel of his own time (though he was a great admirer of Sterne); and in taking Homer as a standard, he was implicitly equating literature with oral recitation (he speaks in several places of the difference between literature and painting as being that between the ear and the eye). But Lessing's observations, all the same, did focus attention on the relation between the properties of language and the structure of narrative; and this helped me to define with more or less precision what had been happening in the modern novel. If, as Lessing did, one assumed as a norm that artists should adapt their material to the requirements of their physical-perceptual medium, it was clear that the avant-garde novel was overtly defying any such norm, and indeed going in quite the opposite direction.

This is where I stopped at the time, without asking myself any more questions and without worrying about the possible relations of these new developments to the past. In recent years, however, renewed attention has been focused on the problem I had broached in the 1940s and Lessing had broached much earlier: the relation of language to literary structure. Such attention has been prompted partly by the intensive researches of linguistic theory into the syntagmatic and paradigmatic properties of language, as well as by the animated discussion provoked by the experiments of the *nouveau roman*. In addition, the early work of the Russian Formalists has now become accessible in European languages; and their attempt to establish a poetics of prose forms in the 1920s anticipated many of the more current concerns. All this has created the basis for a more general theory of spatial form in narrative, which is gradually beginning to emerge.

Of fundamental importance is the distinction drawn by the Formalists between "story" and "plot." The first term refers to the events of a narrative arranged in the strict sequence of a causal-chronological order; the second, to the structure of these same events as they actually appear in any particular work. It was Victor Shklovsky who first stressed the importance of this distinction; and he did so in an essay on *Tristram Shandy*, which, as he explains, he wrote with the aim of seeing whether he could read this novel as he would a Futurist poem.[28] In other words, it was the obvious abandonment of syntactical sequence in modern poetry that first drew Shklovsky's attention, just as it had done my own, to the possibility of a similar variety of form in the novel.

A bit later, basing himself on Shklovsky, Boris Tomashevsky drew a related but broader distinction between what he called "bound motifs" and "free motifs" in any prose text. The first type are essential to the causal-chronological sequence and cannot be eliminated without destroying the text entirely; the second are relatively independent of such a sequence and can be combined in any order the writer desires. Such "free motifs," Tomashevsky remarks, "are presented so that the tale may be told artistically." In this perspective, "art" may be provisionally defined as the extent to which "free motifs" diversify the constraints of the "bound motifs."[29] For, as Tzvetan Todorov has pointed out, causality and chronology dominate in nonliterary types of prose: "pure causality sends us back to practical discourse, pure temporality to the elementary forms of history (science)."[30] Hence it would appear that the literariness of a narrative work, its specific *artistic* quality, may be defined as the disjunction between story and plot—that is, the manner in which the writer manipulates and distorts causal-chronological sequence. This

28. Shklovsky, "Sterne's *Tristram Shandy*: Stylistic Commentary," in *Russian Formalist Criticism: Four Essays*, trans. Lee T. Lemon and Marion J. Reis (Lincoln: University of Nebraska Press, 1965), pp. 25–57.

29. Tomashevsky, "Thematics," ibid., p. 68.

30. Todorov, *Poétique* (Paris: Seuil, 1968), p. 77; my translation.

would be analogous to the function assigned to the equivalences by Jakobson as a signifier of poetic language. And it follows that every narrative work of art necessarily includes elements that may be called spatial, since the relations of significance between such elements must be construed across gaps in the strict causal-chronological order of the text.

It is obvious that the closer the structure of a narrative conforms to causal-chronological sequence, the closer it corresponds to the linear-temporal order of language. Equally obvious, however, is that such correspondence is contrary to the nature of narrative as an art form. Indeed, all through the history of the novel a tension has existed between the linear-temporal nature of its medium (language) and the spatial elements required by its nature as a work of art. Most of what is known as the "formal conventions" of the novel are an implicit agreement between writer and reader not to pay attention to this disjunction and to overlook the extent to which it exists. Shklovsky provocatively called *Tristram Shandy* the most "typical" novel in world literature (of course it is one of the most *untypical*) because it "laid bare" all the conventions employed by the form and whose nature *as* convention had become imperceptible through long familiarity.

For example, we do not feel jolted when, at the end of a chapter in a conventional novel, the author asks us to shift our attention to events in a parallel plot line occurring simultaneously with those we have just read about. But we *do* feel jolted when Tristram Shandy, depicting his mother listening at a door, freezes that particular scene for about ten pages to follow another train of thought and picks it up again when he is done. Nor does the average reader feel disturbed when, having come across a reference or allusion to a character early in a text, the physical appearance of the personage is delayed until a later stage. But it *does* seem odd that Tristram Shandy is not physically born until about two hundred pages of the novel devoted to his life have already been covered. Sterne, in other words, parodies the conventions by breaking into the continuity of sequences at eccentric points and also by highlighting through exaggeration the anomalies involved in reshaping causal-chronological sequence to serve the purposes of art.

The importance of this Russian Formalist contribution is that it focused attention, for the first time, on the existence of elements of spatial form in *all* narrative (though the Formalists themselves never used such a term). That they were actually talking about spatial form, however, has recently been remarked by Todorov, who improves and updates Tomashevsky in his excellent survey of contemporary poetics. Tomashevsky had noted that texts could be organized in two ways: either "causal-temporal relationships exist between thematic elements"; or "the thematic elements are contemporaneous" and/or "there is some shift of theme without internal exposition of the causal connections." Citing this passage, Todorov calls the first type of structure "the logical-temporal order"; "the second—which Tomashevsky identifies negatively—[is] the spatial order."[31] Spatial form is thus recognized as one of the permanent possibilities for the organization of all literary texts.

From this point of view, the emergence of spatial form in twentieth-century narrative should no longer be regarded as a radical break with tradition. Rather, it represents only what Jakobson would call a shift in the internal hierarchy of the elements composing a narrative structure. Predominant in the past were the "bound motifs" of causal-chronological sequence, which, in conformity with the original oral nature of narrative, ruled over the "free motifs," keeping them under strict control (with a few exceptions, considered abnormal, like *Tristram Shandy* and *Jacques le fataliste*). Beginning with the second half of the nineteenth century, however, this predominance of causal-chronological sequence became seriously weakened. And the most radical proponents of the *nouveau roman*—such as Philippe Sollers and the *Tel Quel* group, who see *Finnegans Wake* as the norm of narrative in the future—hope now to wipe out every trace of causal-chronological sequence once and for all. Like all such extremes, however, this ambition is likely to remain, if not impossible, then at least as peripheral a phenomenon as concrete poetry. Such, at any rate, is my own opinion, for the reasons wryly given by Horacio Oliveira, one of the chief characters in Julio Cortazar's *Hopscotch*, when he is asked to define "the absolute." It is, he says, "just that moment in which something attains its maximum depth, its maximum reach, its maximum sense, and becomes completely uninteresting."[32]

Todorov notes that the spatial order of literary works has been

31. Ibid., p. 68.
32. Cortazar, *Hopscotch*, trans. Rabassa, p. 47.

studied primarily in poetry, and refers to the writings of Jakobson as the most systematic effort made in this direction. Narrative spatial form is still a relatively unexplored domain, despite the fact that, as he points out, "today, literature is turning towards narratives of a spatial and temporal type, to the detriment of causality" (by "temporal" Todorov means "le temps de l'écriture," that is, the reflexive temporality of the literary act itself, not narrative temporality in the old sense).[33] Thus much is to be done in working out the particular modalities of spatial form in narrative as it continues to evolve; and also in defining its relations to the literary tradition. Some of the essays in the present volume seem to me notable contributions to a clarification of such questions. On a more theoretical level, I have found much of interest in the writings of Genette, who, along with Todorov, has in my view made the most interesting suggestions toward what can become the basis of an enlarged theory of narrative spatial form.

X

It is Genette who has seen most clearly the theoretical implications of the *nouveau roman* and who has developed them in the context of a sweeping view of the history of narrative as a whole. In doing so, he returns inevitably to Lessing's old problem (though without specific reference to his predecessor) and carries it forward in the light of the contemporary situation. Discussing the relation between narration and description in his brilliant article "Frontières du récit," he writes: "Narration attaches itself to actions and events considered as pure processes, and thus it puts the emphasis on the temporal and dramatic aspect of *récit*; description on the contrary, because it lingers on objects and things considered in their simultaneity, and because it envisages processes themselves as spectacles, seems to suspend the course of time and contributes to spread the *récit* in space."[34] This is Lessing restated—except that the use of description is no longer seen as an attempt to compete with the effect of painting and is now treated as an indigenous component of narrative.

Nonetheless, Genette, like Lessing, notes an inherent imbalance

33. Todorov, *Poétique*, p. 77.
34. Genette, *Figures II* (Paris: Seuil, 1969), p. 59; my translation.

in the relation of these two narrative components (narration and description) to language:

> The most significant difference between them would perhaps be that narration restores, in the temporal succession of its discourse, the equally temporal succession of events, while description has to model in successiveness the representation of objects co-existing and juxtaposed in space; narrative language would thus be distinguished by a sort of temporal coincidence with its object, while descriptive language, on the contrary, would be irreparably deprived of such coincidence. [p. 60]

But this no longer means that description should be totally subordinate to narration, as Lessing had argued; "this opposition," Genette maintains, "loses much of its force in written literature [visual rather than oral], where nothing prevents the reader from retracing his steps and considering the text, in its simultaneous spatiality, as an *analogon* of the spectacle it describes: the *calligrammes* of Apollinaire or the graphic dispositions of a *Coup de dés* only push to the limit the exploitation of certain latent resources of written expression" (p. 60). Such remarks, as I see them, go a long way toward establishing the theory of spatial form in our modern awareness of the synchronic dimensions of language in a written text; and this awareness is now regarded merely as the extension of a traditional narrative component. Indeed if, as I should like to suggest, one enlarges Genette's terms to think of "description" as including the internal world of the psyche as well as the external world of nature and society, the attempt to convey simultaneity by abrupt time shifts and the use of stream of consciousness may well be considered part of "description" in this amplified sense.

Genette also makes some extremely interesting historical observations on the varying role of these two narrative components. In the classical tradition, the function of description was ornamental and decorative; and Lessing reacted against the excess of such ornamentation as part of his campaign against French Neoclassicism (Boileau, on the other hand, counseled writers of epics, "Soyez riche et pompeux dans vos descriptions"). It was the excess of such ornamentation in the Baroque period, as Genette observes, which "ended by destroying the equilibrium of the narrative poem in its decline." At the beginning of the nineteenth century, description reached a new synthesis with narration in the novel. Far from receding into the background, description took on a new importance in Balzac because its function became explicative and symbolic, no longer merely decorative. "The physical portraits, the descriptions of clothes and furniture, tends, in Balzac and his realist successors, to reveal and, at the same time, to justify the psychology of the characters, of which they are at once the sign, the cause and the effect. Description becomes here, what it never was in the classical period, a major element of the exposition" (p. 59). (Such a use of description, we may note in passing, actually began in the Gothic novel and reached Balzac by way of Scott and the historical novel.)

Genette points out, however, that the more recent evolution of the novel has seen what appears to be the increasing liberation of description from its subordination to narration, though he is not sure that it should be interpreted in this way. "The work of Robbe-Grillet," he writes, "appears perhaps more as an effort to construct a *récit* (an *histoire*) through the exclusive means of descriptions imperceptibly modified from page to page, which may be seen, at one and the same time, as a spectacular promotion of the descriptive function and a striking confirmation of its irreducible subordination to narration" (p. 59). Whether one can still speak of description as *subordinate*, in a work composed exclusively of the variation of descriptive fragments, seems very doubtful. But disagreement on this point does not detract from the usefulness of Genette's categories, whose value is that they help us to view the history of spatial form in terms of the changing relationships between description and narration.

Another section of the same essay offers an additional vantage point from which to survey the same problem. Genette here shifts from the inner-textual interplay between narration and description to that of the relation between text and narrator, using some linguistic observations of Émile Benveniste as his point of departure. Benveniste distinguishes between what he calls *récit* and *discours* in terms of whether the presence of a locutor is grammatically indicated. *Récit* tends to eliminate any such reference, whether explicit or implied; *discours* brings the personal source of utterance to the foreground, or at least does not try to conceal such a presence. *Récit* is the pure form of objective narration; *discours* the pure form of subjective narration; neither, however, ever is found in a pure state, and they "contaminate" each other all through the history of narrative. But here again, all the same, there is another imbalance: Genette maintains that *discours* is the widest and most universal category of linguistic expression, which can easily contain and include passages of *récit* without strain. *Récit*, on the other hand, "is a particular mode, *set apart*, defined by a certain number of exclusions and restrictive conditions (avoidance of the present, of the first person, etc.)" (p. 66; italics in text). As a result, *récit* is comparatively a more artificial and limited form; even though it cannot avoid including *discours*, the latter always appears as a violation of its norms.

Récit, obviously, aims so far as possible at being the pure form of causal-chronological sequence; but it is constantly being interfered with by *discours*, which calls attention away from the flow of events to the narrator and the process of narration. Genette analyzes this phenomenon without relating it to the issues that he raised when speaking of narration and description; but the two points of view are obviously connected. For just as description tends to spatialize narration, so *discours* inevitably exercises a discreet spatializing effect, on the micro-narrative level, by its constant interruption of the rhythm of pure chronicity. This explains why an increase of interest in man's subjective and emotional life, when translated into terms of literary form, automatically seems to lead to an increase in the spatialization of narrative (sentimentalism in the mid-eighteenth century, the time of the epistolary novel and Sterne, and the influence of Freud and Bergson at the beginning of the twentieth). *Récit*, according to Genette, celebrated its greatest triumphs in the nineteenth-century novel with Balzac and Tolstoy; but it has now been almost entirely replaced by *discours* in the avant-garde novel of the 1920s and its continuator in French literature, the *nouveau roman*. Proust is, of course, the obvious exemplar (though curiously he is not mentioned in this context), but Genette does refer to Joyce and Faulkner as writers who transfer the *récit* "to the interior *discours* of their principal characters." In the *nouveau roman*, the tendency is "to absorb the *récit* into the present *discours* of the writer in the course of writing" (pp. 67–68). The increasing spatialization of the novel, as we see, is clearly correlated with the growing preponderance of *discours*; and spatial form can thus be regarded as a function of the fluctuating historical relations between these two linguistic modes.

Genette's *Figures III* contains a study of narrative structure, "Discours du récit," which seems to me the most substantial contribution to the poetics of the novel since Wayne Booth, and of equally classic stature. This is not the place to discuss the work in detail; but a glance at the index reveals a large number of technical terms ("achronie," "structure achronique," "anachronie," "anisocronie," "isochronie," "analepse," "prolepse") all of which refer to various ways in which temporality and causal-chronological sequence are manipulated in a narrative text. The examples come mostly, though not exclusively, from Proust; and they constitute, so far as my knowledge goes, the most acute and systematic account of such structures ever attempted in criticism. What Genette has written is, for a good part, a study in spatial form; and students of the subject have a good deal to learn from his pages.

Even more, one of his other essays, "La littérature et l'espace," contains the best analysis I know of the broader horizon against which the idea of narrative spatial form must now be seen. Bergson, at the beginning of the century, had accused language of betraying "reality" by spatializing the temporality of consciousness; and linguistics for the past half-century has confirmed Bergson's ideas without sharing his hostility. "In distinguishing rigorously between the word and language-system," Genette writes, "and in giving first place to the latter in the *play* of language—defined as a system of purely differential relations, in which each element is conditioned by the place it occupies in a general ensemble and by the vertical and horizontal relations that it maintains with related and neighboring elements—it is undeniable that Saussure and his continuators have brought to the foreground a mode of being of language that one must call spatial, although we are dealing here, as Blanchot has written, with a spatiality 'whose originality cannot be grasped in terms either of geometrical space or the space of practical life'" (pp. 44–45).

Nor is it only linguistics, one may add, which has contributed to focus such sharp attention on this spatial aspect of language. Genette says nothing about the work that has been done, primarily by English and American writers, in exploring oral literature and folk poetry and in speculating on the vast changes that have occurred in literary consciousness as a result of the transition from oral to written literature. One thinks here essentially of the work of Albert Lord, but also of such names as Marshall McLuhan and Walter J. Ong, who have stressed the wider cultural ramifications of this transition. The theories of such writers support Genette's remark that "this spatiality of language considered as an implicit system, the system of language which commands and determines every act of speech, is in some way made manifest, placed in evidence, and moreover accentuated in a literary work by the use of a written text" (p. 45).

Genette then goes on to outline, in broad strokes, the contemporary view of the literary work that has gradually evolved as a result of the increasing awareness of the crucial nature of this evolution from speech to writing:

> One has long considered writing, and particularly the writing called phonetic such as we conceive and utilize it, or believe we utilize it, in the West, as a simple means for the notation of speech. Today, we are beginning to understand that it is a bit more than that, and Mallarmé already had said that "to think, is to write without flourishes." Because of the specific spatiality to which we have referred, language (and thus thought) is already a kind of writing, or, if one prefers, the manifest spatiality of writing may be taken as a symbol for the profound spatiality of language. And, at the very least, for we who live in a civilization in which literature is identified with the written, this spatial mode of its existence cannot be considered accidental or negligible. Since Mallarmé, we have learned to recognize (to re-cognize) the so-called visual resources of script and of typographical arrangement, and of the existence of the Book as a kind of total object; and this change of perspective has made us more attentive to the spatiality of writing, to the atemporal disposition of signs, words, phrases and discourse in the simultaneity of what is called a text.

Finally, the result has been to change our notion of what it means to read:

> It is not true that reading is only that continual unfolding accompanying the hours as they pass of which Proust spoke with reference to his boyhood; and the author of *La recherche du temps perdu* no doubt knew this better than anyone—he who demanded of his reader an attention to what he called the "telescopic" character of his work, that is, to the relations at long distance established between episodes far removed from each other in the temporal continuity of a linear reading (but, it should be noted, singularly close in the written space, in the paginated thickness of the volume), and which requires for its consideration a sort of simultaneous perception of the total unity of the work, a unity which resides not solely in the horizontal relations of continuity and succession, but also in the relations that may be

called vertical or transversal, those effects of expectation, of response, of symmetry, of perspective, which prompted Proust himself to compare his work to a cathedral. To read as it is necessary to read such works (are there any others?) is really to reread; it is already to have reread, to have traversed a book tirelessly in all directions, in all its dimensions. One may say, then, that the space of a book, like that of a page, is not passively subject to the time of a linear reading; so far as the book reveals and fulfills itself completely, it never stops diverting and reversing such a reading, and thus, in a sense, abolishes it. [pp. 45–46]

It is very gratifying for me to observe how many of Genette's ideas echo my own of thirty years earlier (without direct influence, as he has been kind enough to inform me in a letter), while developing them far beyond what would have been possible for me at that time. And such convergence, as well as such continuity, seems to me to prove that the idea of spatial form in literature is much more than simply a provocative critical paradox. It is a concept which satisfies the Hegelian requirement that ideas should grasp the inner movement of cultural reality itself.

Space and Spatial Form
in Narrative:
A Selected Bibliography
of Modern Studies

Jeffrey R. Smitten

A bibliography on this topic can hope only to be illustrative, not definitive. The area it must cover is enormous; since space and spatial form are properties of narratives written at any time and in any language, the criticism the compiler must review is without limits. To deal with this mass of material, some arbitrary but, I hope, not illogical boundaries have had to be set.

I INCLUSIONS

Most of the nearly three hundred items here are discussions of narrative. The term *narrative* has been defined broadly to include the novel, short story, drama, romance, and narrative poem, as well as such recent innovations as "surfiction" and the *nouveau roman*. It also includes such nonfiction works as travel books. In one or two instances I have included studies of spatial form in lyric poetry, because of the importance of their theoretical insights—as well as some works of critical theory that have implications for the study of narrative.

The bibliography is limited to twentieth-century criticism. Although space and spatial form are properties of earlier narratives, these critical concepts have been developed only in this century. For earlier periods, adumbrations of spatial form and concern with represented space in narrative are sometimes found in conjunction with the *ut pictura poesis* theory. For a bibliography on this topic, see John Graham, "Ut Pictura Poesis: A Bibliography," *Bulletin of Bibliography*, 29 (1972), 13–15, 18.

The bibliography is international, although when English translations exist, the original edition in another language has usually not been cited. Easily available collections of a critic's essays have been cited in preference to the enumeration of his essays' first appearance. Essays that have been incorporated into books, or dissertations that have been published as books or articles, have not been listed. Reprints of books and articles have been given for only a few items of major importance.

The following types of studies have been included: (1) developments and applications of Joseph Frank's theory of spatial form; (2) discussions of the representation of space in narrative; (3) discussions of simultaneity and/or stasis in narrative (whether or not "space" or "spatial form" figure as terms in the study); (4) the use of superimposition of texts, either intratextual or intertextual, as a critical method (again whether or not "space" or "spatial form" is used as a critical term).

II EXCLUSIONS

All studies making only passing references to or casual citations of Frank's "Spatial Form in Modern Literature" (of which there are many in American criticism) have been excluded, as well as studies making only passing references to represented space, simultaneity, stasis, spatialization of time, superimposition, etc.

The most difficult exclusion to make has been the host of studies that imply spatial form in narrative but that do not confront directly the theory of spatial form. Virtually any study based upon New Criticism will imply some degree of spatiality in the literary work discussed, because the study assumes the work has the status and qualities of an object. Similarly, studies employing a Structuralist or Formalist methodology often will imply a spatial conception of the work or works discussed. But to avoid swamping the bibliography with such material, I have excluded all studies in which the idea of spatiality is only implicit.

Another especially difficult exclusion has been the fruitful and suggestive collateral studies that often lie behind studies of space and spatial form. In particular, works in philosophy, science, film, art, and architecture have been very influential in stimulating and developing the concepts of space and spatial form in literature. At the same time, however, there is no logical limit for such studies, so any listing of this collateral material would be highly subjective and incomplete in any sense. Moreover, the publication of *Aspects of Time*, ed. C. A. Patrides (Manchester: University of Manchester Press, 1976) has in part removed the necessity of such a listing, since it contains a useful bibliography of works dealing with time (and therefore, often enough, space) in the fine arts, science, and philosophy. This listing in fact happens to contain most of the important collateral studies commonly cited in discussions of space and spatial form. For additional material in this vein, see the bibliographies to Sharon Spencer, *Space, Time and Structure in the Modern Novel*, and Joseph A. Kestner, *The Spatiality of the Novel*, both listed below. For some of the cultural background to Frank's "Spatial Form in Modern Literature," see the essay by James M. Curtis in this volume; chapter 3 of Ronald Foust's unpublished dissertation "The Place of Spatial Form in Modern Literary Criticism" (listed below); Maurice Beebe, "What Modernism Was," *Journal of Modern Literature*, 3 (1974), 1065–1084; and Ihab Hassan, "POSTmodernISM: A Paracritical Bibliography," in his *Paracriticisms* (listed below).

Except for studies treating simultaneity and/or stasis in narrative, all studies discussing only temporal manipulation with no extended analysis of space or spatial form have been excluded. Quite obviously, temporal manipulation is closely tied to spatial form, and questions of time in narrative often imply or bear upon those of space. But temporal manipulation is not necessarily the same thing as spatial form (as Ivo Vidan has shown in his essay in this volume), and a discussion of time need not involve a discussion of space or stasis. Thus unless the study explicitly confronts the issues of space and spatial form, it has been excluded. Patrides' *Aspects of Time* is a useful starting point for anyone interested in the problem of time in literature. See also the bibliography of time in English fiction in David Leon Higdon's *Time and English Fiction* (London: Macmillan, 1978).

In the early stages of compiling this bibliography, I received help from Ann Daghistany and J. J. Johnson, for which I am grateful.

BOOKS AND ARTICLES

ALLDREDGE, BETTY. "Spatial Form in Faulkner's *As I Lay Dying.*" *Southern Literary Journal,* 11, No. 1 (1978), 3–19.

ANDERSON, CAROL REED. "Time, Space, and Perspective in Thomas Hardy." *Nineteenth-Century Fiction,* 9 (1954), 192–208.

ARNHEIM, RUDOLF. "A Stricture on Space and Time." *Critical Inquiry,* 4 (1978), 645–655.

ASTALOS, GEORGES. "Théâtre floral spatial: La pluridimensionalité ou la pulverisation de l'action dans l'espace." *Degrés,* 4 (1973), 1–18.

BACHELARD, GASTON. *The Poetics of Space.* Trans. Maria Jolas. Boston: Beacon Press, 1969.

BAKHTIN, MIKHAIL. *Problems of Dostoevsky's Poetics.* Trans. R. W. Rotsel. Ann Arbor: Ardis, 1973.

———. "Zeit und Raum im Roman." *Kunst und Literatur,* 22 (1974), 1161–1191.

BALUTOWA, BRONSLILAWA. "Space—Setting—Things in the English Short Story 1900–1925." *Kwartalnik Neofilologiczny,* 23 (1976), 433–447.

BANCQUART, MARIE-CLAIRE. "L'espace dans *Madame Bovary.*" *L'information littéraire,* 25 (1973), 64–73.

BART, HEIDI CULBERTSON, and BENJAMIN F. BART. "Space, Time, and Reality in Flaubert's *Saint Julien.*" *Romanic Review,* 59 (1968), 30–39.

BARTHES, ROLAND. *Critical Essays.* Trans. Richard Howard. Evanston: Northwestern University Press, 1972. See esp. "Objective Literature."

BEACH, JOSEPH WARREN. *The Twentieth-Century Novel: Studies in Technique.* New York: Century, 1932. See esp. section 5.

BEZNOS, MAURICE J. "Aspects of Time According to the Theories of Relativity in Marcel Proust's *A la recherche du temps perdu:* A Study of the Similarities in Conceptual Limits." *Ohio University Review,* 10 (1968), 74–102.

BLACKSTONE, BERNARD. "'The Loops of Time': Spatio-Temporal Patterns in *Childe Harold.*" *Ariel,* 2, No. 4 (1971), 5–17.

BLANCHOT, MAURICE. *L'espace littéraire.* Paris: Gallimard, 1955.

———. *Le livre à venir.* Paris: Gallimard, 1959.

BLEIKASTEN, ANDRÉ. "L'espace dans *Lumière d'août.*" *Bulletin de la faculté des lettres de Strasbourg,* 46 (1967), 406–420.

———. "Faulkner et le nouveau roman." *Langues modernes,* 60 (1966), 422–432.

BLUESTONE, GEORGE. *Novels into Film.* Baltimore: The Johns Hopkins University Press, 1957.

———. "Time in Film and Fiction." *Journal of Aesthetics and Art Criticism*, 19 (1961), 311–315.

BLY, P. A. "The Use of Distance in Galdós's 'La de Bringas.'" *Modern Language Review*, 69 (1974), 88–97.

BOKLUND, KARIN M. "On the Spatial and Cultural Characteristics of Courtly Romance." *Semiotica*, 20 (1977), 1–37.

BORK, ALFRED M. "Durrell and Relativity." *Centennial Review*, 7 (1963), 191–203.

BOTTEA, DOMNICA. "Structură, timp și spațiu in tetralogia lui L. Durrell." *Analele Universitatii Bucresti. Limbi Germanice*, 19 (1970), 175–185.

BOURNEUF, ROLAND. "L'organization de l'espace dans le roman." *Etudes littéraires*, 3 (1970), 77–94.

BROOKE-ROSE, CHRISTINE. "Le roman experimental en Angleterre." *Langues modernes*, 63 (1969), 158–168.

BROWER, REUBEN A. "The Novel as Poem: Virginia Woolf Exploring a Critical Metaphor." In *The Interpretation of Narrative: Theory and Practice*, ed. Morton W. Bloomfield. Cambridge: Harvard University Press, 1970, pp. 229–241.

BULL, REIMER. *Bauformen des Erzählens bei Arno Schmidt: Ein Beitrage zur Poetik der Erzählkunst*. Bonn: Bouvier, 1969.

BULLEN, JOHN SAMUEL. *Time and Space in the Novels of Samuel Richardson*. Logan: Utah State University Press, 1965.

BURROUGHS, WILLIAM. *The Job: Interviews with William Burroughs*, ed. Daniel Odier. New York: Grove Press, 1970. See "Journey through Space-Time."

BUTOR, MICHEL. *Répertoire I*. Paris: Minuit, 1960.

———. *Répertoire II*. Paris: Minuit, 1964. See esp. "L'espace du roman," "Philosophie de l'ameublement," "Recherches sur la technique du roman," "Le livre comme objet." These and other of Butor's essays have been translated in *Inventory*, ed. Richard Howard (New York: Simon and Schuster, 1969).

———. *Répertoire III*. Paris: Minuit, 1968.

———. *Répertoire IV*. Paris: Minuit, 1974.

CARROLL, DAVID. "Diachrony and Synchrony in *Histoire*." *Modern Language Notes*, 92 (1977), 797–824.

CHAFFEE, PATRICIA. "Spatial Patterns and Closed Groups in Lessing's *African Stories*." *South Atlantic Bulletin*, 43, No. 2 (1978), 45–52.

CHAMPIGNY, ROBERT. *Ontology of the Narrative: An Analysis*. The Hague: Mouton, 1972.

CHATMAN, SEYMOUR. *Story and Discourse: Narrative Structure in Fiction and Film*. Ithaca: Cornell University Press, 1978. See esp. pp. 63–79, 96–107.

COHN, DORRIT. "Psyche and Space in Musil's *Die Vollendung der Liebe*." *Germanic Review*, 49 (1974), 154–168.

CONCALON, ELAINE D. "La symbolique de l'espace dans *Hérodias*." *South Atlantic Bulletin*, 40, No. 1 (1975), 23–28.

COPE, JACKSON I. *The Metaphoric Structure of "Paradise Lost."* Baltimore: The Johns Hopkins University Press, 1962.

CROSS, RICHARD K. *Flaubert and Joyce: The Rite of Fiction.* Princeton: Princeton University Press, 1971.

CURTIS, JAMES M. "The Function of Imagery in *War and Peace.*" *Slavic Review,* 29 (1970), 460–480.

―――. "Notes on Spatial Form in Tolstoy." *Sewanee Review,* 78 (1970), 517–530.

―――. "Spatial Form as the Intrinsic Genre of Dostoevsky's Novels." *Modern Fiction Studies,* 18 (1972), 135–154.

―――. "Spatial Form in Drama: *The Seagull.*" *Canadian-American Slavic Studies,* 6 (1972), 13–37.

CURTIS, JERRY L. "Structure and Space in Camus' 'Jonas.'" *Modern Fiction Studies,* 22 (1976–1977), 571–576.

DOLEZEL, LUBOMIR. "A Scheme of Narrative Time." In *Semiotics of Art: Prague School Contributions,* ed. Ladislav Matejka and Irwin R. Titunik. Cambridge: MIT Press, 1976, pp. 209–217.

DORT, BERNARD. "Sur l'espace." *Esprit,* Nos. 263–264 (1958), pp. 77–82.

DOYEN, VICTOR. "Elements towards a Spatial Reading of Malcolm Lowry's *Under the Volcano.*" *English Studies,* 50 (1969), 65–74.

DUNCAN, PHILLIP A. "The Equation of Theme and Spatial Form in Flaubert's 'Hérodias.'" *Studies in Short Fiction,* 14 (1977), 129–136.

DURRELL, LAWRENCE. *A Key to Modern British Poetry.* Norman: University of Oklahoma Press, 1952. See chapter 2.

ENGELBERG, EDWARD. "Space, Time, and History: Towards the Discrimination of Modernisms." *Modernist Studies,* 1 (1974), 7–25.

FAGAN, EDWARD R. "Disjointed Time and the Contemporary Novel." *Journal of General Education,* 23 (1971), 151–160.

FASEL, IDA. "Spatial Form and Spatial Time." *Western Humanities Review,* 16 (1962), 223–234.

FERNANDEZ, RAMON. *Messages.* Trans. Montgomery Belgion. New York: Harcourt Brace, 1927. See pp. 210 ff.

"Fiction Now." *Partisan Review,* 40 (1973), 427–444. See esp. essays by Federman and Klinkowitz.

FITCH, BRIAN T. "Aesthetic Distance and Inner Space in the Novels of Camus." *Modern Fiction Studies,* 10 (1964), 279–292.

FJELDE, ROLF. "Time, Space, and Wyndham Lewis." *Western Review,* 15 (1950–1951), 201–212.

FLEISCHAUER, JOHN F. "Simultaneity in Nabokov's Prose Style." *Style,* 5 (1971), 57–69.

FOLKENFLIK, ROBERT. "A Room of Pamela's Own." *ELH,* 39 (1972), 585–596.

FRANK, ELLEN EVE. *Literary Architecture: Essays toward a Tradition.* Berkeley and Los Angeles: University of California Press, 1979.

FRANK, JOSEPH. "Spatial Form: An Answer to Critics." *Critical Inquiry,* 4 (1977), 231–252.
———. "Spatial Form in Modern Literature." *Sewanee Review,* 53 (1945), 221–240, 433–456, 643–653. Reprinted with some expansion and revision in Frank's *The Widening Gyre: Crisis and Mastery in Modern Literature* (New Brunswick: Rutgers University Press, 1963; reprinted Bloomington: Indiana University Press, 1968). Reprinted in abbreviated versions with varying titles in *Criticism: The Foundations of Modern Literary Judgment,* ed. Mark Schorer et al., New York: Harcourt Brace, 1948; *Critiques and Essays in Criticism, 1920–1948,* ed. Robert Wooster Stallman, New York: Ronald Press, 1949; *Critiques and Essays on Modern Fiction, 1920–1951,* ed. John W. Aldridge, New York: Ronald Press, 1952; *A Grammar of Literary Criticism,* ed. Lawrence Hall, New York: Macmillan, 1965.
———. "Spatial Form: Some Further Reflections." *Critical Inquiry,* 5 (1978), 275–290.
FREEDMAN, RALPH. *The Lyrical Novel: Studies in Hermann Hesse, André Gide, and Virginia Woolf.* Princeton: Princeton University Press, 1963.
FREEDMAN, WILLIAM A. *Laurence Sterne and the Origins of the Musical Novel.* Athens: University of Georgia Press, 1978.
FRIEDMAN, MELVIN J. "The Neglect of Time: France's Novel of the Fifties." *Books Abroad,* 36 (1962), 125–130.
———. *Stream of Consciousness: A Study in Literary Method.* New Haven: Yale University Press, 1955.

GARRINGER, R. L. "Circumscription of Space and the Form of Poe's *Arthur Gordon Pym.*" *PMLA,* 89 (1974), 506–516.
GEJ, N. K. "Vremja i prostranstvo v strukture proizvedenija." *Kontekst,* 1974, pp. 213–228.
GELLEY, ALEXANDER. "Metonymy, Schematism, and the Space of Literature." *New Literary History,* 11 (1980), 469–487.
GENETTE, GÉRARD. *Figures I.* Paris: Seuil, 1966. See esp. "Espace et langage," "Figures," "Proust palimpseste," "Vertige fixé."
———. *Figures II.* Paris: Seuil, 1969. See "La littérature et l'espace," "Frontières du récit." The latter has been translated by Ann Levonas in *New Literary History,* 8 (1976), 1–13.
———. *Figures III.* Paris: Seuil, 1972. "Discours du récit" has been translated by Jane E. Lewin as *Narrative Discourse: An Essay in Method,* Ithaca: Cornell University Press, 1980.
GIOVANNINI, G. "Method in the Study of Literature in Its Relation to the Other Fine Arts." *Journal of Aesthetics and Art Criticism,* 8 (1950), 185–195.
GOPNIK, IRWIN. *A Theory of Style and Richardson's "Clarissa."* The Hague: Mouton, 1970. See pp. 114–116.
GORDON, AMBROSE, JR. "Time, Space and Eros: The *Alexandria Quartet* Rehearsed." In *Six Contemporary Novels,* ed. William O. S. Sutherland. Austin: University of Texas Press, 1962, pp. 6–21.

GRACE, SHERRILL E. "The Creative Process: An Introduction to Time and Space in Malcolm Lowry's Fiction." *Studies in Canadian Fiction*, 2 (1977), 61–68.

GREGOR, IAN. "Spaces: *To the Lighthouse*." In *The Author in His Work: Essays on a Problem in Criticism*, ed. Louis L. Martz and Aubrey Williams. New Haven: Yale University Press, 1978, pp. 375–389.

GRIMM, REINHOLD. "Romane des Phanotyp." *Akzente*, 9 (1962), 464–479.

GUIGUET, JEAN. *Virginia Woolf and Her Works*. Trans. Jean Stewart. New York: Harcourt, Brace and World, 1965. See pp. 382–398.

GUIMBRETIÈRE, ANDRÉ. "Quelques remarques sur la fonction du symbole à propos de l'espace sacralisé." *Cahiers internationaux de symbolisme*, 13 (1967), 33–55.

GULLÓN, RICARDO. "On Space in the Novel." Trans. René de Costa. *Critical Inquiry*, 2 (1975), 11–28.

GUREWITSCH, M. ANATOLE. "Counterpoint in Thomas Mann's *Felix Krull*." *Modern Fiction Studies*, 22 (1976–1977), 525–541.

HAGAN, JOHN. "Déjà vu and the Effect of Timelessness in Faulkner's *Absalom Absalom!*" *Bucknell Review*, 11, No. 2 (1963), 31–52.

HALL, EDWARD T. *The Hidden Dimension*. Garden City: Doubleday, 1966.

HALTRESHT, MICHAEL. "The Dread of Space in *The Secret Agent*." *Literature and Psychology*, 22 (1972), 89–97.

HAMARD, JEAN-PAUL. "L'espace et le temps dans les romans de Lawrence Durrell." *Critique*, No. 156 (1960), pp. 387–413.

HARMON, WILLIAM. *Time in Ezra Pound's Work*. Chapel Hill: University of North Carolina Press, 1977. See esp. "Appendix: Time in the Study of Literature."

HART, CLIVE. *Structure and Motif in "Finnegans Wake."* Evanston: Northwestern University Press, 1962.

HART, FRANCIS R. "The Spaces of Privacy: Jane Austen." *Nineteenth-Century Fiction*, 30 (1975), 305–333.

HARTMAN, GEOFFREY. "Structuralism: The Anglo-American Adventure." In *Structuralism*, ed. Jacques Ehrmann. 1966; rpt. Garden City: Anchor Books, 1970, pp. 137–158.

HARVEY, W. J. *The Art of George Eliot*. London: Oxford University Press, 1961. See pp. 95–108.

HASSAN, IHAB. *Paracriticisms: Seven Speculations of the Times*. Urbana: University of Illinois Press, 1975. See esp. "POSTmodernISM: A Paracritical Bibliography."

HAUSER, ARNOLD. "The Conception of Time in Modern Art and Science." *Partisan Review*, 23 (1956), 320–333.

———. *The Social History of Art*. 2 vols. New York: Knopf, 1951. See volume II, chap. 8.

HOLDRIDGE, DAVID. "Suspended Structures in Proust's *A la recherche du temps perdu*." *Modern Languages*, 52 (1971), 112–118.

HOLLINGTON, MICHAEL. "Svevo, Joyce and Modernist Time." In *Mod-*

ernism 1890–1930, ed. Malcolm Bradbury and James McFarlane. Harmondsworth: Penguin, 1976, pp. 430–442.

HOLTZ, WILLIAM. "Field Theory and Literature." *Centennial Review*, 11 (1967), 532–548.

——. *Image and Immortality: A Study of "Tristram Shandy."* Providence: Brown University Press, 1971. See esp. pp. 90–119.

——. "Spatial Form in Modern Literature: A Reconsideration." *Critical Inquiry*, 4 (1977), 271–283.

——. "Thermodynamics and the Comic and Tragic Modes." *Western Humanities Review*, 25 (1971), 203–216.

INGARDEN, ROMAN. *The Literary Work of Art: An Investigation on the Borderlines of Ontology, Logic, and Theory of Literature*. Trans. George G. Grabowicz. Evanston: Northwestern University Press, 1973. See pp. 222–233.

ISSACHAROFF, MICHAEL. *L'espace et la nouvelle: Flaubert, Huysmans, Ionesco, Sartre, Camus*. Paris: Corti, 1976.

——. "Qu'est-ce que l'espace littéraire?" *L'information littéraire*, 30 (1978), 117–122.

JENNINGS, CHANTAL. "La symbolique de l'espace dans *Nana*." *Modern Language Notes*, 88 (1973), 764–774.

KAPLAN, MILTON A. "Simultaneity in the Arts." *Journal of Aesthetic Education*, 7, No. 3 (1973), 35–41.

KARST, ROMAN. "Franz Kafka: Word-Space-Time." *Mosaic*, 3, No. 4 (1970), 1–13.

KAWIN, BRUCE F. *Telling It Again and Again: Repetition in Literature and Film*. Ithaca: Cornell University Press, 1972.

KAYSER, WOLFGANG. *Das sprachliche Kunstwerk*. Bern: Francke, 1948.

KENNER, HUGH. *Flaubert, Joyce, and Beckett: The Stoic Comedians*. Boston: Beacon Press, 1962.

——. *The Pound Era*. Berkeley and Los Angeles: University of California Press, 1971.

KERMODE, FRANK. "A Reply to Joseph Frank." *Critical Inquiry*, 4 (1978), 579–588.

——. *The Sense of an Ending: Studies in the Theory of Fiction*. New York: Oxford University Press, 1967.

KESTNER, JOSEPH A. *Jane Austen: Spatial Structure of Thematic Variations*. New York: Humanities Press, 1974.

——. "Pindar and Saint-Exupéry: The Heroic Form of Space." *Modern Fiction Studies*, 19 (1973–1974), 507–516.

——. "The Spatiality of Pasternak's 'Ariel Ways.'" *Studies in Short Fiction*, 10 (1973), 243–251.

——. *The Spatiality of the Novel*. Detroit: Wayne State University Press, 1978.

————. "Virtual Text/Virtual Reader: The Structural Signature Within, Behind, Beyond, Above." *James Joyce Quarterly*, 16 (1979), 27–42.

KLINKOWITZ, JEROME. "Gilbert Sorrentino's Super-Fiction." *Chicago Review*, 24, No. 4 (1974), 77–89.

————. *Literary Disruptions: The Making of a Post-Contemporary American Fiction*. Urbana: University of Illinois Press, 1975; rev. ed., 1980.

KNIGHT, CHARLES A. "Multiple Structures and the Unity of *Tom Jones*." *Criticism*, 14 (1972), 227–242.

KNIGHT, G. WILSON. *The Wheel of Fire: Interpretations of Shakesperean Tragedy*. 1930; rpt. London: Methuen, 1961. See pp. 1–16.

KOHLER, DAYTON. "Time in the Modern Novel." *College English*, 10 (1948), 15–24.

KOLEK, LESZEK. "Music in Literature: Presentation of Huxley's Experiment in 'Musicalization of Fiction.'" *Zagadnienia Rodzajow Literackich*, 14 (1972), 111–122.

KRIEGER, MURRAY. "The Ekphrastic Principle and the Still Movement of Poetry: Or *Laokoön* Revisited." In his *The Play and Place of Criticism*. Baltimore: The Johns Hopkins University Press, 1967, pp. 105–128.

————. *Theory of Criticism: A Tradition and Its System*. Baltimore: The Johns Hopkins University Press, 1976.

KUMAR, SHIV K. "Space-Time Polarity in *Finnegans Wake*." *Modern Philology*, 54 (1957), 230–233.

LACY, NORRIS J. "Spatial Form in Medieval Romance." *Yale French Studies*, No. 51 (1974), pp. 160–169.

Landschaft und Raum in der Erzählkunst, ed. Alexander Ritter. Darmstadt: Wissenschaftliche, 1975.

LAPP, JOHN C. "Art and Hallucination in Flaubert." *French Studies*, 10 (1956), 322–344.

LEBAS, GÉRARD. "The Mechanisms of Space-Time in *The Alexandria Quartet*." *Caliban*, 7 (1970), 79–97.

LEITER, LOUIS H. "Echo Structures: Conrad's *The Secret Sharer*." *Twentieth-Century Literature*, 5 (1960), 159–175.

LEWIS, WYNDHAM. *Time and Western Man*. London: Chatto and Windus, 1927; rpt. Boston, Beacon Press, 1957.

LINS, OSMAN. "O espaço narrativo." *Minas Gerais. Suplemento Literário*, 3 August 1974, p. 4.

————. "Possibilidades do espaço no romance." *Minas Gerais. Suplemento Literário*, 8 June 1974, pp. 1–2.

LITZ, A. WALTON. *The Art of James Joyce*. New York: Oxford University Press, 1961. See pp. 53–62.

————. *James Joyce*. New York: Twayne, 1966. See pp. 77–88.

LOTMAN, JURIJ. *The Structure of the Artistic Text*. Trans. Ronald Vroon. Ann Arbor: University of Michigan Press, 1977.

LOVE, JEAN O. *Worlds in Consciousness: Mythopoetic Thought in the Novels of Virginia Woolf*. Berkeley and Los Angeles: University of California Press, 1970. See pp. 44–48.

LYNEN, JOHN F. *The Design of the Present: Essays on Time and Form in American Literature.* New Haven: Yale University Press, 1969.

MAACK, ANNEGRET. "Das Simultanerlebnis der Wirklichkeit: Zur Struktur von Virginia Woolfs Romam *Jacob's Room.*" *Literatur in Wissenschaft und Unterricht,* 10 (1977), 88–103.

MATORÉ, GEORGES. *L'espace humain: L'expression de l'espace dans la vie, la pensée et l'art contemporains.* Paris: La Colombe, 1962.

McGINNIS, WAYNE D. "The Arbitrary Cycle of *Slaughterhouse-Five:* A Relation of Form to Theme." *Critique* (Georgia), 17, No. 1 (1975), 55–67.

McGUINNESS, A. E. "The Ambience of Space in Joyce's *Dubliners.*" *Studies in Short Fiction,* 11 (1974), 343–351.

McLAURIN, ALLEN. *Virginia Woolf: The Echoes Enslaved.* Cambridge: Cambridge University Press, 1973.

McLUHAN, MARSHALL. "Space, Time and Poetry." *Explorations,* No. 4 (1955), pp. 56–62.

McNEIR, WALDO F. "*The Tempest:* Space-Time and Spectacle-Theme." *Arlington Quarterly,* 2, No. 4 (1970), 29–58.

MARCOTTE, EDWARD. "Intersticed Prose." *Chicago Review,* 26, No. 4 (1975), 31–36.

———. "The Space of the Novel." *Partisan Review,* 41 (1974), 263–272.

MAURIAC, CLAUDE. "'Le temps immobile': Essai de transposition et de composition romanesque." *Cahiers internationaux de symbolisme,* 9–10 (1965–1966), 45–55.

MAYOUX, JEAN-JACQUES. "Le roman de l'espace et du temps." *Revue anglo-american,* April 1930, pp. 312–326.

MEIJER, J. M. "Situation Rhyme in a Novel of Dostoevskij." In *Dutch Contributions to the Fourth International Congress of Slavicists.* The Hague: Mouton, 1958, pp. 115–128.

MELLARD, JAMES M. "*Déjà vu* and the Labyrinth of Memory." *Bucknell Review,* 16, No. 2 (1966), 29–44.

MENDILOW, A. A. *Time and the Novel.* London: Nevill, 1952; rpt. New York: Humanities Press, 1965.

MERCIER, VIVIAN. *The New Novel from Queneau to Pinget.* New York: Farrar, Straus and Giroux, 1971.

MEYER, HERMAN. "Raum und Zeit in Wilhelm Raabes Erzahlkunst." *Deutsche Vierteljahrsschrift für Literaturwissenschaft und Geistegeschichte,* 27 (1953), 236–267. Reprinted in *Zur Poetik des Romans,* ed. Volker Klotz, Darmstadt: Wissenschaftliche, 1969, pp. 239–279.

———. "Raumgestaltung und Raumsymbolik in der Erzählkunst." *Studium Generale,* 10 (1957), 620–630. Reprinted in his *Zarte Empirie: Studien zur Literaturgeschichte,* Stuttgart: Metzler, 1963, pp. 33–56.

MEYERHOFF, HANS. *Time in Literature.* Berkeley and Los Angeles: University of California Press, 1955.

MICKELSEN, DAVID. "*A rebours:* Spatial Form." *French Forum,* 3 (1978), 48–55.

MIEL, JAN. "Temporal Form in the Novel." *Modern Language Notes,* 84 (1969), 916–930.

MINK, LOUIS. "History and Fiction as Modes of Comprehension," *New Literary History,* 1 (1970), 541–558.

MITCHELL, W. J. T. "Spatial Form in Literature: Toward a General Theory." *Critical Inquiry,* 6 (1980), 539–567.

MORSE, J. MITCHELL. "Karl Gutzkow and the Novel of Simultaneity." *James Joyce Quarterly,* 2 (1964), 13–17.

MOURGUES, ODETTE DE. *Racine: Or, the Triumph of Relevance.* Cambridge: Cambridge University Press, 1967. See chapter 2.

MOURIER, MAURICE, and MARIE-CLAIRE ROPARS. "L'espace du texte." *Esprit,* No. 12 (1974), pp. 769–773.

MUIR, EDWIN. *The Structure of the Novel.* London: Hogarth Press, 1928.

NELSON, CARY. *The Incarnate Word: Literature as Verbal Space.* Urbana: University of Illinois Press, 1973.

Nouveau roman: hier, aujourd'hui, ed. Jean Ricardou. 2 vols. Paris: Union générale d'éditions, 1972. See esp. essays by Mansuy, Rossum-Guyon, the Caminades, Lotringer, Bishop, Simon, Ollier, Raillard, and Ricardou.

O'BRIEN, R. A. "Time, Space, and Language in Lawrence Durrell." *Waterloo Review,* 6 (1961), 16–24.

ORTEGA Y GASSET, JOSÉ. "Time, Distance and Form in Proust." Trans. Irving Singer. *Hudson Review,* 11 (1958), 504–513.

PARIS, JEAN. "Notes sur Balzac." *Modern Language Notes,* 89 (1974), 699–732.

PAUL, KURT. "Fictional Simultaneity: A Unique Sense of Time in Modern Narration." *Centerpoint,* 2, No. 2 (1977), 11–16.

PAULSON, RONALD. "Hogarth and the English Garden: Visual and Verbal Structures." In *Encounters: Essays on Literature and the Visual Arts,* ed. John Dixon Hunt. New York: Norton, 1971, pp. 82–95.

PEARCE, RICHARD. "Bring Back That Line, Bring Back That Time." *Tri Quarterly,* 42 (1978), 250–263.

PETSCH, ROBERT. *Wesen und Formen der Erzählkunst.* Halle: M. Niemeyer, 1942.

POULET, GEORGES. *The Interior Distance.* Trans. Elliott Coleman. Baltimore: The Johns Hopkins University Press, 1959.

———. *The Metamorphosis of the Circle.* Trans. Carley Dawson and Elliott Coleman. Baltimore: The Johns Hopkins University Press, 1966.

———. *Le point de départ.* Paris: Plon, 1964.

———. *Proustian Space.* Trans. Elliott Coleman. Baltimore: The Johns Hopkins University Press, 1977.

———. *Studies in Human Time.* Trans. Elliott Coleman. Baltimore: The Johns Hopkins University Press, 1956.

PRAZ, MARIO. *Mnemosyne: The Parallel between Literature and the Visual Arts*. Princeton: Princeton University Press, 1970. See chapter 7.

PRUSOK, RUDI. "Science in Mann's *Zauberberg:* The Concept of Space." *PMLA*, 88 (1973), 52–61.

PRUVOT, MONIQUE. "L'espace imaginaire de Melville dans les *Encantadas* et les significations de trois symboles thériomorphes." *Revue des langues vivantes*, 44 (1978), 15–27.

PURDY, DWIGHT HILLIARD. "Conrad's Spacecraft." *Renascence*, 28 (1976), 203–213.

RABKIN, ERIC. "Spatial Form and Plot." *Critical Inquiry*, 4 (1977), 253–270.

RADCLIFF-UMSTEAD, DOUGLAS. "The Transcendence of Human Space in Manzonian Tragedy." *Studies in Romanticism*, 13 (1974), 25–46.

RAHV, BETTY T. *From Sartre to the New Novel*. Port Washington: Kennikat, 1974. See pp. 4 ff.

RAHV, PHILIP. *Literature and the Sixth Sense*. Boston: Houghton, Mifflin, 1969. See esp. "The Myth and the Powerhouse," "Fiction and the Criticism of Fiction."

REDDICK, BRYAN D. "Point of View and Narrative Tone in *Women in Love*: The Portrayal of Interpsychic Space." *D. H. Lawrence Review*, 7 (1974), 156–171.

RICARDOU, JEAN. *Pour une théorie du nouveau roman*. Paris: Seuil, 1971.

———. *Problemes du nouveau roman*. Paris: Seuil, 1967.

———. "Time of Narration, Time of Fiction." Trans. Joseph Kestner. *James Joyce Quarterly*, 16 (1978), 7–15.

RICE, DONALD B. "The Exploration of Space in Butor's *Où*." In *Twentieth-Century French Fiction: Essays for Germaine Brée*, ed. George Stambolian. New Brunswick: Rutgers University Press, 1975, pp. 198–222.

RICHTER, HARVENA. *Virginia Woolf: The Inward Voyage*. Princeton: Princeton University Press, 1970. See pp. 228–231.

RINGE, DONALD A. *The Pictorial Mode: Space and Time in the Art of Bryant, Irving, and Cooper*. Lexington: University of Kentucky Press, 1971.

ROBBE-GRILLET, ALAIN. *Pour un nouveau roman*. Paris: Minuit, 1963. Trans. Richard Howard, *For a New Novel: Essays on Fiction*. New York: Grove Press, 1965.

ROBERT, PIERRE R. *Jean Giono et les techniques du roman*. Berkeley and Los Angeles: University of California Press, 1961. See chapter 2.

RONSE, HENRI. "Le labyrinthe, espace significatif." *Cahiers internationaux de symbolisme*, 9–10 (1965–1966), 27–43.

ROSE, ALAN. "The Spatial Form of *The Golden Bowl*." *Modern Fiction Studies*, 12 (1966), 103–116.

SAN JUAN, EPIFANIO, JR. "Spatial Orientation in American Romanticism." *East-West Review*, 2 (1965), 33–55.

SCHAAR, CLAES. "Linear Sequence, Spatial Structure, Complex Sign, and Vertical Context System." *Poetics*, 7 (1978), 377–388.

SCOTT, NATHAN. *The Broken Center: Studies in the Theological Horizon of Modern Literature*. New Haven: Yale University Press, 1966. See pp. 25–76.

————. *Negative Capability: Studies in the New Literature and the Religious Situation*. New Haven: Yale University Press, 1969. See pp. 112–144.

SEGRE, CESARE. "Space and Time of the Text." *Twentieth-Century Studies*, No. 12, 37–41.

SELLIN, ERIC. "Simultaneity: Driving Force of the Surrealistic Aesthetic." *Twentieth-Century Literature*, 21 (1975), 10–23.

SHATTUCK, ROGER. *The Banquet Years: The Origins of the Avant Garde in France, 1885 to World War I*. Rev. ed. New York: Vintage, 1968.

————. *Marcel Proust*. New York: Viking, 1974.

————. *Proust's Binoculars: A Study of Memory, Time, and Recognition in "A la recherche du temps perdu."* New York: Random House, 1963.

Shosetsu no Kukan, ed. Yasumasa Okamoto, Iwao Iwamoto, and Kazumi Yamagata. Tokyo: Asaki, 1977.

SHOWALTER, ENGLISH, JR. "Symbolic Space and Fictional Forms in the Eighteenth-Century French Novel." *Novel*, 8 (1975), 214–225.

SMITTEN, JEFFREY R. "Approaches to the Spatiality of Narrative." *Papers on Language and Literature*, 14 (1978), 296–314.

————. "Flaubert and the Structure of *The Secret Agent*: A Study in Spatial Form." In *Joseph Conrad: Theory and World Fiction*, ed. Wolodymyr T. Zyla and Wendell M. Aycock. Lubbock: Texas Tech Press, 1974, pp. 151–166.

————. "Spatial Form as Narrative Technique in *A Sentimental Journey*." *Journal of Narrative Technique*, 5 (1975), 208–218.

————. "*Tristram Shandy* and Spatial Form." *Ariel*, 8, No. 4 (1977), 43–59.

SMOCK, ANN. "The Disclosure of Difference in Butor." *Modern Language Notes*, 89 (1974), 654–668.

SOMER, JOHN. "Geodesic Vonnegut: Or, If Buckminster Fuller Wrote Novels." In *The Vonnegut Statement*, ed. Jerome Klinkowitz and John Somer. New York: Delacorte Press, 1973, pp. 221–254.

SOMVILLE, PIERRE. "Temps et espace dans l'expérience esthétique." In *Proceedings of the Sixth International Congress of Aesthetics*, Acta Universitatis Upsaliensis, Figura Nova Ser. X, Uppsala, 1972, pp. 647–648.

SOUVAGE, JACQUES. *An Introduction to the Study of the Novel*. Gent: E. Story-Scientia, 1965.

SPANOS, WILLIAM. "The Detective and the Boundary: Some Notes on the PostModern Literary Imagination." *Boundary 2*, 1, No. 1 (1972), 147–168.

————. "Heidegger, Kierkegaard, and the Hermeneutic Circle: Towards a Postmodern Theory of Interpretation as Dis-closure." In *Martin Heidegger and the Question of Literature: Toward a Postmodern Literary*

Hermeneutics, ed. William V. Spanos. Bloomington: Indiana University Press, 1979, pp. 115–148.

————. "Modern Drama and the Aristotelian Tradition: The Formal Imperatives of Absurd Time." *Contemporary Literature,* 12 (1971), 345–373.

————. "Modern Literary Criticism and the Spatialization of Time: An Existential Critique." *Journal of Aesthetics and Art Criticism,* 29 (1970), 87–104.

————. "'Wanna Go Home, Baby?': *Sweeney Agonistes as* Drama of the Absurd." *PMLA,* 85 (1970), 8–20.

SPENCER, MICHAEL. "Architecture and Poetry in 'Reseau Aerien.'" *Modern Language Review,* 63 (1968), 57–65.

SPENCER, SHARON. "Novelist's Dance of Numbers." *Par Rapport,* 1 (1978), 41–45.

————. *Space, Time and Structure in the Modern Novel.* New York: New York University Press, 1971; rpt. Chicago: Swallow, 1974.

SPIEGEL, ALAN. "Flaubert to Joyce: Evolution of a Cinematographic Form." *Novel,* 6 (1973), 229–243.

STAROSTE, WOLFGANG. "Die Darstellung der Realität in Goethes *Nouvelle.*" *Neophilologus,* 44 (1960), 322–333.

————. "Raumgestaltung und Raumsymbolik in Goethes *Wahlverwandschaften.*" *Etudes germaniques,* 16 (1961), 209–222.

STATES, BERT O. "The Hero and the World: Our Sense of Space in *War and Peace.*" *Modern Fiction Studies,* 11 (1965), 153–164.

STEDMOND, JOHN M. *The Comic Art of Laurence Sterne: Convention and Innovation in "Tristram Shandy" and "A Sentimental Journey."* Toronto: University of Toronto Press, 1967. See pp. 11–29.

STERNBERG, MEIR. *Expositional Modes and Temporal Ordering in Fiction.* Baltimore: The Johns Hopkins University Press, 1978.

STOEHR, TAYLOR. *Dickens: The Dreamer's Stance.* Ithaca: Cornell University Press, 1965. See pp. 19–33.

STOLL, ELMER E. *From Shakespeare to Joyce.* Garden City: Doubleday, 1944. See "Time and Space in Milton."

Studies in the Novel, 9, No. 4 (1977). Special issue on Huxley's *Point Counter Point.*

SUKENICK, RONALD. "Twelve Digressions toward a Study of Composition." *New Literary History,* 6 (1974–1975), 429–437.

Surfiction: Fiction Now . . . and Tomorrow, ed. Raymond Federman. Chicago: Swallow, 1975. See esp. essays by Federman, Sukenick, Kostelanetz, and Oxenhandler.

SUTTON, WALTER. "The Literary Image and the Reader: A Consideration of the Theory of Spatial Form." *Journal of Aesthetics and Art Criticism,* 16 (1957), 112–123.

SYPHER, WYLIE. *Rococo to Cubism in Art and Literature.* New York: Random House, 1960. See pp. 295–311.

TALON, HENRI. "Space, Time, and Memory in *Great Expectations.*" *Dickens Studies Annual,* 3 (1974), 122–133.

TIMPE, EUGENE F. "The Spatial Dimension: A Stylistic Typology." In *Patterns of Literary Style*, ed. Joseph Strelka. University Park: Pennsylvania State University Press, 1971, pp. 179–197.

TOBIN, PATRICIA DRECHSEL. *Time and the Novel: The Genealogical Imperative*. Princeton: Princeton University Press, 1978.

TODOROV, TZVETAN. *The Poetics of Prose*. Trans. Richard Howard. Ithaca: Cornell University Press, 1977. See esp. "The Grammar of Narrative," "How to Read?"

———. *Poétique*. Paris: Seuil, 1968.

———. "The Structural Analysis of Literature: The Tales of Henry James." In *Structuralism: An Introduction*, ed. David Robey. Oxford: Oxford University Press, 1973, pp. 73–103.

TOLIVER, HAROLD. *Animate Illusions: Explorations in Narrative Structure*. Lincoln: University of Nebraska Press, 1974. See pp. 3–16.

TROY, WILLIAM. *Selected Essays*, ed. Stanley Edgar Hyman. New Brunswick: Rutgers University Press, 1967. See "Time and Space Conceptions in Modern Literature," "Virginia Woolf and the Novel of Sensibility."

USPENSKY, BORIS. *A Poetics of Composition: The Structure of the Artistic Text and Typology of a Compositional Form*. Trans. Valentina Zavarin and Susan Wittig. Berkeley and Los Angeles: University of California Press, 1973.

VACHON, ANDRÉ. *Le temps et l'espace dans l'oeuvre de Paul Claudel*. Paris: Seuil, 1965.

VANCE, EUGENE. "Spatial Structure in the *Chanson de Roland*." *Modern Language Notes*, 82 (1967), 604–623.

VERNON, JOHN. *The Garden and the Map: Schizophrenia in Twentieth-Century Literature and Culture*. Urbana: University of Illinois Press, 1973.

VON BROEMBSEN, F. "Mythic Identification and Spatial Inscendence: The Cosmic Vision of D. H. Lawrence." *Western Humanities Review*, 29 (1975), 137–154.

WEIGEL, JOHN A. *Lawrence Durrell*. New York: Twayne, 1965. See chapter 5.

WEIMANN, ROBERT. *"New Criticism" und die Entwicklung Burgerlicher Literaturwissenchaft*. Halle: M. Niemeyer, 1962.

WEISGERBER, JEAN. "A la recherche de l'espace romanesque: *Lazarillo de Tormes*, *Les Aventures de Simplicus Simplicissimus*, et *Moll Flanders*." *Neohelicon*, 3, Nos. 1–2 (1975), 209–227.

———. "Aspects de l'espace romanesque: *Moll Flanders*." *Revue des langues vivantes*, 40 (1974), 503–510.

———. "Aspects de l'espace romanesque: *L'histoire du Chevalier Des Grieux* et de *Manon Lescaut*." In *Etudes sur le XVIIIe siècle II*, ed. Roland Mortier and Hervé Hasquin. Brussels: Université de Bruxelles, 1975, pp. 89–107.

––––––. "Nouvelle lecture d'un livre ancien: L'espace dans l'*Histoire de Tom Jones, enfant trouvé.*" *Cahiers roumains d'études littéraires,* No. 1 (1975), pp. 69–86.

WELLEK, RENÉ, and AUSTIN WARREN. *Theory of Literature.* 3d ed. Harmondsworth: Penguin, 1963. See pp. 212–225.

WIDMER, KINGSLEY. "Timeless Prose." *Twentieth-Century Literature,* 4 (1958), 3–8.

WILLIAMS, ARNOLD. *Flower on a Lowly Stalk: The Sixth Book of the "Faerie Queene."* East Lansing: Michigan State University Press, 1967.

WIMSATT, WILLIAM K., JR., and CLEANTH BROOKS. *Literary Criticism: A Short History.* New York: Knopf, 1957. See pp. 683–686.

WITT, MARY ANN. "Eugene Ionesco and the Dialectic of Space." *Modern Language Quarterly,* 33 (1972), 312–326.

WRIGHT, TERENCE. "*Under the Volcano*: The Static Art of Malcolm Lowry." *Ariel,* 1, No. 4 (1970), 67–76.

WYNNE, CAROLYN. "Aspects of Space: John Marin and William Faulkner." *American Quarterly,* 16 (1964), 59–71.

ZANTS, EMILY. *The Aesthetics of the New Novel in France.* Boulder: University of Colorado Press, 1968.

ZINK, KARL E. "Flux and the Frozen Moment: The Imagery of Stasis in Faulkner's Prose." *PMLA,* 71 (1956), 285–301.

ZIOLKOWSKI, THEODORE. *Dimensions of the Modern Novel: German Texts and European Contexts.* Princeton: Princeton University Press, 1969. See chapter 6.

UNPUBLISHED DISSERTATIONS

Note: *DAI* stands for *Dissertation Abstracts International.* Before 1967 the publication was called *Dissertation Abstracts (DA).*

ALLEN, EVERETT MAYNARD. "The Presentation of Space in the Published German 'Hoerspiel' Text." *DAI,* 35 (1974), 2976A.

BIRRELL, GORDON EASTRIDGE. "Spatial and Temporal Structure in the 'Maerchen' of Novalis and Tieck: An Approach to the Problem of Genre in Early Romanticism." *DAI,* 29 (1969), 2249A–2250A.

BROWN, ROBERT EDWARD. "Walk in the World: A Journey in the Space of William Carlos Williams' 'Paterson.'" *DAI,* 31 (1971), 3540A.

BURROWS, CAROLYN. "The Faces of Chronos: Temporal Innovations in the Technique of the Novel." *DAI,* 30 (1969), 1163A–1164A.

CAVANAUGH, HILAYNE E. "Faulkner, Stasis, and Keats's 'Ode on a Grecian Urn.'" *DAI,* 38 (1977), 2783A–2784A.

CORRIDORI, EDWARD L. "The Quest for Sacred Space: Setting in the Novels of William Faulkner." *DAI,* 32 (1972), 5224A.

DOBBS, ELIZABETH ANN. "Space in Chaucer's *Troilus and Criseyde.*" *DAI,* 37 (1976), 960A.

DOWNING, BARBARA SCHWARTZ. "Symbolic Space in the Novels of Flaubert." *DAI*, 28 (1968), 4169A.

DOYLE, LINDA SHEIDLER. "A Study of Time in Three Novels: *Under the Volcano, One Hundred Years of Solitude,* and *Gravity's Rainbow.*" *DAI*, 39 (1978), 1547A.

FOUST, RONALD. "The Place of Spatial Form in Modern Literary Criticism." *DAI*, 36 (1976), 6671A–6672A.

GANIM, JOHN MICHAEL. "Mutable Imagination: Time, Space, and Audience in Medieval English Narrative." *DAI*, 35 (1974), 2221A.

GLASS, FRANK P. "Thematic Uses of Space in Contemporary Theatre." *DAI*, 35 (1974), 3158A.

HANDELSMAN, RICHARD LYNN. "Spatial Metaphors in Arnold Bennett." *DAI*, 36 (1975), 901A–902A.

HIRSCHMAN, JACK A. "The Orchestrated Novel: A Study of Poetic Devices in the Novels of Djuna Barnes and Herman Broch and the Influence of the Works of James Joyce upon Them." *DA*, 22 (1962), 3220.

KING, JOHN STEPHEN. "Space in Thomas Mann's *Buddenbrooks, Der Zauberberg,* and *Doktor Faustus.*" *DAI*, 38 (1977), 296A.

KOMAR, KATHLEEN LENORE. "The Multilinear Novel: A Structural Analysis of Novels by Dos Passos, Döblin, Faulkner, and Koeppen." *DAI*, 38 (1977), 2101A.

KUMM, KARL W. G. "Michel Butor: A Spatial Imagination." *DAI*, 31 (1971), 5409A.

LANNON, JOHN MICHAEL. "William Faulkner: A Study in Spatial Form." *DAI*, 33 (1973), 5184A.

LEWIS, KATHLEEN BURFORD. "The Representation of Social Space in the Novel: *Manhattan Transfer, Naked Year,* and *Berlin Alexanderplatz.*" *DAI*, 37 (1976), 2849A–2850A.

LEWIS, NANCY WHYTE. "Lawrence Durrell's *Alexandria Quartet* and the Rendering of Post-Einsteinian Space." *DAI*, 37 (1977), 7143A–7144A.

LYNGSTAD, SVERRE. "Time in the Modern British Novel: Conrad, Woolf, Joyce, and Huxley." *DA*, 27 (1966), 1374–1375A.

NEIDHARDT, FRANCES ELAM. "Verbal-Visual Simultaneity in Faulkner's *The Sound and the Fury:* A Literary Montage Filmscript for Quentin." *DAI*, 39 (1978), 1165A.

NELSON, CARY ROBERT. "The Incarnate Word: Studies in Verbal Space." *DAI*, 31 (1971), 6623A. See the chapter on *Religio Medici.*

PECK, HENRY DANIEL. "The Pastoral Vision: A Study of the Aesthetic Space of James Fenimore Cooper's Fiction." *DAI*, 35 (1975), 4448A–4449A.

PHILLIPS, JOSEPH M. "The Uses of Scientific and Philosophical Concepts of Space and Time in James Joyce's *Finnegans Wake.*" *DAI*, 32 (1972), 6999A.

RAABERG, GLORIA GWEN. "Toward a Theory of Literary Collage: Literary Experimentation and Its Relation to Modern Art in the Work of Pound, Stein, and Williams." *DAI*, 39 (1978), 2932A–2933A.

REHN WOLFMAN, URSULA MARIA. "Ecriture/Lecture: Jeu d'espace littéraire pictural, sculptural: Samuel Beckett—Alberto Giacometti." *DAI,* 38 (1977), 2163A.

SHINE, CAROL ELLEN BOLDUAN. "Montage: A Critical Technique in Selected Modern Novels and Narrative Films." *DAI,* 39 (1978), 2A.

SPANGLER, ELLEN STEWART. "The Book as Image: Medieval Form in the Modern Spatialized Novel of Marcel Proust and His Contemporaries." *DAI,* 37 (1976), 2865A–2866A.

STEELE, THOMAS J. "Literate and Illiterate Space: The Moral Geography of Cooper's Major American Fiction." *DAI,* 29 (1969), 4570A.

THOMAS, ROBERT KEDZIE. "The Tree and the Stone: Time and Space in the Works of Henry David Thoreau." *DAI,* 31 (1970), 1776A.

THOMSON, ALLAN. "Space-Time in James Joyce's Thought: A Study of the Role of the Artist in History." *DA,* 22 (1961), 265.

WILD, FREDERIC MAX, JR. "'A Plank in Reason': Time, Space, and the Perception of the Self in the Modern Novel." *DAI,* 34 (1973), 2665A.

Contributors

JAMES M. CURTIS is Associate Professor of Russian at the University of Missouri. He has published a number of essays on spatial form in Russian literature and on comparative literature and critical theory. His scholarly interests also include American popular culture.

ANN DAGHISTANY received her Ph.D. degree from the University of Southern California, where she was an NDEA fellow. She is a specialist in comparative literature, with particular interest in the archetypes and stereotypes of women in world literature. Currently she is an Assistant Professor of English at Texas Tech University.

RONALD FOUST teaches at the University of Maryland, where he took his Ph.D. with a dissertation on the subject of spatial form. He has written essays on contemporary American writers and fantasy literature. He is currently working on a theory of Gothic fiction while planning a book-length theory of American fiction based upon a conjunction of the principles of pragmatism and phenomenology.

JOSEPH FRANK is Professor of Comparative Literature and Director of the Christian Gauss Seminars in Criticism at Princeton University. Some of his numerous essays have been gathered together in *The Widening Gyre* (1963). He has also edited R. P. Blackmur's *A Primer of Ignorance* (1967). Most recently he has been working on a biography of Dostoevsky, the first volume of which (*Dostoevsky: The Seeds of Revolt, 1821–1849*) appeared in 1976.

J. J. JOHNSON is a specialist in contemporary fiction and has published essays on Evelyn Waugh and John Hawkes, among others. He received his Ph.D. degree from Vanderbilt University and now lives in Austin, Texas.

JOSEPH KESTNER received his doctorate in English and comparative literature from Columbia University, where he was a President's Fellow and a Woodrow Wilson Fellow. He is the author of *Jane Austen: Spatial Structure of Thematic Variations* (1974) and *The Spatiality of the Novel* (1978). His critical essays have appeared in *Studies in the Novel, Poétique, The Wordsworth Circle,* and the *James Joyce Quarterly,* among other journals. He has translated essays by Jean Ricardou and Tzvetan Todorov. Having taught at Princeton University and The City University of New York, he is currently an Associate Professor in the Graduate Faculty of Modern Letters, The University of Tulsa.

JEROME KLINKOWITZ is Professor of English at the University of Northern Iowa. He is the author of *The American 1960s* (1980), *The Practice of Fiction in America* (1980), *Literary Disruptions* (1975; expanded 1980), and *The Life of Fiction* (1977); co-author of *Vonnegut in America* (1977), *The Vonnegut Statement* (1973), and of descriptive bibliographies of Donald Barthelme (1977) and Kurt Vonnegut (1974). He is editor of *The Diaries of Willard Motley* (1979), *Writing under Fire: Stories of the Vietnam War* (1978), and *Innovative Fiction* (1972). His graduate training was received at Marquette University and the University of Wisconsin, and he lectures frequently at universities in Hungary, Poland, and France.

DAVID MICKELSEN received his Ph.D. in comparative literature from Indiana University. His scholarly interests include the European and Latin American novel, the Symbolist movement, Faulkner, and censorship; and he has published articles on the fortunes of French Symbolism in Denmark, on *Histoire d'O,* and on spatial form in *A rebours.* An Associate Professor of English at the University of Utah, he spent 1980–81 teaching American literature on the Ivory Coast.

ERIC S. RABKIN is Professor of English at the University of Michigan and Director of the Collegiate Institute for Values and Science. His books include *Narrative Suspense* (1973), *Form in Fiction* (with David Hayman, 1974), *The Fantastic in Literature* (1976), *Science Fiction: History, Science, Vision* (with Robert Scholes, 1977), *Arthur C. Clarke* (1979), and *Fantastic Worlds: Myths, Tales, and Stories* (1980).

JEFFREY R. SMITTEN received his Ph.D. from the University of Wisconsin and is a specialist in eighteenth-century literature. He is co-editor of the journal *The Eighteenth Century: Theory and Interpretation* and has published a number of essays dealing with Sterne, Johnson, Conrad, and critical theory. He is Associate Professor of English at Texas Tech University.

Ivo Vidan is Professor of English and American Literature at the University of Zagreb, Yugoslavia. He was graduated from Zagreb University and received the Ph.D. at the University of Nottingham, England. Professor Vidan has lectured in several universities and participated at scholarly gatherings in various European countries and in the United States. He is an editor of a Yugoslav critical journal, and his publications include three books on modern literature (*The Unreliable Narrator, The Stream of Consciousness Novel, Texts in Context*) in Serbo-Croatian, and a number of scholarly and critical articles in English on Conrad, on American nineteenth-century writing, and on comparativist topics.

Index

SPATIAL FORM
in NARRATIVE

Designed by G. T. Whipple, Jr.
Composed by Eastern Graphics
in 10-1/2 point Times Roman, 2 points leaded,
with display lines in Times Roman.
Printed offset by Thomson-Shore, Inc.
on Warren's Number 66 Text, 50 pound basis.
Bound by John H. Dekker & Sons
in Holliston book cloth
and stamped in Kurz-Hastings foil.

Library of Congress Cataloging in Publication Data
Main entry under title:

Spatial form in narrative.

    Bibliography: p.
    Includes index.
    Contents: Introduction : Spatial form and narrative
theory / Jeffrey R. Smitten — The novel as artifact /
Jerome Klinkowitz — Romantic irony, spatial form, and
Joyce's Ulysses / Ann Daghistany and J.J. Johnson —
[etc.]
    1. Fiction—Technique—Addresses, essays, lectures.
2. Narration (Rhetoric)—Addresses, essays, lectures.
3. Fiction—20th century—History and criticism—Addresses, essays, lectures. I. Smitten, Jeffrey R., 1941–
II. Daghistany, Ann, 1942–
PN3383.N35S64   808.3   81-3244
ISBN 0-8014-1375-3   AACR2